FEAR AND COURAGE
in the Democratic Party

By Glenn Hurowitz

*To the Hackley History Department —
thank you for all
the years of education; they
helped make this book possible!*

[signature]

Maisonneuve Press
Washington, DC

FIRST EDITION

Cover and text design by Aimee Wood. Logo design by Shannon Ryan.

Library of Congress Cataloging-in-Publication Data

Hurowitz, Glenn, 1978

Fear and courage in the Democratic Party / Glenn Hurowitz.

  p. cm.

Includes bibliographical references and index.

ISBN 978-0-944624-48-7 (alk. paper)

  1. Democratic Party (U.S.) 2. Progressivism (United States politics) 3. United States--Politics and government--1989- I. Title.

JK2316.H87 2007

324.2736--dc22

          2007046255

To Amanda.
To my parents.
To a living planet.

TABLE OF CONTENTS

PREFACE
★★★★

"The senator agrees with you, but he's not sure about the politics," the senior Democratic Senate aide told me. "But if the politics changes, the Senator would definitely like to vote your way – so good luck; we're behind you." The aide was explaining to me why his boss, a Democrat who represented a rural, Republican-leaning state, hadn't supported higher fuel efficiency standards for cars and trucks in a recent vote. The aide told me that though the senator agreed with the environmental group I was working for that increased auto mileage made sense for the environment, for national security and for his rural constituents (who drove longer distances than average and stood to save thousands of dollars in gas bills from increased auto mileage), he was afraid that his constituents might not support his stance, especially after being bombarded with auto industry ads on the airwaves.

It was a response I would hear over and over again from Democrats as I went from leading local and state level environmental campaigns to helping direct those campaigns at the national level. When Democrats voted against us, it was rare to hear them say they disagreed with us on the merits. Instead, they'd tell us they were afraid: afraid that their constituents wouldn't support a pro-environment position; afraid of defying President Bush and the Republican noise machine; or they'd even admit they were afraid of angering this or that corporate lobby and losing campaign contributions to the Republicans. To be sure, on a basic level, I found their explanations infuriating: shouldn't leaders do the right thing, even when doing so might entail some political risk? But even when I put myself in their shoes and tried to look at their positions from the perspective of a purely self-interested politician, these explanations still seemed to make little sense: polls consistently show strong support in all parts of America for stronger environmental protections – it's one issue that unites grassroots Republicans and Democrats. What's more, in my experience, politicians who were willing to confront powerful interests in tough battles came out of those battles more, not less, popular.

When I looked outside the environmental movement, I saw the same thing. Starting with President Clinton, through the 1990's, and down to the present, Democrats shied from a full-throated campaign for government-financed universal health care, not because they disagreed with experts' assessment that it was the best and most affordable way to provide health coverage to the greatest number of people, but because they were afraid of taking on the HMOs and insurance companies. Many Democrats supported President Bush's tax cuts for the ultra-rich, not because they thought giving billionaires a tax break while the working and middle classes were feeling economic insecurity was a good idea, but because they were afraid of opposing President Bush, no matter how worthy the cause. And of course, dozens of Democrats failed to speak out against Bush's rush to war in Iraq, not because they thought George Bush would bring peace and democracy to the Middle East, but because they were afraid that Republicans would paint them as weak. Again, I found their explanations morally and politically bankrupt: not only were they the wrong decisions, they also served to empower the very corporations and special interests out to defeat Democrats.

The consequences of these failures to confront have been severe: environmental and human disasters like Katrina, a health care system that is at once wasteful and cruel, rising economic inequality and debt, an enduring war in Iraq, and still-rising hatred of America abroad. On the political front, the situation is equally dire. Despite the palpable failures of Republican governance, Republicans managed to keep Democrats out of Congress for 12 long years and managed to hold the White House for the last seven years. Even as the spectacle of Republican corruption, incompetence, and foreign adventure forced Americans to turn to the Democrats, the party has been largely unable to turn the 2006 midterm election mandate to either their policy or political advantage. They've been unable to stop the war and unable to accomplish much of anything else either – seeing their policy objectives stymied by a combination of stalwart Republican obstruction and Democratic unwillingness to challenge Republicans even with the political wind at their back.

There has been no shortage of explanations of these Democratic failings. The author Thomas Frank posited in his 2004 blockbuster bestseller *What's the Matter With Kansas?* that the Republican ascendancy could be explained largely by Democrats' abandonment of the populist economic agenda that was the foundation of the party, allowing corporate Republicans to swoop in, pay lip service to a populist anti-abortion, anti-gay agenda and persuade working and service class Americans to vote against their own economic interests. In *God's Politics*, the Reverend Jim Wallis recommended that Democrats learn to communicate better with religious Americans. The Berkeley linguist George Lakoff, in his 1996 book *Moral Politics* and later in *Don't Think of an Elephant* blamed Democratic failures in large part on their inability to articulate a coherent message – and suggested ways they could more effectively dominate the field of debate. Psychologist Drew

Westen followed that up with a discussion of how Democrats could win more support by utilizing principles of political psychology when they craft their speeches and advertisements in his book *The Political Brain*. Bloggers Jerome Armstrong and Markos Moulitsas Zúniga discussed how to remedy the Democrats' relative infrastructural and tactical weakness in their 2006 book *Crashing the Gate*. Most recently, *New York Times* Magazine writer Matt Bai blamed Democratic failures largely on a lack of "big ideas" in his book *The Argument*.

All of these diagnoses have a great deal of truth to them. Heeding their often brilliant analysis and advice will be essential to any Democratic resurgence. But they're all based on the notion that Democrats are at some level stupid; that they lack the knowledge or expertise to practice politics effectively. This book takes a very different line: that the problems diagnosed above are not themselves the source of Democratic failings, but rather symptoms of a deeper problem: a lack of courage. It is not a crisis of competence that we face, but rather a crisis of confidence. It will be impossible to implement any of these solutions until Democrats gain the backbone to do so.

Let me explain: it's not so much that large numbers of Democrats suddenly swallowed the free market Kool-Aid and, overnight, started believing in Republican Voodoo economics; rather, they became afraid that voters would no longer support a populist economic agenda. It's not so much that Democrats lack the ability to communicate effectively or are ignorant of basic political psychology, but that they are afraid that using the hard-edged messages that work will turn off some small group or another. It's not so much that Democrats lack the smarts or tactical expertise to build an effective party infrastructure, but that they shy from deploying that infrastructure with the aggressive, confrontational spirit necessary to beat an opponent as ruthless as the modern Republican Party. And it's not so much that Democrats lack big ideas, but that they are afraid that actually articulating those big ideas will provoke big enemies.

We can't sugar coat the depth of this crisis or the difficulty of solving it. Making the fearful fierce is not as easy as raising money, starting think tanks, training political organizers, or writing a political ad. To be sure, restoring courage to the party will require new leadership. But on a deeper level, it will require a grassroots moral revolution within the party and the broader progressive movement. It is my hope that this book charts a course towards that revolution, not just for political leaders, but for people around the country and even around the world desperately seeking a new, more courageous, and more winning politics.

INTRODUCTION:
THE POLITICS OF FEAR
★★★★

"Trim your sails," said Barack Obama.

"I can't make a mistake," said Hillary Clinton.

Uh-oh.

The Spineless Dem is rising again.

This Potomac jellyfish just won't die. Democrats have nominated equally butter-boned candidates before. You'd think they'd have learned: these Gumby donkeys lose and lose. It should be obvious: fear of your own convictions, of your own hopes and dreams, not to mention those of your followers, just isn't that fetching. And crumbling into a quivering mass of blow-dried coiffure, $1000 suits, and vague bromides in the face of determined right wing attacks doesn't just lose elections. It allows extremist Republicans to start wars, attack basic rights, and imperil the planet while making their own backers richer and Democrats weaker.

Yet so many Democrats still believe that a Politics of Fear is the only path to victory. Some of the country's smartest and most talented politicians remain slaves to this creed of cowardice. What is it about this Politics of Fear that is so attractive and so powerful? Is caution really the only way Democrats can have a shot at winning?

The answer, thankfully, is no. Forty years of political science research show that being a proud progressive makes political sense for Democrats. So do the lives of the handful of courageous progressives who have persevered and triumphed in an era dominated by the Politics of Fear. This book explores that research and some of those lives, as well as the lives of some formerly powerful – and often quite talented – politicians who rode the Politics of Fear to catastrophic defeats.

So that's the good news: courage works. But the bad news is that the Politics of Fear has become so ingrained in the Democratic Party that it's going to take more than just evidence to finally slay the Spineless Dem. This monster's power is no accident. Like many great and powerful things in American politics, it was birthed in a crowded hotel room. And that's where our story begins.

A Lie is Born

On March 10, 1989, a powerful clique of centrist Democrats, corporate lobbyists, and incognito Republicans gathered in the Philadelphia Franklin Plaza Hotel. They were the leaders of the Democratic Leadership Council (known as the DLC) – an organization founded four years earlier with the mission of moving the Democratic Party firmly to the right – and they were in trouble. They'd been trying to sell, on the merits, their agenda of tax cuts for the rich, cutbacks in environmental protections, and a more moderate approach to issues like abortion, affirmative action, and civil liberties. But increasingly, Democrats weren't buying. What the DLC was saying was just too similar to what Democrats believed was the failed Reagan-Bush agenda.

Even more problematically for the DLC, Democrats of all ideological backgrounds were beginning to question their motives. Uncomfortable facts about the organization – like its funding – were drawing more attention. Many of the DLC's backers were the same foundations, corporations, and ideologues who had funded the right wing take-over of the Republican Party in the 1960's, 70's, and 80's: The Lynde and Harry Bradley Foundation (which has given more than $25 million to the right wing think tanks American Enterprise Institute and the Heritage Foundation),[1] hundreds of major corporations like U.S. Tobacco, Philip Morris, Union Carbide, Citigroup, Enron and Pfizer,[2] and even prominent Republicans like Nestle Enterprises CEO James Biggar.[3] Now these groups were funneling money and resources to the DLC to move America's other great political party, the Democrats, sharply to the right. People were starting to notice where all that cash came from. Jesse Jackson spoke for many when he said that DLC stood for "Democrats for the Leisure Class."

The DLC knew it needed a new strategy if it was to persuade both Democratic elites and the Democratic voter base to support a corporate-friendly, centrist presidential candidate in 1992. They decided to reframe the debate. They stopped attempting the Sisyphean task of persuading the liberals, working class voters, and minorities who largely controlled the Democratic primary nominating process that centrist, corporate-friendly policies were good for the country. Instead, they framed their arguments in the one way guaranteed to get the attention of politicians and partisans of any ideological stripe: that advocating centrist policies would help Democrats get elected.

It was a smart move: on this field of debate, they had no opposition. There was then and is now no progressive equivalent to the DLC – a group making a systematic case that progressive policies are not only a good idea for their own sake, but the only agenda that Democrats can ride to victory.[i] This is due to a little bit of naïve idealism on the side of progressives: while the dozens of liberal groups that make up the national progressive movement often issue reports and

[i] I'm happy to report, however, that on June 16, 2005, strategists Stanley Greenberg, Ruy Teixera, and yes – William Galston! – launched The Democratic Strategist (www.thedemocraticstrategist.com), a web magazine that will at least provide a forum for these kinds of debates.

books about why a certain progressive policy will be good for the country and the world, they rarely frame those arguments in the one way that's almost guaranteed to get the attention of elected officials and candidates: this policy will help you get elected. That gap is why this book is necessary – it's long past time for a defense of a progressive agenda not just on the grounds that pursuing it will make the world more peaceful, just, and sustainable, but also that it can bring lasting political success as well.

As a result of the DLC's superior framing, a huge number of formerly progressive Democrats bought the DLC dope. Unfortunately for them (and the country that had to deal with the consequences), the idea that a centrist agenda could help Democrats win was spectacularly and obviously wrong. This was the big con: both the data and common sense show that pursuing progressive policies makes political sense for Democrats.

How wrong were they? To start with, progressive policies were and are more popular than conservative ones. More than 80 percent of voters favor increasing the minimum wage.[4] A majority says that abortion should be completely or mostly legal.[5] Big majorities consistently favor expanded government protection of the environment[6] and a bigger government role in guaranteeing health care (at the same time, however, Republicans can usually count on majorities to favor tax cuts and, at critical moments, reductions in First Amendment and other civil rights).

Issues Don't Matter (Much)

What's more, research done since the dawn of modern political science has shown over and over again that most voters don't cast their votes primarily on issues, but on other factors, like the party of the candidate, his personal qualities, and economic factors. Changing positions on issues to get closer to the supposed midpoint of the electorate doesn't do a whole lot if voters aren't actually voting on the issues. It's like finding out that a girl's favorite color is yellow and deciding to wear lemon-colored suits all the time; she may like the suits, but it's not going to help if you're still a jerk.

So if it's not issues, how do voters make their decisions? To figure it out, I analyzed data from the National Election Survey, the huge biennial poll run by the University of Michigan since 1948, and collaborated with statistician Gregory P. Nini, to run an analysis using the best, most proven social science mathematical tools[ii]. We used a regression analysis – the standard statistical tool that can determine how closely different factors are correlated – and separate out other factors. That last piece – separating out other influences – is extremely important, and something that just displaying raw poll results won't capture. For instance, 90 percent of Iraq war supporters voted for President Bush in 2004 – but that doesn't mean that those voters voted for Bush because of their support for the Iraq war. It could mean (as evidence suggests that it does), that they support the Iraq War because they support President Bush.[iii] That phenomenon occurs all the time: it's why, for instance, many Republicans who opposed President Clinton's war with Serbia, have enthusiastically supported President Bush's foreign adventure in Iraq. In their book *Partisan Hearts and Minds*, Donald Green, Bradley Palmquist, and Eric Shickler report how Richard Nixon's decision to open diplomatic relations with China dramatically boosted previously anti-China Republicans' support for engagement. They also talk about how Ronald Reagan supporting lower taxes as a deficit-cutting measure changed Republicans' willingness to accept voodoo economics even though it defied Republican economic orthodoxy.[7] What our analysis helps do is separate out these effects and figure out what factors are really driving the vote.

Indeed, candidates' positions on all issues combined account for only six percent of the election outcome, according to the data.[iv] That means that pandering to the middle by pursuing moderate policies is unlikely to have much impact for the average voter, who is unlikely to be aware of those policies or to factor them heavily into his or her decision.

In comparison, economic conditions account for 15 percent of a voter's decision; a voter's perception of a candidate's personal qualities (particularly whether or not the candidate is considered a "strong leader"), 16 percent; and a candidate's party a whopping 38 percent (Republicans tend to vote for Republicans and Democrats for Democrats).

There are several other factors more important than issues in determining how someone will vote: ideology, race (particularly powerful in the black community, which has never given less than 80 percent of its vote to the Democratic

---

[ii]Our analysis only includes the years 1984-2004, because many of the questions about people's opinions on policy have only been asked since 1984. Nevertheless, our conclusions echo those of pre-1984 analyses as well, showing the remarkable stability in the motivating factors for American voting behavior over time.

[iii]See Gregory B. Markus's September, 1982 article "Political Attitudes in an Election Year: A Report on the 1980 NES Panel Study" in *The American Political Science Review*, p. 538-560 for more insight into this phenomenon.

[iv]See Appendix for full results.

candidate since 1972); voters' perception of economic conditions over the past year (good conditions favor the incumbent); and candidate characteristics, particularly whether or not a voter believes the candidate is a strong leader.[v] In addition, several studies have shown that perceptions of integrity and competence are also quite powerful.[8] Even the weather can have a significant impact. A 2004 paper by Christopher Achen and Larry Bartels estimates that "2.8 million people voted against Al Gore in 2000 because their states were too wet or too dry," and because people traditionally take out latent frustration about the weather on incumbents.[9][vi] The power of these other factors also has major implications for political strategy. It suggests that rather than trying to appeal to voters based on issue stances, Democrats would be well served to figure out what qualities individuals are seeking in a candidate. Is it a particular issue position or is it, more likely, a candidate with a certain set of personal characteristics? Right now, Democratic campaigns focus their surveys on figuring out what issues people care about – that's certainly interesting and helpful data, but nowhere near as interesting as finding out what factors, whether issues or something else, most influence their vote – and focusing their appeals on convincing voters that a candidate has what they're looking for. It means that candidates can take quite unpopular positions without suffering major negative political consequences. So long as they do it with sincerity, integrity, and passion, they're unlikely to lose many votes because of it.

---

[v]It's important to understand where this overriding voter focus on factors other than issues comes from. First off, lots of voters just don't have a great incentive to spend lots of time focusing on learning about issues. It really does take a lot of time to learn about how the different parties' tax, health care, environmental, defense, etc. policies will affect you. And the truth is, once a voter goes to all that trouble, that knowledge isn't likely to make a tremendous amount of difference – each person only has one vote, and the likelihood of that vote being decisive is low – so there's a huge cost for little reward for people to become intimately familiar with the positions of different candidates and civic issues in general.

There are ways for voters to increase their chances of voting for politicians who will act in their best interests even if they have only limited knowledge about politics. One of the most common ways is by asking a politically knowledgeable friend for his or her opinion about who to vote for and acting on it. Indeed, government and politics is one of the top three subjects about which people ask for advice (along with restaurant recommendations and cooking recipes.) Smart political strategists are quickly realizing how important word of mouth is in persuading people to vote or get involved in a political campaign – and are increasingly targeting their outreach toward what pollsters Ed Keller and Jon Berry call "The Influentials" – the 10 percent of Americans who other Americans turn to for advice (*The Influentials*).

Voters can also use non-substantive signals from the candidate to figure out which candidate is more likely to act in their interests, without going to all the trouble of learning about their issue positions. In 1976, for instance, Gerald Ford walked into a Mexican restaurant in Texas and tried to eat a tamale with the corn husk still on it. Ford's gaffe didn't mean that his policies would be better or worse for Mexican-Americans, but it could reasonably signal to a Chicano voter that someone who didn't know how to eat a tamale might not be sufficiently connected to the Mexican-American community to effectively address its concerns (Popkin, Samuel. *The Reasoning Voter*).

Why don't issues have more of an impact? One reason is that voters tend not to have strong opinions about even the most contentious policy issues of the day. This is the dirty little secret of every poll and focus group. If you ask people their opinion on an issue, most people will give it, or make one up. Many people will even offer opinions about issues that don't exist. In one famous University of Cincinnati study, a team led by professor George Bishop asked poll respondents their opinions about imaginary laws. They found that more than 30 percent of people could consistently be persuaded to give an opinion on fabricated bills such as the "Agricultural Trade Act of 1983."

Even when it comes to questions like Iraq or the war on terror which attract enormous media attention, the same is largely true. Here again, one finds a relatively limited influence of a candidate's policy positions on the vote. A recent study in the journal *Political Behavior* found that although opinions about the Iraq war could have some significant effect, party identification was still the much more powerful factor.[10] Having said that, it is possible for big events like war and natural disaster to have huge effects on a candidate's political prospects – but not in the way Democratic politicians and strategists usually think (or act like they think). Judgments are made less on whether or not a candidate holds the identical position to voters and more on some combination of an evaluation of how much they succeeded in the past in handling the issue and how much they're likely to succeed in handling the issue in the future. The perception that George Bush handled September 11th well clearly had a major positive impact on his approval ratings; the perception that he totally fouled up Hurricane Katrina clearly had a major negative impact. But it's important not to confuse approval of performance with positions on specific policy issues – very few people have strong opinions about exactly what should be done about Katrina or terrorism. To the extent they're both concerned and knowledgeable, they're worried about the outcome, not the specifics of how different politicians plan to get there.

The softness of most voters' issue positions has enabled Republicans to make previously unpopular policies about invading Iraq, immigration and taxes embraced almost overnight through aggressive advocacy and concerted public relations campaigns. Even in those cases where voters have strong opinions about issues, it doesn't mean that they know the candidates' positions about those issues. A recent study by the Annenberg Public Policy Center showed that even in the 2004 presidential election (which registered some of the highest levels of voter knowledge in history), 25 percent of people couldn't answer correctly whether it was George W. Bush or John Kerry who favored making the tax cuts permanent, and 37 percent didn't know which candidate wanted to allow prescription drugs to be imported from Canada.[11] In less supercharged elections and in congressional races (which receive less media coverage), it's common for 50 percent of voters or more to be unable to correctly identify candidates' issue positions even on big questions like war, abortion, health care. Indeed, only about 1/3 of the American people are even able to identify their senators![vii][12] What's more, when political scientists Michael Alvarez and Charles Franklin asked Americans how certain they were about their own positions on the issues, while 77.7 percent said they were "very certain" about their position on abortion, only 41.8 percent said the same thing about their position on taxes – an uncertainty that is even greater on other, less prominent issues.[13]

While Democrats have very little to gain from shifting issue positions, doing so can cause considerable damage. If they're seen to be shifting their agenda out of political expediency and not out of conviction, it hurts them when voters are considering whether or not Democrats are "strong leaders" or "have integrity," two measures that matter to voters far more than a candidate's issue positions.

Moving to the middle can also turn off the millions of progressives who make phone calls, donate money, and blog for the Democrats. These progressives – and the organizations that represent them – do watch the issues very closely. No matter how lame a Democratic candidate is, they may not switch their vote to a Republican. But if they're not inspired, they can take out it on Democrats in other important ways: not showing up to vote, voting for a protest candidate, or doing something other than help Democrats with their time and money[viii] Indeed, several analyses of recent congressional elections by Professors Neil Wollman and Leonard Williams have found that liberal ideology seems to boost a candidate's chances of winning re-election; at worst, it has no effect. During the 1994 Republican "tidal wave" that was widely blamed on excessive Democratic liberalism, they found that even in the most "marginal" districts – those where the incumbent had won with less than 55 percent of the vote in 1992, 85 percent of Democratic liberals won re-election, while only 43 percent of moderates did. Their analysis of the 2006 election, however, found that ideology – right or left – had no discernible impact on the outcome of different races.[14]

[vii]In fairness, there's a somewhat higher rate of voters' ability to recall a senator or congressman's name when presented with it on a ballot. This, in part, explains incumbents' natural advantage: voters are more likely to recall his name than his opponents.

[viii]My discussion of voter behavior was originally published in slightly different form in *The Baltimore Sun* on January 28, 2007 in the article "Move to Middle Hurts Democrats."

But whether their Politics of Fear was groundless or not was of little concern to the DLC. It was their ticket to power. They were certainly not going to let the facts stand in the way. Because their assertions that Democrats should fear a progressive agenda contradicted accepted political science, the DLC needed a political scientist willing to give a sheen of legitimacy to their fraud. To do so, the DLC turned to William Galston, who had been issues director for the failed 1984 Mondale campaign and also worked on long-time Republican Congressman John Anderson's 1980 independent presidential run. He had previously been known not as a voter behavior expert as much as a policy wonk who pushed corporate friendly ideas like allowing companies to pay their employees less when their profits declined.

Galston delivered for the DLC big time. In a speech at the Philadelphia DLC meeting, and later in "The Politics of Evasion," a paper based on the speech co-written with operative Elaine Kamarck, Galston made his case that the electorate had moved permanently and irretrievably to the right, and that the only way for politicians to avoid annihilation was to move with it. Galston and Kamarck blamed the Democrats' 1980, 1984, and 1988 presidential defeats on what they said was the liberalism of the Democratic candidates and especially on the "liberal fundamentalism" of the Democratic Party as a whole – in particular their defense of a progressive economic policy and civil rights. "Democrats must now come face to face with reality," they wrote. "Too many Americans have come to see the party as inattentive to their economic interests, indifferent if not hostile to their moral sentiments and ineffective in defense of their national security."[15] You may be thinking that this nominally "Democratic" explanation for Democratic defeats sounds a lot like the Republican explanation for Democratic defeats – that right wing ideas are just better and more appealing. You're not far off the mark. Perhaps unsurprisingly given their funding sources, Galston and Kamarck's critique essentially recycled Republican attacks.

Their argument also contradicted most political observers' assessments of the 1980, 1984, and 1988 presidential races. Conventional wisdom blamed those defeats on a number of factors: Reagan's popularity, economic conditions, and the weakness of the Democratic campaigns.[ix] Many other observers

---

[ix]See especially Shanks, J. Merrill and Miller, Warren E. "Partisanship, Policy and Performance: the Reagan Legacy in the 1988 Election" in *British Journal of Political Science*. Vol. 21, No. 2 (April 1991)., p. 129-197 *and* "Policy Direction and Performance Evaluation: Complementary Explanations of the Reagan Elections" in *BJPS*, Vol. 20, No. 2, April 1990, p. 143-235.

doubted exactly how liberal Carter, Mondale, and Dukakis had been (Carter, for instance, initially supported the DLC). But Galston and Kamarck argued instead that those resisting their bid for center-right control of the Party were wrongly putting their principles above political expedience: "The politics of evasion…continues unabated today, years after the collapse of the liberal majority and the New Deal alignment," they wrote. "Its central purpose is the avoidance of meaningful change. It reflects the convictions of groups who believed that it is somehow immoral for a political party to pay attention to public opinion."[16] It urged Democrats to reevaluate their support for traditional affirmative action programs, welfare programs, its foreign policies, and at least the way it formulated the debate about abortion rights. The paper dismissed the idea that a stronger progressive movement, better candidates, and improved communication by Democrats could make enough of a difference. The only way for Democrats to avoid political annihilation, they wrote, was to shift their values, their policies, and their programs firmly to the right.

Slaves to Failure

Though I hope readers will recognize the absurdity of the Politics of Fear on its face – that movements that sell their souls for political expedience rarely maintain the credibility and passion necessary to win in politics – I'm sad to report that the Democratic Party has not. Indeed, as I chronicle in the second chapter, the Politics of Fear became the organizing theory of Democratic politics in the 1990's when DLC Chairman Bill Clinton won the presidency – and remains so to this day. And it's the reason Democrats sometimes act so ignobly. It's not that they're intrinsically bad or cowardly. It's that they remain slaves to a deeply flawed political strategy that says that courage would ruin their political chances of success. As a result, even as they act cravenly, they can rationalize it by saying that those acts are necessary to their political survival – and that despite any one particular surrender, they're at least better than the Republicans.

It is my hope that this book banishes that rationalization to the trash heap of bad ideas where it belongs with global warming denial, the muu-muu, and the 2004 Joe Lieberman presidential campaign. I hope that it persuades Democrats and progressives at all levels that being politically courageous is not only good, but also good for you politically. And if top Democrats don't listen, I hope that this book shows how vulnerable they are – and how they can be beaten by those eager to ride a progressive agenda towards a new, more powerful movement and

Democratic Party.

The Heroes

The good news is that there are progressive politicians and activists out there who have the persistence, enthusiasm, and killer instinct as necessary for success in politics as it is in Nature. I profile three of these progressive heroes in this book. The first, Minnesota senator Paul Wellstone, rode his political courage to extraordinary political success, despite having little money, odd manners, and bad hair. Wellstone repeatedly defied the high priests of the Politics of Fear – casting high profile votes against welfare reform and the Iraq War when the polls and the pundits predicted that those votes would doom him. Instead, he found his support surge as voters responded positively to his courageous stances, even when they disagreed with those stances. Even since his tragic death in 2002, his courage has continued to inspire activists and politicians alike. Most notably, the 2008 presidential candidates are hotly competing to claim Wellstone's mantle of representing the "Democratic wing of the Democratic Party."

The second hero, though not a person, shows how courage works in the Internet age. MoveOn.org went viral when it stood up to the Republican attempt to impeach President Clinton over his private life – tapping into a vein of progressive anger at Republicans at a time when national Democrats were doing little to defend their president against the right-wing witch hunt. And then MoveOn did it again and again by aggressively taking on President Bush over the Iraq War, the 2004 election, and his attempt to stack the federal judiciary with rightist extremists. It was providing the courage that Washington Democrats weren't. As a result, it reaped enormous financial and political benefits from millions of people hungry for that kind of leadership. Indeed, it became so rich and powerful that many centrist Democrats were reduced to begging it for money in 2006.

The final heroes are Nancy Pelosi and the Democrats of 2006. Pelosi brought to Congress a much more aggressive style and a much greater willingness to confront Republicans than her predecessors, positioning Democrats to take advantage of Republican failures when the time came. Of course, since taking Congress, Pelosi and the Democrats haven't been able to achieve all of their lofty aims, stymied by Republican obstructionism on the one hand and the still-present grip of fear on too many members of the Democratic caucus. However, their victories have begun an essential, though too slow, process of transformation for the Democratic Party.

It is these heroes who, I hope, represent the bridge between the courageous progressivism of the past and the dominant progressive movement of the future. But the bad news is that these heroes are still a minority – courageous giants persevering in the face of the climate of fear that has consumed the Democratic Party.

The Weasels

And so I discuss two politicians who let fear ruin otherwise extraordinary careers. The first, Bill Clinton, is widely considered the greatest political talent of his generation. But he had a crippling fear of confrontation that, throughout his career, left his progressive friends feeling betrayed and his right-wing enemies emboldened. That fear created the circumstances that allowed Republicans to take over Congress in 1994 and unleash a right-wing assault on progressive America. That assault ultimately targeted Clinton himself, dragging him through the mud and paralyzing his domestic agenda while Republicans attempted to impeach him. Their past experience with Clinton made Republicans think that no matter how much abuse they doled out, Clinton would not fight back. Of course, the Republicans ultimately overreached, forcing even Clinton to start swinging, however momentarily. And it was at those rare moments of confrontation that Clinton himself proved the political value of courage. When he was finally forced to confront Republicans in the fight over the federal government shutdown and most famously, over his impeachment, he saw his approval ratings surge to record levels. But he would always retreat to the presidential equivalent of the fetal position, leaving progressives uninspired and uninvolved. That weakness in the party and the movement ultimately paved the way for George W. Bush's victory.

Tom Daschle had a similarly fraught relationship with confrontation. He came from South Dakota, one of the most Republican states in the nation, and he'd honed his "Dakota Democrat" political strategy to an art form. At home, he talked moderate. In Washington, he voted liberal. Above all, he brought home the bacon. But when Senate Democrats chose him to be their leader because they wanted someone who would present a non-confrontational image, the stage was set for a political disaster. Daschle ultimately became torn between the national Democratic Party's need for an aggressive leader who would boldly challenge George Bush and his own political need to appear independent from that party to Republican South Dakotan voters. It was an impossible position and he ended up doing neither well: when he capitulated to national Republicans, he looked weak and allowed them to pass very damaging legislation. And when he stood up to them, he couldn't count on the support of people in his home state. And so, despite all his power and prestige, in 2004, he became the first Senate party leader turned out of office in more than 50 years.

The Path of Courage

The point of this book is not to pass judgment on the heroes and weasels chronicled here, but instead to show, in detail, how courage can produce political success for Democrats and progressives the world over. Despite the lack of any systematic effort at making a political (rather than policy) argument for a progressive agenda, courage in the Democratic Party is on the rise. It's ascendant because grassroots and netroots Democrats are using their increasing leverage to persuade and force Democrats to show more backbone.

As a result, there are many progressive Democratic politicians who are adopting – albeit slowly – the politics of courage. You can see it in the increasing willingness of Democratic politicians to stand up to the Republicans and articulate an alternative vision. You can see it in Democratic National Committee Chairman Howard Dean's "50 State Strategy" – his investment of organizers, money, and resources in building the Democratic Party in all the states, not just the conservative or liberal ones. And you can even sometimes see it on Capitol Hill, where new Speaker Nancy Pelosi has demonstrated the gumption to face down Republicans and some recalcitrant Democrats to pass much of the progressive agenda Democrats ran on in 2006.

But the battle is far from over – the 2008 presidential primaries will, in many ways, constitute a battle between those who practice the failed Politics of Fear and the leaders with the long run strategy for victory who are infusing the American and global progressive movements with the courage needed to deliver the peaceful, just, and living society that the country and planet deserve.

PAUL WELLSTONE

★★★★

March 12, 1991 – "Senator Millstone," his fellow senators were calling their freshman colleague from Minnesota, Paul Wellstone. On this day, Wellstone felt the description might just be an apt one. In just two months in office, he had gone from being the toast of his state and progressives nationwide to scoring an abysmal approval rating of 35 percent in the latest Minnesota poll. Inside the Beltway, he was faring little better. Few of his fellow senators would even spend time with him, much less join him at a news conference or cosponsor a piece of legislation with him. The Washington punditocracy all agreed that he had made one of the most politically disastrous debuts in Washington history.

How had it come to this? Just a few months before, the shaggy-haired leftist college professor had astounded the country by being the only challenger to unseat an incumbent senator that election year of 1990. And he'd gotten elected his way, the courageous way, the way he'd always done politics since his days protesting the Vietnam War as a 25 year old tenured professor: proud of his progressive values, saying what he believed, promising to fight a corrupt system, relying primarily on grassroots organizing, economic populism, and a few clever television shots at his opponent. And his election proved that being courageous worked! Despite low name recognition, being outspent 7 to 1 and a reputation as a leftist radical, he'd gone up against Rudy Boschwitz, a 12-year incumbent with the biggest war chest in the Senate and a 70 percent approval rating, and won. At the end of his campaign speeches, Wellstone would say, "This time, vote for what you believe in" and he intended to do the same in Washington.

Buoyed by his victory, he'd come to the Capitol brimming with confidence. He planned on remaking Congress the same way he had won his dramatic electoral victory – through courageous stands other politicos were too chicken to take, stirring oratory, and prairie fire political campaigning. Building relationships with his fellow senators and other Washington power-brokers wasn't high on his agenda. It was exactly this kind of backroom politics that he had run against, and was now determined to eradicate. Nor did he prioritize getting his office running smoothly and helping Minnesotans navigate the federal government – with world-historical issues like the first Gulf War on the agenda, how could making sure Minnesota grannies got their Social Security checks on time compete?

The result was a disaster. Even his parking made enemies. Wellstone rode into Washington on his green campaign bus and violated parking rules by rolling up to the front of the Capitol, taking up three parking spots – and irking everyone who heard about it in a perks-conscious capitol. During the highly ritual-ized swearing-in ceremony, he foisted a tape recording of Minnesotans objecting to an invasion of Iraq onto an irritated Vice President Dan Quayle (whom he was meeting for the first time). Then, at a reception with President Bush, Well-stone cornered Bush *three times* to needle him about the impending invasion of Iraq, prompting Bush to ask an unnamed Minnesota congressman, "Who is this chickenshit?" in a widely publicized remark.[1] Wellstone's colleagues and his con-stituents might have passed off these faux pas as rookie mistakes had it not been for Wellstone's biggest blunder. On January [2], he held a highly controversial news conference to protest the impending Gulf War outside the Vietnam Veterans' memorial. Wellstone's conference outraged many veterans, who felt that Well-stone was trying to take advantage of their comrades' sacrifices for political pur-poses. "For a politician to intrude on our very special place, to use our memorial for his own political gain, is an outrage, to say the least," said Larry Rivers, execu-tive director of the powerhouse Veterans of Foreign Wars. "He certainly would know the deep feelings the Vietnam War created among Americans and certainly would know the strong feelings of veterans toward a memorial we had to build ourselves."[2] Senators began to avoid Wellstone in the halls of the Capitol. They never seemed to be able to clear their schedules to appear with him at events, and were unwilling to put their names on press releases or legislation along with him. Back in Minnesota, bumper stickers reading, "Don't blame me. I voted for Wellstone, but I didn't think he could win" cropped up on cars across the state. [3] According to conventional Beltway wisdom, Wellstone was politically dead.

And yet, by the time of his tragic death 13 days before Election Day 2002 in his bid for a third term, Wellstone not only had dug himself out of his hole, but had become a Washington star – a leader of the national progressive move-ment, respected and admired by his colleagues, with important legislative wins under his belt. He had done it not by conforming to the punditocracy's formula for a successful politician, but by riding his courageous fights for his principles to extraordinary political success. Over and over, he cast courageous votes even when they defied popular opinion in his own state. And over and over, he saw his popularity surge as a result. Wellstone repeatedly violated senatorial decorum and tradition, loudly denounced his fellow senators' actions, and tangled up the Senate in infuriating procedural delays. Yet, just as his popularity would rise when he defied the polls, he found his colleagues' respect for him rise when he defied them too.

That incredible story – how Paul Wellstone went from one of the most disastrous debuts in American political history to become a national progressive hero, someone who voted his conscience, trumpeted his values, fought hard for them using every tool available to him, and often triumphed in a conservative political era – is the story of this chapter. **It is a story that will, I hope, inspire those readers who also find themselves facing seemingly insurmountable odds. For Wellstone's career proves that courage can overcome unpopularity, contempt, lack of resources and even bad hair.**

Organizing for Credibility

On that March day in 1991 when the poll came out showing just how unpopular he was, Wellstone knew he was floundering. But he knew just as clearly that his path to success would not and could not be that of just another insider Washington Democrat – keeping quiet, waiting patiently for a committee chairmanship, not gumming up the works by making a big stink about issues like workers' rights, the environment, or peace. "I was a good anti-incumbent candidate because I represented, in some way, the opposite of what people don't like about politics," Wellstone told *The National Journal*. "Rocking the boat [while in office] creates some risk in public service. But there is a greater risk to me in not being outspoken. I need to feel good about myself."[4] The whole reason he'd run was to fight this system to make a real difference – and quick – for his constituents, for the country, and for the world. He knew that achieving his lofty goals would require a new kind of senator and a new kind of leadership, but apparently not the kind of leadership he'd been practicing in his first three months. He needed courage, but not courage alone. He also needed Washington savvy and a grassroots movement around the country that would provide the political backing necessary in his great fights.

The great thing about Washington savvy is that you can hire it. While it's certainly helpful to know for yourself where the bodies are buried and how to bury them, it's almost as good to employ someone who can discreetly whisper these secrets into your ear at the right moment. And Wellstone quickly staffed up with some very savvy insiders. But achieving Wellstone's other great ambition – building the progressive political movement - wasn't going to be a matter of just hiring the right cunning insider. It would require Wellstone to inspire his constituents with his achievements, his votes, his every action and every word. Just recognizing the desirability of such a social movement was a rare asset among Washington Democrats – and gave Wellstone a big advantage. His colleagues tended to see the path to success as the right combination of big money donations, slick ads, charisma, home state pork barrel spending, and policy stands calibrated to where polls told them undecided voters stood. Courage might not be a huge asset if you're just trying to coax money out of the pockets of a few big contributors – corporate lobbyists don't care too much about your style or your soul, they care about whether or not you'll deliver on their agenda. But for Wellstone, the courage that could build a political movement was absolutely essential.

Entering politics as an ultra-liberal, anti-corporate political science professor, it goes without saying that, early on, Wellstone wasn't wrestling with ethical conflicts about how Big Money could corrupt him. Nobody with Big Money was *trying* to corrupt him. And although he possessed a certain quixotic charisma, he could also be politically and socially tone deaf in a way that caused him to be alternately too shrill, too soft-spoken, or just plain inappropriate in both his personal interactions and his speeches. For instance, early in his 1990 Senate campaign, he was invited to an early-morning meeting at a high-powered downtown Minneapolis law firm to address a political "giving club" of wealthy Democratic lawyers. It was a golden opportunity for an underfunded candidate like him. But when he walked off the elevator on one of the top floors of Minneapolis's prestigious Pilsbury Center skyscraper to go into the meeting, he was drenched in sweat, and still wearing the muscle shirt he had put on for his morning workout. He then launched into a screaming polemic against Big Money, complete with wild gesticulation, that might have been appropriate for an audience of 500 rank-and-file union members, but was not structured to appeal to the 12 seated, muted, and aghast corporate lawyers at 7:30 am.[5] As a result of moves like this, the Minnesota political establishment viewed him as little more than a hyperactive academic gadfly, and wasn't exactly stirring itself to pour resources into his candidacy. Without support from the top, the only avenue open to him was grassroots political organizing.

To a great extent, this meant building the infrastructure necessary for a massive grassroots political operation – hiring organizers, scheduling meetings with local leaders, recruiting volunteers – and Wellstone built one of the most impressive tactical grassroots operations in America. But as anyone who has worked on a campaign knows, having good mechanics in a field operation isn't enough – with all the distractions of modern life and competition between many causes and candidates, attracting the large numbers of people necessary to form a great political movement requires genuine enthusiasm and a sense that one's involvement will make a difference.[x]

Luckily, Paul Wellstone could fire people up, and awaken in them a sense of their own potential like few other politicians. He could also keep that fire burning – an especially important ability for a senator, who only has the opportunity to rally the troops for an election campaign every six years. Wellstone stoked his movement's fire by constantly engineering confrontations with his opponents. "You've got to start a fight to win one," he'd tell his followers. Because he viewed political combat as essential to political success, he rarely shied from a political battle. It was that thirst for confrontation that helped draw people hungry for a politician with guts to him.

Of course, Wellstone had quickly proven with his anti-war theatrics that confrontation alone is not enough. First, you need to build popular support so people will have the faith to follow you into battle. To start winning veterans' trust, he finally focused on his basic constituent services duties, helping individual veterans get health and disability benefits from the federal government. He also took the extra step of making veterans issues one of his priority legislative issues. He set up a series of "listening sessions" with veterans around the state during his weekends home from Washington. He was true to the sessions' title: instead of giving speeches, he mainly just listened to veterans talk about their lives, the issues they cared about, and their personal struggles. Their war stories moved him, but so did their tales of difficulty adjusting to life back home, getting health care, or just making ends meet. He quickly came to realize how much his actions at the Memorial had hurt veterans who felt that it was their sacred ground. Though it was hard for him, he made a formal apology at a meeting of St. Paul veterans on April 3.[6] On June 17, Wellstone even swallowed some pride and spoke alongside Vietnam War commanding general William Westmoreland at a dinner to raise money for a Vietnam Veterans' Memorial in Minnesota, and once again apologized for his insensitivity.[7] Pretty soon, memories of his blunder had faded, and veterans started looking to the Wellstone office for help getting their benefits.

In most congressional offices, when someone called to ask for help getting veterans benefits, a Social Security check, or to voice an opinion about an issue, they were shunted to the most junior-level person in the office. If a case was particularly serious, or held the potential for getting publicity, a senior staffer or

---

[x]For a great account of the mechanics of Wellstone's field operation, and a great deal of else about the Wellstone political magic, see Wellstone Action's excellent book, *Politics the Wellstone Way: How to Elect Progressive Candidates and Win on Issues*, edited by Wellstone biographer and campaign worker Bill Lofy (Minneapolis: University of Minnesota Press, 2005).

even the Member of Congress himself might write a letter or make a few calls to help the constituent, or even organize a news conference. Many congressional offices were quite adept at performing these "constituent services" and often won the gratitude of people who called in for help. But Wellstone's office went much further. They saw constituents seeking help as a major opportunity to build the Wellstone movement. When someone contacted Wellstone's Senate office with trouble getting Medicare or to voice an opinion on say, an environmental issue, they'd get advice and aid like in the other offices. But the staffer would also categorize callers by issue. Then, they'd invite everyone who'd called in on a particular issue to a meeting with Wellstone in Minnesota.

At the meetings, Minnesotans would sometimes learn for the first time that there were many others out there struggling with the same issues. The Wellstone staff made sure that the problems were presented as systemic ones with systemic solutions: a constituent's problems affording health care would be related to the lack of universal health care and low wages. Another's anger about a smell in the local lake would be related to polluter influence in Congress. The Wellstone staff would do everything they could to organize these people to take collective action to solve their problems. They'd introduce these constituents to statewide or national groups also working on these issues – helping build progressive organizations.

There were clear political benefits to this organizing. Constituents organized by the Wellstone office often stayed involved in politics, and, more specifically, stayed involved through the Wellstone office. Many intimately realized just how well Wellstone was working for them on their issue, and started to follow Wellstone's efforts with a great deal of investment. When campaign time came around, they were more likely to believe that politicians in general could make a difference, and that Paul Wellstone in particular could make a difference on the issue they cared about – making them much more likely to vote, volunteer, or donate to Wellstone's campaigns. Additionally, progressive organizations were often grateful for the influx of volunteers that Wellstone had brought to their organizations – and more likely to lend him their resources on Election Day.

Championing Atomic Veterans

Although Wellstone did this kind of organizing on a great number of issues and with a great number of constituencies, he kept a special focus on veterans. He hoped to do more with veterans than just hold meetings and exhort them to start organizing. But first, he needed an "organizing vehicle": a cause that would excite veterans and inspire them to get and stay involved politically. One day in January, 1994, that cause sailed into his office when a staffer received a letter from Smoky Parrish, a Republican former mayor of the tiny town of Hackensack, Minnesota. Parrish's letter – and those that followed it – told the harrowing story of "Operation Tumbler Snapper" – a series of U.S. government nuclear tests he had participated in during his 1950s Army service.

One of the goals of the tests was to discover how exposure to radiation and the devastation of nuclear wasteland would affect troops. To find answers, top Army personnel directed Parrish and thousands of other troops to wait in trenches or holding zones between five miles and one mile from the H-bomb detonation sites – close enough to feel the force and heat of the nuclear explosion, and see the intense sun-like light of the blast even with their eyes covered. Immediately following the test explosion, the soldiers would run into an uncovered jeep and race to ground zero as quickly as possible. Often, when the soldiers arrived, the tanks, trucks, houses, and animals near ground zero were still burning, and sheep, dogs, and other test animals slightly outside the zone of death wandered around blinded and bleating in pain and confusion. The Army forbade the test subjects to talk about the tests – threatening those who did with court-martial.[8] They also made no effort to track the long-term health impacts of radiation on the veterans of these tests.

As the atomic veterans got older, they started to suffer diseases that could be associated with radiation – leukemia, dozens of types of cancer, deterioration of the spinal cord, and other radiation-linked diseases such as deterioration of the spinal cord. Of course, all of these conditions can have other causes too, and the Veterans' Affairs Department required veterans to prove their disease was directly linked to radiation exposure. This task was difficult because neither the Army nor the Department of Energy kept track of radiation that troops inhaled or that penetrated their skin. As a result, out of 19,885 claims from veterans for benefits related to radiation exposure, the Veterans' Affairs Department had granted benefits to fewer than 2,000.[xi][9]

Parrish was one of those to whom benefits had been denied. His wife had suffered two miscarriages and three stillbirths after Parrish's return from the Army, but she had given birth to a healthy son before he left for his service. Parrish

---

[xi]The Clinton Administration's Advisory Committee on Human Radiation Experiments calculated that only a few hundred deaths were likely to result from radiation exposure to the nuclear tests and the occupation of Hiroshima and Nagasaki, though they acknowledged that the number could be much higher due to the scanty data.

himself suffered from pulmonary problems, severe and debilitating headaches, and partial blindness in one eye that could be related to his radiation exposure.

For Parrish and many atomic veterans, even more painful than their physical ailments was the feeling that America had forgotten them. This was the perfect opportunity for Wellstone to help right a wrong and begin his work of rallying and organizing veterans. One of his first actions was to organize a meeting in Minnesota for atomic veterans – many of whom came from Parrish's 216th Army Chemical Company. Wellstone heard the veterans' and their widows' stories – of cancers, sterility, and birth defects – and frequently of how the Veterans' Affairs Department denied their requests for benefits. He promised to work to do what he could for them in Washington, but, more importantly, Wellstone urged the veterans to organize other atomic veterans across the country and build the kind of pressure needed to get the federal government to act.

The veterans listened to Wellstone's advice. Parrish helped organize the "Forgotten 216th" – an organization of his former comrades dedicated to winning justice for themselves and for atomic veterans everywhere. The Minnesota veterans also played a significant role in the National Association of Atomic Veterans, which had been created to help atomic veterans in 1979. Suddenly, veterans around the country who had been suffering from illnesses potentially related to radiation were banding together – and getting results.

At the same time that Wellstone was building his movement through this kind of constituent grassroots organizing, he was also looking to expand his more traditional Washington power base. He got a huge boost for his efforts in March, 1995, when the Democratic leadership gave him a spot on the Veterans' Affairs Committee – giving him a launch pad for his efforts on behalf of veterans, and added credibility in a re-election bid. With his new committee imprimatur, Wellstone quickly established himself as the Senate's leader on atomic veterans. He succeeded in passing a resolution declaring July 16 – the anniversary of the first nuclear test at Alamogordo, New Mexico – "National Atomic Veterans Day."[10] Although the legislation was non-binding, it gave many atomic veterans hope that real government action to help them was possible.[11]

Of course, neither they nor Wellstone were satisfied with symbolic action. In 1997, he introduced the "Justice for Atomic Veterans Act" to mandate that atomic veterans who suffered from brain, lung, and colon cancer automatically get benefits without having to prove that the cancers had been caused by the atomic tests. But in taking on this fight, he faced resistance from both a Republican Party determined to deny vulnerable first-term Democratic senators policy victories, and persistent opposition from the Clinton administration – which in the wake of the right-wing takeover of Congress in 1994 wanted to control all kinds of spending in order to convince voters that it no longer represented "big government." The Clinton administration also claimed that it remained unconvinced about the links between the atomic tests and cancers that veterans were suffering.[xii]

Wellstone remained dogged in the face of these obstacles. He repeatedly wrote letters to the Veterans' Affairs Department urging them to expand the list of atomic veterans' diseases. He would even show up at technical hearings on the matter to try and advance the cause. He ultimately convinced the Republican-controlled Senate Veterans' Affairs committee to hold an official hearing about atomic veterans on April 21, 1998. His persistent campaigning slowly won over senators on both sides of the aisle, but the administration remained resistant. Finally, in retaliation, Wellstone unleashed a series of public attacks on the Clinton administration's unwillingness to provide benefits to atomic veterans suffering from cancer and other diseases – sending out one news release describing the White House's actions as "indefensible."[12] His willingness to criticize his fellow Democrat in the White House gave Wellstone credibility with his Republican colleagues, and helped win their support for a Senate resolution calling on the administration to expand coverage for atomic veterans. Despite everything, the Clinton administration was so reluctant to increase spending, even on veterans, that it refused to meet Wellstone's demands. But his work had had a positive result: by the time Clinton left office, Wellstone had created a very powerful atomic veterans movement – and significantly bolstered the broader veterans' movement as well.

As a result, when the George W. Bush administration came into office, it was presented with a powerful movement of veterans demanding justice. Veterans were a key ingredient of the Bush coalition, and the Bush administration was loath to defy them, even though Republicans were looking to slash domestic government spending more generally. The Bush administration adopted a much more accommodating attitude than Clinton had. As a result, Wellstone publicly and repeatedly lavished praise on Bush's new Veterans' Affairs secretary, Tony Principi – a marked contrast to his frequent denunciations of the Clinton admin-

---

[xii]Some Clinton administration officials had private misgivings about this position. On the same day that he testified to the Veterans' Affairs Committee about the reasons for the administration's opposition to expanding coverage for atomic veterans, Undersecretary of Health Kenneth W. Kizer wrote a memo to then-Veterans Affairs' secretary Togo West urging the Clinton administration to change its position and support Wellstone's legislation.

istration's failures to provide support. At last, his persistent movement-building paid off in a big victory. In 2002, the Bush administration enacted his Justice for Atomic Veterans Bill by administrative fiat and expanded the list of cancers qualifying for veterans' benefits to include lung, colon, bone, brain, central nervous system, and ovarian cancers. It was a huge victory and one that would have been unlikely without Wellstone

By the time of Wellstone's 1996 re-election campaign, The Vietnam Veterans of America, the Paralyzed Veterans of America, the Disabled American Veterans, the National Association of Atomic Veterans, and the Military Order of the Purple Heart had all given Wellstone awards for his service to veterans. Perhaps more tellingly, Wellstone was getting the enthusiastic support of people like Republican atomic veteran Smoky Parrish. Indeed, Parrish was so impressed by Wellstone's fights with and for atomic veterans that he joined the Wellstone campaign in 1996 and helped organize veterans all over the state to support Wellstone. When, during that campaign, Republicans accused Wellstone of hostility to the armed forces and veterans because Wellstone opposed, on free-speech grounds, amending the Constitution to prohibit flag burning, these veterans swung into action to publicly defend Wellstone – boosting his campaign at a critical moment.

Wellstone brought laser-like focus to building a political movement because he saw that on that work hung not only his success or failure in his fights for re-election, but also the success or failure of his vision for a better world. Unlike conventional Democrats, he never saw politics primarily as a contest whose outcome was determined by the more skillful execution of modern political tactics: which team of professional political consultants could more artfully word an advertisement, effectively repackage old policy ideas as new, or nominate a more charismatic candidate. Instead, he saw politics as the titanic clash of the world's great political movements, where the outcome was determined by the relative strength of those movements. Which side had more people and more passion? Which side had more money? Which side had the force of right on its side? *Which side had more power?* If he wanted to create what he always referred to as a "better Earth on Earth," he needed to shift that balance in his favor.

Confrontation Pays Off

In early 1992, Wellstone put his aggressive style – and the strength of his growing movement – to the ultimate test in a showdown with party leaders. Republicans and Democrats had agreed on a $25 billion taxpayer bailout for corrupt Savings and Loans institutions. Many taxpayer watchdogs opposed the bailout because it rewarded corporate malfeasance. But the powerful banking industry argued that it was necessary to avoid a crisis of confidence in America's financial system – and had convinced a majority of senators to support it. Few senators, however, wanted to go on record giving away such a large amount of taxpayer money to the savings and loans operators responsible for the crisis, so they agreed to pass the bill by anonymous voice vote. Wellstone, however, felt on principle that senators should be forced to go on record so that voters could hold them accountable. When Democratic Majority Leader George Mitchell motioned for a voice vote, Wellstone defied Senate protocol and objected to his own leader. The Democratic reaction was instantaneous. His fellow Democrats physically surrounded him and cajoled, threatened, and even insulted him in an attempt to get him to give in and let them off the hook. "What makes you so self-righteous," one asked; "Who do you think you are?" "If you make us vote on this, I'm not going to forget." Wellstone didn't flinch. He insisted on the vote – and got it. The next morning, Wellstone received a phone call from Florida Republican Connie Mack. "We were watching you from our side of the aisle," Mack told Wellstone. "We saw them beating up on you and were wondering if you would break. You didn't, and it took a lot of guts!"[13]

With this taste of success, Wellstone was emboldened to push the confrontation envelope even further. In June, 1992, a series of tornadoes leveled towns throughout central Minnesota and the notoriously slow Bush administration disaster relief bureaucracy failed to guarantee assistance. In response, Wellstone refused to let a high-profile $1 billion bill for the reconstruction of riot-torn Los Angeles proceed until he received promises that Minnesota would get the help it needed for tornado damage. Appropriations Committee Chair Ted Stevens was apoplectic – he was normally irascible, and he'd put a tremendous amount of energy into shepherding the Los Angeles riot relief bill to the floor. He was not about to have it be held up by an ultra-liberal freshman senator from Minnesota. He unleashed his temper on Wellstone on the Senate floor, imploring Wellstone to let the bill go forward: "I am on my feet basically to urge the Senator not to hold up this bill," a phrase that, from Stevens, would normally chill the most stout-hearted of senators. But the Bush administration couldn't afford to have its Los Angeles riot reconstruction bill held up, and within hours sent Wellstone the assurances he sought. Wellstone let the bill go forward. Immediately afterwards, the formerly furious Stevens – notorious for holding grudges – headed straight for Wellstone. "That is exactly what I would have done for Alaska," Stevens said.

"That's the way you get things done around here."[14]

Taking Back Lunch

By this point, Wellstone had regained much of the ground he had lost from his disastrous debut. In addition to his work with veterans, Wellstone had won the passionate support of the environmental movement and the admiration of his colleagues by almost single-handedly taking on powerful members of the Democratic leadership to stop an energy bill that would have handed over billions of dollars in subsidies to polluters. But he wasn't about to coast or focus his work too narrowly. Instead, he chose as his next major fight something guaranteed to deeply annoy nearly every member of the Senate – banning the Washington power lunch.

It was one thing to argue with a senator on energy policy, and quite another to attack the manner in which he lunched. Capitol Hill lunches loomed large in the public imagination in 1992 and 1993. Lobbyists for huge corporations frequently took members of Congress out to fancy feeds at Capitol Hill restaurants like La Colline ("The Hill" in French), picked up the tab, and took advantage of loopholes in congressional regulations to throw in even pricier gifts as well – like golfing, ski, and tennis trips to America's most luxurious resorts. These lobbyists almost never had to disclose any of the gifts. In some ways, these "free martini" lunches had become a symbol for other clearly criminal and unethical abuses happening in Congress at the same time – 269 members of the House of Representatives had improperly overdrawn their bank accounts, others were kiting checks, or stealing from their campaign accounts. Democratic Ways and Means Chairman Dan Rostenkowski was laundering money and keeping phantom employees on his payroll. A typical January 1992 poll found that 57 percent of Americans had an unfavorable impression of Congress, with only 30 percent approving of the job Congress was doing.[15]

With public pressure for reform so high, this was a major opportunity for Wellstone and his allies to limit the influence of the corporate lobbyists in the way of his progressive agenda. It was rare for progressive public interest organizations to take senators out to lunch or bring them on junkets – sometimes they didn't have the money, sometimes they thought doing so was improper, and sometimes didn't feel they could justify engaging in such a back-door process to their citizen memberships. By limiting the opportunities for corporate schmoozing with members of Congress, Wellstone would level the lunch table. He decided that he would try to shame his fellow Members of Congress into avoiding contact with corporate lobbyists by proposing an amendment requiring that lobbying firms disclose every gift they gave to each Members of Congress – meaning that voters would be able to decide for themselves if, for instance, it was appropriate for Louisiana senator J. Bennett Johnston or others to enjoy $250 lunches with an oil lobbyist at La Colline.

Even some Democratic champions of limiting lobbyist gifts urged Wellstone to drop it – few of them wanted to see their opponents running advertisements with reenactments of their own lunches with industry lobbyists or a list of gifts they'd received from unsavory operators. But Wellstone was insistent, in part because that kind of accountability was precisely what he wanted to encourage – so that his fellow senators would think twice about allowing corporate lobbyists to monopolize their time.

And so, against the private objections of his colleagues, he called for a vote on the amendment and nearly all senators fell into line – unwilling to cast a vote that would allow their opponents to charge that they were keeping gifts from shady lobbyists secret. The measure passed by voice vote. Standing up to the leadership and the corporate lobbyists won Wellstone major national accolades, including an editorial mash note from *The New York Times* that dubbed him "The Wellspring of Lobby Reform." Once again, Wellstone was seen taking on the Washington establishment and winning. For voters disgusted with that establishment, it was instant cred: proof that Wellstone was one of them, and a very effective one at that.

"I'm a Fat White Guy and I Could Feel It"

But when Republicans took over Congress in 1994, opportunities for Wellstone to force through positive changes became much scarcer. Republicans were determined to shut Democrats out of substantive deliberations, and were hell bent on eviscerating the Democratic Party and the progressive movement. Above all, that meant weakening America's labor movement, which showered Democrats with millions of dollars in donations every year and whose campaign door-knocking and calling operations were the only real vestige of the national Democratic Party's grassroots arm. If Republicans could stop workers from joining unions and make it easier to fire already unionized workers, it would be an important step toward their goal of making the Democrats a permanent minority.

For Wellstone, their attacks on worker rights were personal. Long before he became a fixture at Minnesota picket lines, Wellstone was a labor man. Growing up, his mother had worked in the cafeteria at his school in Arlington, Virginia. Wellstone later recalled how other students would make fun of how the cafeteria workers dressed and spoke. He would try to hide the fact that they were making fun of his mom. But as he grew older, he began to take pride in her struggle to earn money for their family. Even as a senator, he would always insist on meeting the cafeteria staff in any school he visited. So when Republicans tried to restrict workers' rights, it wasn't an abstract everyman he was thinking of, it was his own flesh and blood.

No matter the depth of his feeling, defending people like his mother wouldn't be easy. Corporations that had hired scabs and union-busting thugs 60 years before to keep out unions and had failed had discovered a new way to keep out unions and their high-wage jobs: send heavily unionized manufacturing jobs to southern states that restricted workers rights, or abroad to low-wage, often tyrannical countries in Latin America and Asia. As a result, union membership had plummeted nationwide (including in Minnesota) – from a national high of 32.5 percent in 1953 to 16.1 percent in 1991 – with more declines on the way.[xiii] As if these global economic forces weren't strong enough, both the Reagan and Bush I administrations and now the Republican Congress did all they could to stop the government from protecting workers' rights to unionize. Employers started forcing workers to sit through anti-union presentations, and engaging in dirty tricks like giving union leaders extra work or just firing them outright. Workers knew they faced retribution, and, as one organizer told Wellstone, "You have to be a hero to organize your own workplace."[16]

Wellstone wanted to make sure that unions were accessible to everyone, not just heroes. This idea was so important to him that he frequently took time off from his other senatorial duties to visit groups of workers in Minnesota. Usually, he wasn't urging them to support his campaign or even boasting about what he was doing for them in Washington. Instead, he was taking time to talk about why they should join a union. While other senators dialed wealthy donors for dollars, Wellstone phone-banked workers. One on one, he'd tell them how union workers made better wages and had better conditions. Or he'd call employers and urge them to meet union demands or come up with a mutually acceptable compromise – putting himself, his office, and his reputation on the line. That sometimes meant enduring corporate sniping and generous campaign contributions to Wellstone's Republican opponents from powerful corporations.

But it also meant that he became an inspiration to workers across the country. I witnessed one burly union leader break down in tears as he showed me newspaper photos of Wellstone walking the picket line with

---

[xiii]Even as inflation adjusted Gross Domestic Product skyrocketed 32 percent between 1980 and 1991, wages increased only 16 percent during the same period – with the bulk of the increase coming from higher compensation for executives

his union. Through it all, Wellstone was aided by a down-to-earth personality, sincerity, and total lack of affect that appealed to most blue-collar union members who might otherwise have been suspicious of an ultra-liberal former college professor. As longtime steelworker Marty Henry recounted when I met him on the Iron Range in 2005, "When you got hugged by Paul, you knew it – he had that wrestling stuff. I mean, I'm a fat white guy and I could feel it…If he knew you were a steelworker, he knew who you were."[xiv][17]

Wellstone's interactions with the labor movement weren't all sweetness and Joe Sixpack to Joe Senator love. Wellstone knew that successful organizing involved having the courage to confront one's supporters almost as much as confronting one's opponents. Otherwise, it would be impossible to shake them of their apathy. With workers, this was particularly important. They had jobs requiring long hours, families to take care of, had been defeated in previous attempts to organize, were illegal immigrants scared of deportation, or had been betrayed by Democratic politicians who used them to get elected and then forgot about them afterwards. It could add up to a lot of fear, or at least ambivalence. And so when he felt they'd become dispirited or just plain lazy, he'd tell them so – with all the force he could muster, if necessary.

At one point, Wellstone felt steelworkers in northern Minnesota's Iron Range weren't doing enough to protect themselves from increasingly high-cost foreign competition. And so, during one of his frequent visits there, Wellstone gathered a group of steelworkers into a room. Then, he started pounding on the table and yelling, "Get off your asses and organize!" His exhortations had the intended effect. When he left, one of the steelworkers asked the others, "Are we so stupid that he has to come here and holler at us?" – they knew that they were not and immediately came up with an action plan.[18] "No politician ever talked to us like that before," said another steelworker. Because of interactions like these, rank and file union members often gave Wellstone more support than union leadership. That support gave Wellstone the courage to push aggressive legislation like his "Right to Organize Act," which proposed tripling penalties for labor law violations and allowing union organizers onto company premises, even though the bill went beyond what even the AFL-CIO was proposing.[19]

Wellstone's work with union members paid big dividends in his election campaigns. Even during his first Senate campaign, when many labor leaders were reluctant to endorse a long-shot leftist college professor, Wellstone could count on the fervent support of rank and file union members across the state. They

---

[xiv]In truth, Marty, while solid, is hardly obese.

helped him win at the state Democratic convention, in the Democratic primary, and enthusiastically volunteered for time-intensive field operations. Their support also gave him room to maneuver when Republicans tried to cut into Wellstone's labor base by using wedge issues that would divide them.

The Wellstone Movement, Confronted

Willingness to use confrontation was a relatively rare quality on the Democratic side, but it was far from unusual among Republicans – and Republicans were far from shy about employing it against Wellstone. They especially chose fights that would peel away working class and lower-middle class socially conservative voters. Republicans picked fights on abortion, guns, gays, environmental issues, President Clinton's private life, and other targets of opportunity with an impressive creativity – and frequent success. Indeed, they were able to pick some fights that put Wellstone's courage to the test – and caused even some of his strongest supporters to question it. As Wellstone's campaign for re-election in 1996 approached, Republicans took their pugnacity to a level that topped even their own past excesses. And they had a willing attacker in former Senator Rudy Boschwitz, who remained bitter over his loss to Wellstone in 1990 and was eager for a rematch.

One of the first big fights Boschwitz and the Republicans picked was welfare. It was a logical choice: at this moment in American political history, welfare recipients were an easy political target. An April 2, 1995 *Minneapolis Star-Tribune* poll found that more Minnesotans – 57 percent – blamed welfare recipients for the country's problems than any other group (trailed by immigrants at 49 percent, religious extremists at 45 percent, liberals at 33 percent, and gays and lesbians at 32 percent)[20] – even though welfare accounted for less than one percent of the federal budget. It was a powerful emotional issue with the ability to divide the Democratic coalition. Many working and middle class voters resented the idea that even a little of their hard-earned tax-dollars were going to people who weren't doing any work – even if the actual picture of an average welfare recipient was a single mom who needed welfare support to help feed and clothe her children.

Despite welfare's unpopularity, Wellstone was one of its biggest champions. In the early 1970's, he had spent more than a year working with single mothers on welfare in Rice County, Minnesota, where he was a professor at Carleton College, and had even written a book about his experiences, *How the Rural Poor Got Power*. He was unapologetic about championing society's most vulnerable members.[21]

Conventional wisdom said that Wellstone's support for welfare would be an albatross around his neck. Not only were the overwhelming majority of

Minnesotans in favor of draconian welfare reform, but the Democratic president was hardly offering much defense of traditional welfare programs. President Clinton had come into office promising to "end welfare as we know it" by imposing time limits on welfare recipients. Although he had vetoed two earlier Republican attempts at gutting welfare, he certainly wasn't providing any rhetorical covering fire for Wellstone's defense of traditional welfare.

In the spring of 1996, Republicans in Congress decided to put President Clinton's promise to "end welfare as we know it" to a final test. They once again passed a welfare bill, but this time dropped many of the harshest provisions, though they still included major cuts. Clinton wasn't the only target: Boschwitz took to calling Wellstone "Senator Welfare." His campaign even put up billboards outside Wellstone's office featuring "Welfare Man" – a caricature of a welfare lout with a cartoon superhero cape and tights. Just to make sure Minnesotans got the message, the Republicans ran an ad statewide saying that Wellstone had voted to massively increase welfare spending.[22] Boschwitz's effort to take advantage of Wellstone's support for welfare was part of a national Republican effort to do the same to other Democrats facing re-election. And it worked. One by one, all Democrats facing re-election announced their support for the Republican welfare overhaul.

But Wellstone was not intimidated – and was not swayed by the minor revisions to the welfare bill. He told a reporter, "You could stick a gun to my head, and I'm not going to vote for a bill that will hurt children."[23] He spoke out repeatedly against the bill – culminating in an appeal to the Senate Democratic caucus – but in the political climate, it fell on deaf ears. The Senate passed the bill 78-21, and President Clinton signed it. Republicans pounced. "He's way to the left of President Clinton on this," Boschwitz campaign spokesman Josh Ullyot said of Wellstone immediately after the vote.[24]

Wellstone didn't shy from the issue for the rest of the campaign. He even publicly criticized President Clinton at the Democratic National Convention for signing the welfare bill. And a funny thing happened. Instead of having his support collapse after casting a very unpopular vote, his support rose. In the wake of the debate, Wellstone started getting "strong leader" ratings in the high 50's. Even his approval rating among conservatives jumped eight points after the vote to 41 percent.[25]

A Radical's Compromises

Many of the socially conservative voters that Republicans were targeting through initiatives like welfare reform lived in Northern Minnesota's Iron Range

– a heavily unionized area dependent on iron mining. It's a special place – the Range borders the Boundary Waters Canoe Area Wilderness in Minnesota – one of the only areas in the entire country where it's possible to go canoeing and enjoy wilderness without having the experience spoiled by motorboats. But many Northern Minnesota residents, including many union members, *liked* bringing their motorboats into the backcountry. For some hard-working steel-workers, the liberty to do what they wanted in the great outdoors was about the only freedom they felt they had in lives that often seemed totally at the mercy of global economic forces, heartless corporate executives, and the ever-present chance of a dangerous accident in the mines or at the furnace. So Wellstone's pro-environment record and willingness to consider restrictions on motorboats was a potential liability for him in this otherwise Democratic area.

Republicans attempted to capitalize on the issue by convincing some Iron Rangers to put up signs with the initials of the Boundary Waters Canoe Area – BWCA – all around the region, with the phrase "Beat Wellstone Come Autumn" written in smaller letters below it. When Wellstone toured the region on campaign swings, campaign officials would sometimes get warnings that hostile Republicans would try to disrupt their appearances. The tension reached its highest level on one Wellstone visit to an iron mine in Virginia, Minnesota. There were rumors of violent threats to Wellstone. When Wellstone arrived at the mine, a group of anti-Boundary Waters workers who had climbed to the roof of the plant unfurled a giant banner emblazoned with the "Beat Wellstone Come Autumn" slogan. Even one of the most virulent of his opponents, miner James R. Maki, told me later that, "I thought it was rather courageous of him coming in there." [26]

Despite his courage in confronting his opponents at the mine, Wellstone largely sidestepped the issue. Instead of taking a firm stand, he proposed setting up a joint commission that would attempt to forge an agreement between environmentalists, motorboat users, and other key stakeholders – after the election. His plan was accepted and the commission was created – but was in the end unable to reach any agreement. It did, however, take a divisive issue off the table from Republican attacks.

The episode can be seen as an example of Wellstone's belief that compromise, or even capitulation, was sometimes necessary in politics. Early in his career, Wellstone had reached that conclusion when he became involved in a famous strike at the Hormel meat packing plant in Austin, Minnesota. It became clear that the company was going to bring in outside workers and break the strike if the two sides didn't cut a deal soon. Wellstone urged the union to come to an agreement with management rather than risk the loss of their jobs. They didn't listen to his advice, the company got the governor to send in the National Guard, and hundreds of workers found themselves unemployed. In his autobiography, Wellstone wrote about the necessity of compromise by retelling a story about Senator Estes Kefauver:

> Myles Horton, founder of the Highlander Folk School and one of our country's great radicals… and some coal miners were meeting with their senator from Tennessee, the great progressive Estes Kefauver. They insisted he support a strong labor bill. He listened and then said, "I'll vote for this, but I want you to know that it is my honest judgment as a politician that if I support this I won't be reelected. If I am not reelected I can't do many of the things I can do for you. But if you want me to vote this way I'll do so. So given what I just said to you, tell me what you want me to do." Myles said they all told him to vote against the labor bill![27]

For Wellstone the politician, compromise was sometimes required, but he wasn't about to make a habit of it!

Victory, the Wellstone Way

More typically, of course, Wellstone was one of the few national Democratic politicians willing to stand up to Republicans, big corporations, or whomever he thought was standing in the way of the better world he sought to create.

Despite all his colleagues' predictions that his courageous stands would backfire – that he'd turn off socially conservative voters, that he wouldn't be able to raise any money because he'd defied corporate lobbies, that he didn't present a good image by not going along to get along, Wellstone actually entered the final stage of his re-election in 1996 in excellent position. Not only did he have great name recognition, concrete legislative accomplishments, and a record of good constituent services – he also had a lot of money. By being one of the few, if not the only, members of the Senate willing to both articulate progressive values and, more importantly, fight hard for them, Wellstone had developed a national following among progressives. He received big, direct contributions from labor unions, environmental groups, and human rights organizations, as well as thousands of small contributions from progressives all over the country thirsty for a courageous champion.[xv][28] By the end of his cam-

---

[xv]These donations only include those over $200. Smaller contributions are not required to be reported to the FEC.

paign, he'd raised $7.5 million, more than five times what he'd raised in 1990. This time around, he even out-fundraised Boschwitz.[xvi] The election proved that fighting corporate America was at least as much of a cash cow as kissing up to it.

Wellstone's fights didn't just bring him cash. His energetic combat with Republicans and big corporations had given him an awesome army of enthusiasts on the ground that even the richest, most powerful corporation couldn't deliver – no matter how much one kissed up to their executives. His army was made up of people who found in Wellstone for the first time a progressive politician who articulated their values, fought for them in the Senate, and very likely had recruited them to get involved in politics in the first place.

In a sense, Wellstone acted as his own field director. Though he had one of the best – perhaps the best – voter organizing and turnout efforts in the country, he never relied primarily on that machine. Because his actions as a senator and his words as an advocate excited thousands of potential volunteers – and rarely left them feeling betrayed – he drew thousands of people to his movement before his talented political organizers ever made one phone call. And when they did start calling, emailing, and canvassing to recruit people, it was a comparatively easy pitch. It didn't take a lot of charm or rhetorical dexterity to convince the people that formed Wellstone's potential volunteer pool that Wellstone was fighting for them and would continue to do so if reelected. They'd been hearing and reading about his fights in the newspaper, from their friends, and from the organizations they belonged to for years. Because these volunteers' enthusiasm was so real, it was also infectious – people talked up his candidacy to their friends, colleagues, neighbors, members of their religious congregations, clubs, and others.

These powerful social networks gave Wellstone a critical edge – by the time of Wellstone's second run for the Senate in 1996, television advertising was already losing its power of persuasion, in a process that would accelerate rapidly with increased use of the Internet over the next six years. People felt bombarded with marketing messages on television, on the radio, in print, at the supermarket, on the highway, and even in church – and increasingly tuned it out. It meant that people turned more and more for advice to the friends and neighbors they trusted – believing their friends' opinions more than 150 percent more than advertising in studies of influence.[29] To some extent, this social networking also inoculated the electorate against the barrage of attack advertising the Republi-

---

[xvi]Boschwitz's campaign, however, probably had higher overall *spending* – it was aided by a $1.5 million advertising campaign by the Republican National Senate Committee and other large independent expenditures; Democrats and Democratic-leaning groups also made heavy independent expenditures, but they were estimated to be far smaller than the Republican ones.

cans unleashed on Wellstone. If a friend, or even a neighbor, was vouching for Wellstone, voters were a lot less likely to believe even the most insipid attack ad.

As a result, although Boschwitz and Wellstone were about even in public opinion polls going into Election Day, Boschwitz knew that Wellstone's political movement would bring a much higher percentage of his supporters to the polls – and that Boschwitz needed a major knock-out punch to overcome this disadvantage. On the Friday before Election Day, Boschwitz invited an Iron Range Veterans of Foreign Wars local Commander, Bob Niskala, to join him at a news conference and accuse Wellstone of burning a flag. But when reporters pressed Niskala to offer evidence to back up his accusation, Niskala couldn't provide any, nor even a specific time and date that the event took place, saying finding such evidence "takes too much investigating."[30] Nevertheless, Boschwitz demanded that Wellstone respond to the accusation. Wellstone did – and angrily denied the story. Over the final election weekend, Wellstone supporters in the veterans' community traveled the state of Minnesota to demand an apology. It was no coincidence – it was the product of all of Wellstone's years of organizing the veterans' movement. The Boschwitz campaign's wild charge backfired – and Wellstone won the election by nine percentage points.

A *Minneapolis Star-Tribune* exit poll taken on Election Day demonstrated how Wellstone was able to persuade voters to back him even when they disagreed with him. The poll found that a whopping 81 percent of Minnesota voters either supported the welfare bill that Wellstone had opposed, or believed that the bill *hadn't gone far enough* to cut people off welfare. But Wellstone was still able to win the votes of 59 percent of the people who thought the welfare bill got it right, and even 34 percent of the hard core anti-welfare voters who thought the welfare bill didn't cut welfare enough![31] These voters were either voting on other issues, or valued qualities like courage over any particular issue. It was a classic Wellstone exercise of courage – he had gone against all political wisdom, not yielded to pressure, and found his support surge as a result. It was proof that courage worked.

The Democratic Wing of the Democratic Party

The national stature that Wellstone gained through all his fights – and his impressive margin of victory – allowed him to set his sights even higher than the U.S. Senate. In a private meeting with staff in the last days of the 1996 campaign, he told them, "Let's win this first and then we need to start thinking about a presidential campaign."[32] It was an extraordinary aspiration for someone who, not so long ago, had been sweating through his muscle shirt screaming at corporate lawyers at the top of the Pilsbury Tower.

Soon after his election, Wellstone departed on a national poverty tour, following the route that Robert F. Kennedy had taken on his own poverty tour 30 years earlier. On April 8, 1998, he became the first candidate to formally establish a presidential exploratory committee for the 2000 election. He visited Iowa and New Hampshire on several occasions to make his case for a progressive presidency. On one trip to Iowa, he coined the phrase that would come to capture the spirit of his political philosophy and movement – and endure after him in the presidential campaign of Howard Dean. At a meeting of Johnson County Democrats, Iowa gubernatorial candidate Tom Vilsack shouted out, "Paul, why do you keep coming to Iowa?" and Wellstone responded, "I come to Iowa to represent the Democratic wing of the Democratic Party!" The 300 people in attendance went wild – and Wellstone knew he had a winner.

Indeed, as he traveled around the country and picked up momentum, he was met almost everywhere with an enthusiasm none of the other candidates could generate. In August, 1998, he electrified a meeting of the Iowa AFL-CIO with a rousing attack on the vagaries of unfettered global capitalism, decrying "hard-driving tyrants on the production line," "callous profiteers" and denouncing corporate lobbyists as the "bottom-dwellers of commerce".[33] Despite his success on the campaign trail, he wasn't moving in the polls. In national surveys of Democrats in January, 1999, he remained stuck at one percent. Of course, it didn't matter much so early in the election cycle. There were still almost two years until Election Day and the media hadn't yet launched major coverage of the contenders for the Democratic nomination. Prairie fire candidacies usually took off in the spring. In retrospect, the sudden surge behind Howard Dean's candidacy in 2004 shows that Democratic voters could have gotten behind an unapologetically progressive candidate (or one who, in Dean's case, at least was articulating progressive values despite a more centrist record).

But that was not to be. Wellstone had experienced serious back pain since his days as a college wrestler – and it had been getting worse, forcing him to walk with a pronounced limp. He had had spinal surgery in early 1998, but it hadn't helped. As he traveled around the country, the physical demands of a presidential campaign wore heavier on him. When making long car rides, he was forced to recline the passenger seat and lie on his stomach to alleviate the pain. During plane rides, he walked the aisles introducing himself to his fellow passengers so he wouldn't have to experience the pain of sitting until the cabin crew insisted that he take his seat. Doctors had been unable to diagnose his ailment and when he returned to the Mayo Clinic, they advised him that he could not continue a presidential campaign without seriously jeopardizing his well-being (he was later diagnosed with multiple sclerosis). So, on January 9, Wellstone withdrew from the race just as it was about to intensify.[xvii]

When the 2000 election concluded, it was time for Wellstone to remobilize his forces for his own 2002 senatorial re-election campaign. But there was a problem – the day *after* he had been elected in 1990 he had pledged to serve for only two terms and then return to teaching. Running again would require breaking this promise – and defying the 53 percent of voters who said in a January *Star Tribune* poll that he had a moral obligation to keep it. But Wellstone decided that with the Senate equally divided between Democrats and Republicans, and George Bush poised to sign right-wing legislation passed by a right-wing Congress, there was too much at stake in Washington, and no Democrat poised to take up his role as the Senate leader of the progressive movement. "Now is not the time to walk away from this fight," Wellstone said. His switch jeopardized his reputation for absolute integrity – one of the primary qualities that had allowed him to overcome Minnesotans' disagreements on policy with him. Republicans were quick to point it out. "His greatest strength was that even if you disagreed with him, you respected his integrity, and this undercuts his integrity," said former St. Paul Mayor Norm Coleman, who was contemplating running against Wellstone. "Now not only can you disagree with him, but you can question his integrity."[34] Later on in the campaign, Coleman would transform this criticism into a catch phrase: "The Paul Wellstone of 1990 wouldn't have voted for the Paul Wellstone of 2002."

Final Courage

There had been one other big change from Wellstone's two previous election bids – September 11. Wellstone had entered office as the Cold War was ending,

---

[xvii]Even if Wellstone himself couldn't be president, he still wanted to have a hand in the campaign – and endorsed former New Jersey senator Bill Bradley in his primary challenge against Gore. Wellstone made a return trip to Iowa for Bradley, but it had some unintended consequences. Wherever the two went together, Wellstone would appear first and whip the crowd into a frenzy with his passionate populism. Then the lugubrious Bradley would come on stage with a far more modulated message and suck the life out of the room. At every appearance, people would come up to Wellstone afterwards and tell him that they wished it was he who was running instead of Bradley – giving Wellstone a sense of what might have been.

and had served as senator in a time of relative peace. His opposition to excessive defense spending had been seen largely as an example of his willingness to stand up to another big, wasteful corporate lobby – the defense industry. But with America at war, Wellstone fell under the attack that he had put his "peace ideology" before the safety of the American people. At the very least, the war climate made it extremely difficult for Wellstone to focus on the bread and butter economic and social issues like Social Security, health care, and the environment, with which he was more comfortable. Indeed, all the media – and many Minnesotans – seemed to be interested in was whether or not he would vote to give President George W. Bush the authority to unilaterally invade Iraq.

Bush wanted war. With his national approval rating at 64 percent, this was the time to force the issue.[35] After the election, Senate Democrats might be more inclined to vote their consciences rather than on the basis of what polls were telling them was the pro-war mood of the country. But Bush knew few Democrats facing re-election would have the gumption to defy him on a national security issue just a year after September 11. And if any rebellious Democrats *did* defy Bush, that just might turn a pro-Bush, security-obsessed electorate against them. That would put the Republicans that much closer to picking up the one Senate seat they needed to retake control of the Senate.

Bush wasn't afraid to put his star power to the test. He flew around the country to speak at rallies and fundraisers in key congressional campaigns, in hopes that Republican candidates would share in his reflected light – and that he could inspire the Republican base to put pressure on their representatives to vote for the war, and aimed some of his fire at Wellstone. By autumn, the president had already visited Minnesota for a speech in which he attacked nameless senators who had voted for defense cuts, and was promising two more visits in the weeks before Election Day.

For his part, Norm Coleman, Wellstone's now official Senate opponent, was doing everything he could to capitalize on the pro-war mood. In September, he launched a "national defense tour"[36] and traveled around the state attacking Wellstone as an out-of-touch 60's radical whose ideals – and his past votes against military weapons contracts – were costing American lives. The tour culminated at a September 19 event in Minneapolis where the Coleman campaign rolled out retired Air Force Reserve Brigadier General Denny Schulstad, who described Wellstone as "among the worst enemies of America's defense" for voting against military spending programs, like the $2 billion-a-plane B2 Bomber, which had previously been considered a symbol of defense contractor greed.[37]

To make sure Minnesotans got the message – and heard it over and over again – the Republicans released a new attack ad on September 30 blasting Wellstone for endorsing cuts for weapons systems and accusing him of voting against "pay raises for our soldiers 13 times and against health benefits for our veterans." The ad concluded, "If he's not fighting for them, ask Wellstone, who *are* you fighting for?"[38] The war campaign wasn't just confined to television or the media – it had real popularity. Across Minnesota, "Liberate Iraq" yard signs were popping up, vying with the peace signs that usually dominated. A September 1 *Minneapolis Star-Tribune* poll found that 54 percent of Minnesotans supported the war (with only 32 percent opposing), before the administration had begun its major push for war – a number that had increased to 63 percent support in Fox News election poll.[39]

Even Wellstone Senate allies were on the war path. All month, Connecticut Democratic Senator Joe Lieberman (with whom Wellstone had recently led the successful effort to stop oil drilling in the Arctic National Wildlife Refuge in Alaska) hit the cable news circuit to bang the war drums for Bush. "Every day Saddam remains in power is a day of danger," he told a news conference on September 19.[40] Having just been the Democrats' vice presidential candidate, Lieberman was still considered a respected Democratic Party leader and not the apostate he would become. The media replayed Lieberman's words over and over again as evidence that the war had strong bipartisan support. There *were* a few prominent voices urging peace or caution – but what voices there were had a hard time getting equal play in the media. Three Democratic senators not facing re-election – West Virginia's Robert Byrd, Massachusetts's Ted Kennedy, and Wisconsin's Russ Feingold – were as close to a peace caucus as Democratic senators came, but even their opposition was tempered by moderating clauses, tributes to what they saw as Bush's good intentions, uncertainty, and their general acceptance of the idea that Iraq was a menace and that unilateral action might at some point become warranted.[xviii] On balance, the climate in Washington, around the country, and in Minnesota swirled in a maelstrom of war fever.

The rising pressure was too much for most of Wellstone's fellow Democrats. Even those who had major doubts about giving Bush such unrestricted authority fell one-by-one into the pro-war column. Early on, presidential hopeful North

---

xviiiThe right-wing media machine attacked even these comparatively tepid opponents with a vitriol that exceeded even their own acerbic norms. Fox News host Sean Hannity took to calling the 84 year-old Byrd "KKK Byrd," a reference to Byrd's brief and shameful association with the Ku Klux Klan in the late 1940's, something Byrd had repeatedly apologized for and distanced himself from, and that, in any event, was irrelevant to his stance on the prospect of war in Iraq in 2002.

Carolina Senator John Edwards argued for an Iraqi invasion on the floor of the Senate, raising the specter of Hussein arming terrorists to bolster his case (Edwards would go on to repudiate his vote following the 2004 election).[41] Even liberal senator Tom Harkin – Wellstone's best friend in the Senate – a veteran Navy pilot who had, in 1969, first become prominent for publishing pictures in *Life* magazine of South Vietnamese political prisoners being tortured by the U.S.-backed regime – was silent.

On the morning of October 2, it became clear that the Democratic Party leadership would line up behind Bush as well. House Democratic Leader (and presidential hopeful) Richard Gephardt joined other Democrats and Bush in the Rose Garden at the White House to endorse formal language giving Bush the authority to unilaterally invade Iraq. Gephardt and others supporting this resolution were clear – they were willing to put their trust in George W. Bush's willingness not to cash the blank check Congress was giving him.

Now, it was Wellstone's turn to decide. It wouldn't be an automatic choice. Not only did he face a rising tide of pro-war political pressure, he was genuinely torn about the decision. Despite his opponents' characterizations of him as a reflexive pacifist, Wellstone understood that force was sometimes necessary to stop great crimes and great criminals like Saddam Hussein. This was a man, after all, who had used chemical weapons against his own people, bulldozed 40,000 Kurdish villages, committed one of the great environmental and human crimes of the 20th century by draining the Everglades-size marshes of southern Iraq, had invaded Kuwait, launched the Iran-Iraq war, and was even now giving $10,000 cash rewards to the families of Palestinian suicide bombers in Israel. As the son of Jewish immigrants, Wellstone had learned the lesson of the Holocaust at an early age – that if democracies fail to stand with resolve – and force – against tyrants who would persecute minorities and rob people of their human rights, genocide could be the result. The post-Holocaust Jewish cry, "Never Again!" became his own. Even in 1990, when Wellstone had so outspokenly opposed the first Persian Gulf War, he had made clear repeatedly that he was willing to entertain the use of military force – but only if economic sanctions on Iraq were given more time to have effect. In 1998, he had supported the Iraqi Liberation Act, which stated that the policy of the United States was to overthrow the Saddam regime, and authorized the Pentagon to give military training and up to $97 million worth of arms to anti-Saddam rebel groups. Wellstone had also been one of the earliest advocates of using U.S. military strength – unilaterally if necessary – to stop Serb dictator Slobodan Milosevic's genocidal attacks against Croats, Bosnian Muslims, and Kosovars in the former Yugoslavia.[42]

But at the same time that Wellstone wanted to challenge Hussein, he also wanted to avert war: his political life had begun in the crucible of anti-Vietnam War protest, and he had never lost his love of peace nor his suspicion of American military adventures overseas. He also wanted to make sure that America stayed focused on stopping future terrorist attacks. Perhaps most of all, Wellstone didn't entirely trust Bush, whom he thought had improperly pressed his political advantage from the September 11 attacks. How could he trust that Bush – who had already withdrawn America from the Kyoto Protocol to stop global warming, the anti-ballistic missile treaty, and who showed contempt for the United Nations – would sincerely work to win international cooperation in any invasion and occupation of Iraq?

To aid in his decision, Wellstone drew on all resources available to him as a U.S. Senator and member of the Senate Foreign Relations Committee. He warned them to leave political considerations out of the equation: on an issue of war and peace involving so many lives, he was determined to do the right thing regardless of the political consequences. His staff did their job. Chief of Staff Colin McGinnis brought in working level officials from the CIA and super-secret Defense Intelligence Agency to brief Wellstone on the threat from weapons of mass destruction. The picture they painted was a very different one from that being reported in most mainstream media and hyped every day by President Bush – rather than reporting that Hussein's "weapons of mass destruction" were what CIA Director George Tenet would later characterize as a "slam-dunk," they presented a far more ambiguous picture. They reported that it was unclear to what extent Hussein had either attempted to or was able to develop weapons of mass destruction after U.N. weapons inspections had concluded in 1998.[43]

Despite Wellstone's instructions to leave politics out of the decision, they inevitably reared their head. On September 16, campaign manager Jeff Blodgett received an email from a senior Democratic Senatorial Campaign Committee staffer implying that if Wellstone voted against the war resolution, it could impact the DSCC's willingness to give Wellstone the financial resources he needed to win. It "makes me almost physically ill to even contemplate our spending 9m [$9 million] on a candidate who decides to commit [political] suicide [by voting against the Iraq war] -- however principled and otherwise defensible," the official wrote.[44] Despite anti-war students staging sit-ins at his St. Paul office, and the rise of a Green Party challenger, the crescendoing support for the war made Wellstone believe that voting against the war would cost him his Senate seat. But when decision time came, he followed his own instructions and kept politics out of it.

At the end of the day, he decided that he just couldn't trust Bush with war making authority when Bush's own officials didn't back the administration's pro-war claims. Without evidence of a grave threat from Iraq – or real international backing for the effort to overthrow the Saddam regime – America needed to focus on winning the war against Islamic fundamentalist terror. He asked himself if he would be willing to send his own three children to war against Iraq under Bush's command – and the answer was no. Though Wellstone had made his decision, it didn't mean he rested easy. Shortly afterwards, Wellstone told Chief of Staff Colin McGinnis that he worried his anti-war vote would make him lose the election – and worried about what would happen to his staff who would lose their jobs. McGinnis replied, "But Paul, this is why people came to work for you – because you're willing to be a stand-up guy."[45] Wellstone banged on the table, yelled "That's Right!" and left the room. "I don't think he ever looked back," McGinnis said later about the talk.[46]

And so, on October 3, just one day after Democratic leader Gephardt appeared in the Rose Garden to announce his support of the war, Wellstone appeared on the Senate floor to announce that he would oppose giving Bush the authority he sought to start a war with Iraq. Just like the pre-election welfare vote of 1996, Wellstone was the only Democrat running for re-election who voted against the resolution – again defying the advice and predictions of the financiers, the pundits, and even many of his closest advisors. "I was asked this morning if this would hurt me politically," he told the *Los Angeles Times* in one interview. "I don't have any idea. But what would hurt me for sure would be to utter words on the floor of the Senate that I don't believe or to vote for something I am against, especially on a question of life and death."[47]

Wellstone's announcement was big news. But so was the Republican reaction. Norm Coleman flew to Washington and called a press conference outside the Senate to denounce Wellstone's action. "Senator Wellstone is simply wrong, simply wrong, when he refuses to join in a broad bipartisan effort to stand with the president of the United States to determine how to best deal with that threat," he said. The Coleman campaign kept pounding that message on the stump and on the airwaves. The only thing Wellstone could do now was campaign hard and hope that Minnesotans would support his lonely stand, or at least support him in spite of it.

His hope was fulfilled. In the wake of his vote, Wellstone began a dramatic upswing in the polls, just as his welfare vote had propelled him upward in 1996. Before the vote, the September 21 MSNBC-Zogby poll showed Wellstone down six points in the polls at 41 percent to 47 percent. But in the next poll, Wellstone had shot ahead to gain a nine point lead over Coleman 46-37. Wellstone's internal tracking polls also showed him with a six point lead – 44 to 38, up from a 46-43 advantage in August. Minnesotans had decided that this was indeed the Wellstone they had come to love – the one who would do what he thought was right no matter the political calculus.

These were to be the last polls in the race. Wellstone and Coleman had a final debate in St. Cloud on October 21. President Bush was planning on making two visits to Minnesota before the election to energize the Republican base; Wellstone's legendary grassroots operation was drawing an increasing number of get-out-the-vote volunteers, fired up by the closeness of the race, the national stakes, and Wellstone's stand against the Iraq war. On October 25, Wellstone, his wife Sheila, daughter Marcia and campaign aide Tom Lapic took off from St. Paul to travel to northern Minnesota for the funeral of the father of Wellstone supporter State Representative Tommy Rukavina. They would never make it. About two miles from the airport, the Wellstones' small plane suddenly crashed into a boggy forest, killing everyone on board. Across the country, Democrats, progressives, and Americans of all stripes mourned the loss of one of the most courageous senators in history.

But life, and politics, inevitably continued. In the wake of the crash, former Vice President and Minnesota senator Walter Mondale took Wellstone's spot on the ballot and appeared headed for a solid victory over Coleman. Mondale led Coleman 52-39 in internal polls in the days after the crash. Both Republicans and Democrats assumed that Mondale would coast to victory on a tide of sympathy and nostalgia for Wellstone and respect and affection for Mondale, Minnesota's widely beloved senior statesman. But then a second disaster struck the Democrats – highlighting the perils of Wellstone-style decentralized grassroots politics in an era when every misstep of every follower, no matter how humble, could be transformed into a major scandal through the power of the media.

At an October 29 public memorial service for Wellstone, the crowd of 20,000 grieving Wellstone partisans turned what had been planned as a solemn event into a raucous political rally. The crowd booed Republican politicians like Trent Lott as they entered the arena, while giving Democrats rousing greetings. The event got totally out of control when Wellstone's grief-stricken best friend, Rick Kahn, turned his already partisan eulogy into a bizarre appeal to Republicans to end their campaign and back Mondale. Then, Wellstone's son Mark, who had largely avoided politics despite his father's avocation, led the crowd in a chant of "We Will Win!" This was red meat to the crowd of bereaved Democratic activists who had come to honor their hero – and they went wild. But outside of the arena, on television, where it mattered, many Minnesotans reacted with anger to what they perceived as Democratic efforts to exploit Wellstone's death for political gain. Angry viewers flooded television stations, Republican head-quarters, and the Coleman campaign offices with irate calls about the rally. They lined up the next day around the block at Coleman headquarters in St. Paul to volunteer – giving the previously anemic Coleman grassroots operation a sud-den boost and infusing Coleman himself with a new energy. In the week and a half leading up to Election Day, Minnesota's television stations played Kahn's grieving partisan rant over and over again. Despite a vigorous campaign from Mondale, voters punished him for what they saw as his party's trampling on the "Minnesota nice" tradition of civil, respectful politics. Coleman squeaked out a dramatic come-from-behind victory, winning by two percentage points – and giving Wellstone's political legacy an unlikely Republican coda.

We'll never know definitively who would have won, but it's likely that though Coleman would have benefited from the general Republican surge in the final days of the 2002 campaign, the combination of Wellstone's lead going into the weekend, and his superior turnout operation, would have won Wellstone a very narrow victory.

Legacy of Courage

Despite his loss, Wellstone's legacy didn't end with his name pasted on a cou-ple of schools, a highway, or even an aircraft carrier (though Minnesota now boasts two Paul Wellstone schools, the Paul and Sheila Wellstone Community Building Center, a Sheila Wellstone Center for domestic violence prevention, and there are four Wellstone Muscular Dystrophy Centers around the country, as well as numerous awards named in Wellstone's memory). His primary legacy won't even be the legislation he passed – or blocked. Many of the courageous stands he is remembered for – and which are recorded here – were part of losing battles, ones which he never really had a shot at winning. It was Wellstone's fate to live in an era in which the right-wing was ascendant and most progressives were consumed by a near-paralyzing fear of their opponents and even of their own constituencies. There were limits to what he – or anyone in his lonely position – could accomplish.

But Wellstone left behind something more powerful than an aircraft carrier – the seeds of a nationwide, progressive political movement infused with his courage. At its epicenter is Wellstone Action, an organization run by former Wellstone staff and led by Jeff Blodgett, Wellstone's three-time campaign manager. The organization runs "Camp Wellstone" trainings all over the country, teaching progressives how to win as candidates, how to be effective political organizers, and how to make as big an impact as possible as citizen activists. So far, the organization has trained more than 10,000 people in Wellstone-style politics and movement-building. Like many other training programs, the camps train attendees in specific tactical skills like fundraising and public speaking. But they also teach two extremely rare lessons from Wellstone's legacy. The first is that winning elections is not just a battle of media, money, and mobilizing activists; it's the product of the strength of a political movement. Campaigning for political office, while extremely important in its own right, is largely a vehicle for getting people involved in political movements. When powerful enough, those progressive movements can win election after election and change the laws that mold society. This can be a hard lesson to swallow: many future candidates go into the trainings thinking that campaigns are primarily battles between the individuals on the ballot, and they come to the camp to make themselves better candidates. However, at Camp Wellstone, the candidates are told that they are representatives of their movements and not vice versa, and repeat the line "It's not about me," over and over. The other lesson is the importance of confrontation. Camp attendees learn how to become progressive warriors who can do battle with Republicans and confront their own supporters to inspire them to act as well. There's even a book – *Politics the Wellstone Way* – compiled by Wellstone Action Communications Director (and Wellstone biographer) Bill Lofy which gives a nuts and bolts guide to running and winning campaigns and building social movements. And it works – so far, more than 200 Camp Wellstone graduates have won political office.[48]

"I wondered about this man"

After Election Day 2002, 45 senators eulogized Paul Wellstone on the floor of the Senate. Among them was West Virginia's Robert Byrd, who was first elected senator in 1958, and who served as Democratic leader for 12 years. In his speech, Byrd recalled the fateful Memorial Service:

> I was at that dread gathering. I was struck by the size of that tremendous gathering of people singing songs, speaking. **I wondered about this man, what kind of hold he must have had on the hearts of the**

people of Minnesota to draw a huge audience like that in a memorial service.[49]

To an average Washington Democrat, the strength of the Wellstone movement *was* a wonder. Though Wellstone had touched many with his quixotic charm, his empathy, and his down-to-earth style, in many ways he was the opposite of what Democratic conventional wisdom said should be successful: he was short, ultra-progressive, acted largely without regard to polls. On television – and in person – he often appeared crazed, overly polite, or just plain awkward. And while he had passed some important pieces of legislation, it wasn't like there was a truly major bill with his name on it that had had transformed American society. Most of his accomplishments were achievements of obstruction – requiring him to do things that might seem destructive rather than constructive: holding up popular bills for pet issues, threatening to shut down the Senate, being impolite and negative. He would outrage his fellow senators with his tactics. Even when he did block a particularly odious bill, Republicans would try and try again – and often figure out a way around him.

And yet – here they were: 20,000 people so inspired by Wellstone that they could forget themselves and turn a somber memorial into a political rally. And here are tens of thousands of Americans coming to Camp Wellstone trainings and learning how to build a progressive movement – and going out and organizing their communities or running for public office. Here are Democratic presidential candidates competing to claim the Wellstone mantle of representing the "Democratic wing of the Democratic party." It is the kind of legacy that very few, if any, U.S. Senators have ever left. But it's the kind of legacy that could be just the beginning as more Democrats and progressives become more like Paul Wellstone.

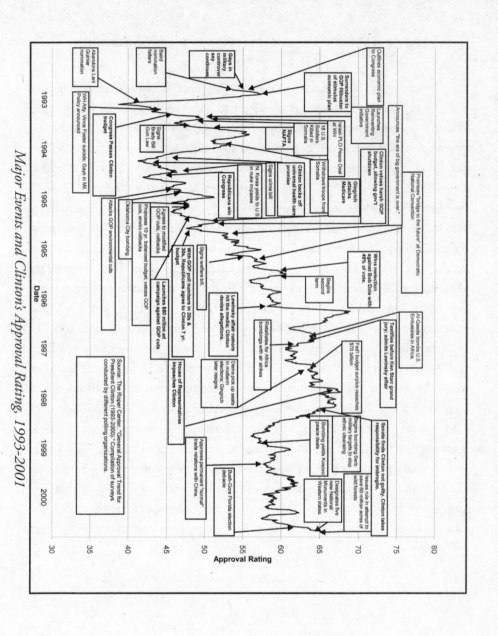

Major Events and Clinton's Approval Rating, 1993–2001

BILL CLINTON:
GUTLESS WONDER

★★★★

W hen Bill Clinton entered office in January, 1993, the Democratic Party was at the zenith of its power. It held a whopping 82 seat majority in the House of Representatives and controlled a 57-43 majority in the Senate. For the first time since Jimmy Carter, there was a Democrat in the White House. The progressive movement was filled with hope and enthusiasm about the new, young president. Clinton had won on a largely progressive agenda – emphasizing his promises to fight for universal health care, environmental protection, a woman's right to choose an abortion, and increased taxes on the ultra-rich. To be sure, Clinton always pitched himself as a "New Democrat" and promised to reexamine policies and practices traditionally associated with liberals. He favored overhauling welfare (while spending more money on it), supported the death penalty, free trade, putting more cops on the street, and "Reinventing Government" by making it more efficient.

Clinton's tremendous personal charm and the hope he represented for a new era in government excited not just progressives, but the vast majority of the country. But along with that charm came a character flaw far more consequential than his proclivity for young interns: his paralyzing fear of confrontation. No matter how hard his enemies hit him, and almost no matter how much he intellectually disagreed with what they were trying to do, Clinton was forever trying to reach out and find common ground with the very people who were out to destroy him, his party, and the progressive movement. But reaching out and trying to accommodate people who were impossible to accommodate turned off the very people who he should have cared about: the progressives who had propelled him to power in the first place and who he would need to keep him there and provide the political support to pass the progressive agenda he had campaigned on. As important as what Clinton did politically was what he didn't do: organize a grassroots political movement. His was an elitist politics of television, ads, media, and above all polling and fundraising. It was not a citizen-based politics at all. And so grassroots progressives largely spent the 1990's either working to make Clinton live up to his own progressive promises, or just fuming about it and sitting politics out entirely, instead of actively working to build the Democratic Party together with Clinton.

These disgruntled progressives would only come out of the woodwork when Clinton's Republican opponents did something so extreme (like slashing the federal budget or threatening to impeach him for actions in his private life) that staying out of politics would mean abandoning not just Clinton to Republican extremists, but the entire federal government. Ironically, it was also in these moments that Clinton, despite his fear of confrontation, did his best. As you can see in the chart at the beginning of this chapter, his biggest surges in popularity came not when he was moving closer to the Republicans, but when he was forced to fight them. And it was in those fights that progressives organized themselves in ways that would provide the nucleus for the resistance to the Bush administration and the ultimate Democratic success in taking back Congress 12 years after Clinton helped lose it.

But as soon as the danger was gone, and Clinton started betraying the very people who had saved him, the reason for their mobilization on his behalf vanished. It was not just Clinton who suffered the consequences of his disloyalty. It was in part his betrayals that caused just enough progressives to stay home or vote for Ralph Nader that put George W. Bush in the White House. Even evaluated on his own terms, his accomodationist strategy was a disaster. His constant shifts and capitulations played right into the Republican caricature of him: that he would do anything to get elected. It was a portrait that damaged him inordinately on independent voters' critical judgment of whether or not he was a strong leader.

As a result, when Bill Clinton left office eight years later, the Democratic Party's power at the dawn of the Clinton era seemed like a distant progressive fantasy: extremist Republicans now controlled both houses of Congress and George W. Bush, probably the most right-wing president in history, had seized the White House. With Clinton's consent, the Republican machine had already succeeded in dismantling many of the great progressive achievements of the 20th century. It had slashed the social safety net, student aid, and funding for environmental protection. With full control of the government under Bush, the Republicans multiplied their assault on Clinton's New Democratic America – slashing support for education, health care, and the environment, passing massive tax cuts for the ultra-rich, and destroying much of the international good will Clinton had cultivated.

Of course, while all this was happening, President Clinton became the first elected Democratic president to win re-election since FDR. And he won big, with a 9 percentage point margin over Republican candidate Bob Dole. But his personal political success translated into little additional power for his party, for the progressive movement, or even his anointed successor, Vice President Al Gore. Indeed, despite all of President Clinton's focus on securing large financial contributions from major corporate donors, George W. Bush outraised Gore

$190 million to $130 million. Clnton presided over the second highest rate of decline in union membership of any post-war president, seeing the unionized workforce decline from 15.8 percent of the workforce to 13.5 percent during his term, a rate of decline exceeded only by Ronald Reagan. With unionized workers voting Democratic at consistently far higher rates than non-unionized workers, this reduced the size of one of the Democrats' most reliable voting blocs. Finally, Clinton saw a dramatic decline in the enthusiasm of the progressive base for the Democratic Party, a shift that led, in part, to Gore's underperformance among progressive Democrats and, notably, the defection of just enough liberals to Ralph Nader to swing the disputed Florida vote to Bush.

This chapter probes how Bill Clinton, a man widely proclaimed the greatest political talent of his generation, could end up presiding over such a large and lasting political collapse with such catastrophic consequences. For in the end, his election and re-election were his greatest political achievements. Even they were matters at least as much of luck as of skill. Clinton was always fortunate in his enemies, whether it was the recession-saddled George H.W. Bush, the overreaching and whiny Newt Gingrich, or his out of touch, uncharismatic 1996 opponent, Bob Dole. Even looking at these victories in the best of lights, from today they seem relatively inconsequential compared to the dramatic weakening of the Democratic Party and the progressive movement during his term in office – a weakening that even under the best of circumstances will take at least a generation to recover from. As I outline in this chapter, Clinton's failure stems from two main sources – his total focus on his own political success to the exclusion of that of his party and the progressive movement, and his fear of fighting for a progressive America.

Getting Rolled

Clinton developed the reputation for a lack of political courage even before his administration started. On December 24, 1992, he nominated Zoe Baird, the general counsel for insurance giant Aetna, to become the first female attorney general in American history. Although consumer advocates criticized Clinton for nominating a corporate lawyer after promising to free government from the grip of special interests, with strong bipartisan support on the Judiciary committee, she seemed headed for an easy confirmation. But on January 13, Clinton officials revealed that Baird and her husband, Yale Law School Professor Paul Gewirtz, had employed two illegal Peruvian immigrants to take care of the couple's infant son and to serve as Baird's driver, and hadn't paid Social Security taxes for them until a month earlier. Although Baird had followed an immigration attorney's advice in withholding the taxes, and sponsored the employees' attempt to gain legal residency, employing the immigrants clearly violated a rarely enforced 1986 immigration law. But Baird had told the Clinton administration and the FBI about the issue before she was nominated, and Clinton decided to nominate her anyway (Clinton later claimed that her statement about illegal immigrants wasn't passed up to him).

Despite the extenuating circumstances, then-House Republican whip Newt Gingrich saw the "nanny issue" as a way to tar the Clinton administration even before it took office and held a news conference decrying Clinton's choice. "You can't have a person who ought to be prosecuted serving in the Cabinet," he said.[1] Gingrich was widely thought of at this point as an extremist fire-brand. Anyway, as a House member, he wouldn't have a vote on Baird's confirmation. Despite Gingrich's attack, the nomination retained its momentum. On January 15, Senate Judiciary Committee Chairman Orrin Hatch, who not only *did* have a vote, but would also oversee the confirmation hearings for the Republicans, enthusiastically endorsed Baird. "It's no big deal," Hatch told *The New York Times*. "No one is above the law, but people make honest mistakes, and that should not deprive her from serving her country. She is a very fine person who has the qualifications to be Attorney General."

At her hearing, Baird apologized repeatedly for hiring the illegal immigrants – and faced more scrutiny from Democrats on the panel than the Republicans, leading to some speculation that Republicans were supporting Baird because of her corporate-friendly reputation and fear that Clinton's next nominee would be tougher on corporate wrong-doing. Meanwhile, Clinton stuck by Baird, sending his press secretary out to defend her. But a January 21 CNN/USA Today/Gallup poll showed that 63 percent of Americans opposed Baird's nomination – a stark lack of support for a president who should have been enjoying a honeymoon with the press and public. Many Americans told pollsters that they were angry that a woman who had earned over $500,000 a year as a corporate executive would be given a free pass for breaking the law, while they had to struggle to balance work and child care without the luxury of a domestic employee – legal or illegal – to help them.[2] This grassroots sentiment filtered onto Capitol Hill. Louisiana Democrats J. Bennett Johnston and Democratic Leadership Council Chair John Breaux joined nine Republicans and announced their opposition to the nomination.

The Baird nomination was vulnerable in large part because there was no movement willing to line up behind her. While Newt Gingrich and Rush Limbaugh enthusiastically trashed her to score points against the new president, progressive America stayed silent. Women's groups had felt spurned when Clinton didn't choose their favorite, DC lawyer Brooksely Born. More substantively, progressives remained angry that Baird had helped Dan Quayle in his "tort reform" campaign – his effort to make it harder for citizens to hold corporations accountable for wrongdoing or pollution. They weren't about to spend their political capital on a special interest lawyer who had been working for the other side while they were fighting on the political front lines in the long dark Reagan-Bush years. That left Clinton alone to fight for her – and as senators and the public turned against her, he was unwilling to wager his political capital on a nomination that might or might not succeed no matter what he did.

With sentiment against the nomination rising, Clinton called an Oval Office meeting to assess the politics of the nomination. White House Counsel Bernie Nussbaum, a tough New York lawyer who had worked on the House Judiciary Committee during the Nixon impeachment proceedings warned Clinton against caving to pressure so early in his term. "When you abandon your people, you send a message that you can be rolled," he told Clinton.[3] Clinton rejected Nussbaum's advice and soon the administration pressed Baird into withdrawing. So Clinton ended up surrendering on the first big fight of the administration – leaving progressives feeling unenthusiastic, the general public again questioning his ethical standards and competence, and Republicans suddenly aware that getting Clinton to give in might be easier than they'd ever imagined.

Of course, if this had just been an isolated incident, it would probably have been written off as a rookie staff mistake – but the capitulations kept coming. After the Baird withdrawal, Clinton settled on Federal Judge Kimba Wood as his next choice for attorney general – and had the appointment leaked to the press as his likely choice. But then, during a vetting session, Wood told administration investigators that she had hired a nanny on an expired visa – but before doing so became illegal under the 1986 law. Unlike Baird, Wood had paid Social Security taxes for the woman. Clinton quickly jettisoned Wood, deciding that Americans might not distinguish between Baird's illegal act and Wood's legal one. To further justify their decision, anonymous Clinton officials told *The New York Times* that they had discovered that Wood had worked for five days as a Playboy croupier in London when she was a student at the London School of Economics.[4] Dropping Wood for acting legally – and then gratuitously exposing her brief work at a Playboy club – once again made Clinton look like he was not only afraid of standing up for himself and his people, but willing to embarrass them to protect himself. This second capitulation brought criticism from women's organizations that had been among his more enthusiastic backers in the general election campaign. They argued that Clinton's capitulation represented a double standard: cabinet member Ron Brown had also admitted to not paying Social Security taxes on his domestic help, but wasn't being asked to leave the cabinet for it. The National Organization of Women launched a campaign to ask all the male cabinet members about their child care arrangements.

The nanny imbroglio led to Clinton's appointment of Janet Reno, a relatively unknown prosecutor from Miami-Dade County. Reno possessed what had become a singularly valuable quality in a nominee for Attorney General – she was female, unmarried and therefore pretty unlikely to have a nanny problem hidden in her past. Clinton's appointment capitulations continued when he abandoned Lani Guinier, a lawyer with the NAACP's Legal Defense Fund and a longtime friend, as his nominee to head the Civil Rights division of the Justice Department. Guinier had written articles in academic law journals urging the United States to move towards a "cumulative voting" system, in which each voter would be given more than one vote and allowed to distribute it among a number of candidates, so that they could more easily express their preference for, for instance, a candidate of their own race. The Republican machine saw Guinier's scholarly consideration of a shift away from strict one man–one vote doctrine as an opportunity to attack Clinton for nominating what they memorably described as a "quota queen." Several friendly senators told Clinton that the nomination would have a difficult time winning approval; after reading Guinier's writings, Clinton decided that he didn't want to defend her philosophy and dropped her. The move earned scorn from both Clinton's allies in civil rights groups and from his opponents on the right. Congressional Black Caucus Chairman Kweisi Mfume told *The New York Times* that "some people who worked to put Bill Clinton in office, who took to heart his pledge to bring about change, to some extent feel betrayed" while Pennsylvania Republican Senator Arlen Specter said, "There are some fights you have to fight even if you may lose them. I think he misreads the Senate, and this is going to do him some harm as he faces a tough battle on the budget."[5]

During the first months of his presidency, Clinton also managed to turn off other key constituencies who had helped put him in the Oval Office. In February 1993, Clinton announced that his administration would implement a policy that environmental groups had long been demanding – charge market rates to ranchers and loggers who had long been exploiting America's public lands at fire-sale prices. When Western senators expressed opposition, he dropped the proposal, angering environmentalists who had helped get him elected. Mike Francis, an official with The Wilderness Society, told *The New York Times*, "I don't think I've ever seen a white flag get put up so fast. The Clinton White House came out charging but, once close enough to see the whites of the enemy's eyes, turned tail."[6] The capitulation even seemed too much for one of the main backers of the lower ranching fees, Montana Democrat Max Baucus, who said after the Clinton change was announced, "Uh-oh. This is a problem. They're going too far."[7]

Most famously, Clinton had promised during the campaign to allow gays and lesbians to serve openly in the military, and had even included the pledge in his campaign book, *Putting People First.*[8] The Bush campaign had decided against raising the issue out of fear of seeming intolerant, while Ross Perot had come out in support of the Bush administration's discriminatory policies, but changed his position the next day after coming under intense criticism from gay rights organizations.[9] One week after the election, NBC News reporter Andrea Mitchell asked Clinton if he would fulfill his promise and Clinton replied that he would, but refused to set a timeline and said he would do so only after consulting with the military leadership.[10] Gay rights advocates, including many who had actively supported Clinton's campaign, urged the President to issue an executive order to force the military to allow gays in, much as Harry Truman had when he racially integrated the military over the top generals' opposition. The military was ripe for it – military brass and rank and file soldiers seemed resigned to, if not supportive of, the change.

But Clinton's refusal to set a timeline on issuing such an order and his pledge to work with military leaders made the generals and their anti-gay supporters in Congress sense weakness. Joint Chiefs of Staff Chairman Colin Powell took the lead, arguing that integrating gays into the military would be "prejudicial to good order and discipline" and recycled remarks that any comparison between discrimination against gays and discrimination against blacks was "invalid" because "skin color is a benign, non-behavioral characteristic. Sexual orientation is perhaps the most profound of human behavioral characteristics."[11] Because of the ongoing debate, coverage of Clinton's decision on gays in the military dominated coverage of the first few weeks of his administration, giving voters the mistaken impression that Clinton was spending an enormous amount of time on the issue, not on the economic problems he had been elected to address.

Indeed, a *Los Angeles Times* poll of military personnel found that even 66 percent of them felt the issue was draining attention from other more important issues facing the military.[12] The generals and conservatives in Congress were able to marshal enough support to force Clinton into accepting the compromise "Don't Ask, Don't Tell" policy that would maintain the ban on homosexuals in the military but prohibit the military from actively pursuing gays. Clinton's hesitancy ultimately led to one of his few outright defeats in Congress in 1993, when Congress passed amendments in the fall removing Clinton's authority to set the military's policy on homosexuals.

Capitulation after capitulation was gradually forming a clear image in the heads of the public, Clinton's friends, and especially his enemies. He became the man who would always blink first, who would abandon his friends in vain attempts to appease those who hated him. With his personal and ideological friends worrying that Clinton would push them overboard to avoid even the smallest fight, they became more and more reluctant to rally to his cause or even work closely with him. And his enemies learned that no matter how far you pushed, it was almost impossible to find a bottom line.

Putting the Bond Market First

On its own, Clinton's performance on gays in the military, like his performance on ranching fees and appointments, probably alone would not have amounted to much. These weren't the kinds of issues that decided elections, presidential legacies, or the fate of parties and political movements. But Clinton's reputation for being easy to roll, and his continued surrenders on matters of great national import, emboldened his opponents and demoralized his supporters in ways that plagued him throughout his presidency.

Clinton tackled the first of these great issues right away – the economy. If there was one issue that had driven Clinton's 1992 electoral "mandate for change," this was it. During the 1992 campaign, the unemployment rate had averaged 7.5 percent and more than three quarters of Americans consistently said they were dissatisfied with President Bush's management of the economy.[13] In order to ride this wave of economic discontent to victory, Clinton ran largely on a progressive economic platform of putting people back to work, raising taxes on the ultra-rich (and lowering them on the middle class and poor), and providing universal health care. Clinton had also promised a $50 billion annual government "investment" in education, new police forces, environmental protection, and the creation of the Internet in its modern form. Even his promise to "end welfare as we know it" entailed having government spend more: he planned on spending billions to give people the training and education necessary to move them off the welfare rolls and into high-quality steady jobs.

To some extent, the progressivism of Clinton's economic platform was a departure for him: Clinton had established his national reputation through his chairmanship of the Democratic Leadership Council, the corporate-funded organization founded with the mission of moving the Democratic Party rightward. And in a series of speeches at Georgetown University that led up to his announcement that he was running for president, Clinton developed a "New Democratic" agenda: support for free trade, a pledge to "reinvent government" by eliminating waste and unnecessary bureaucracy, and criticism of traditional "tax and spend" government economic policies. But as the 1992 campaign developed, the Clinton campaign team quickly discovered that paeans to the corporations responsible for the layoffs were falling flat with an electorate feeling daily economic anxiety. Starting in the New Hampshire primaries, and continuing through Election Day, Clinton's speeches focused far more on the progressive economic pieces of his agenda than on the corporate friendly ones like his conditional support for the North American Free Trade Agreement.

Indeed, Clinton made his campaign slogan "Putting People First" – which he contrasted with the Reagan-Bush government that had "been rigged in favor of the rich and special interests…While the rich cashed in, the forgotten middle class worked harder for less money and paid more taxes to a government that failed to produce what we need: good jobs in a growing economy, world-class education, affordable health care, and safe streets and neighborhoods."[14] Clinton used this class-oriented rhetoric to surf the wave of economic discontent and to portray himself as someone who was in touch with the concerns of ordinary Americans. Now, he had to deliver on his promises.

The economy – and the outgoing Bush administration – made that difficult. On January 6, 1993, Bush budget chief Richard Darman released new budget numbers. They predicted that the 1997 budget deficit would be $60 billion higher than previously forecast. Clinton staffers took to calling the bigger deficits "Darman's revenge." The new numbers spelled trouble for either Clinton's pledge to reduce the deficit in half, his plans to bolster the health of the economy with new government spending, or his proposed middle class tax cut. It was the kind of fundamental choice Clinton faced over and over during his term: he had made three promises and only one or two would be possible to fulfill. Which would he choose?

Each of those promises had likely benefits – and interest groups fighting for them. Wall Street prioritized deficit reduction. According to the Wall Street theory, lower deficits would boost investors' confidence that the government would honor its debts – meaning that the government could offer lower interest rates and still get people to buy government bonds. When interest rates were low, more people would borrow money to invest in buying new houses, new cars, and starting and expanding businesses, fueling the economy and creating jobs. Meanwhile, low interest rates would also keep inflation in check. The Wall Street theory was just that, a theory. Indeed, many economists believe that the link between lower deficits and lower interest rates is tenuous at best.[15] Nevertheless, from Clinton's perspective, this approach had a big advantage that the others didn't: it was the approach favored by Republicans and Wall Street (and conservatives in his own party) and would allow him to avoid conflict with them.

But the other theory, the more classical economic theory most clearly enunciated by early 20th century British economist John Maynard Keynes, was that increased government spending would act as a stimulus to the economy. As long as spending didn't drive the deficit to absurd heights (triggering inflation), this could be an extremely useful way to directly stimulate economic activity. Unlike the Wall Street theory, which relied on investors behaving in a certain way, the government could be sure that its spending would circulate through the economy as it bought goods and hired people. Government spending could also finance programs that on their own did good: hiring cops, providing college students with financial aid, enforcing environmental laws, and providing food to the poor. If properly targeted, it could also bolster the long-term economic health of the country by increasing the country's potential. Labor Secretary Robert Reich was the biggest advocate of this approach. He urged Clinton to fulfill his campaign promise to invest at least $50 billion in improving education, building the nascent Internet, and protecting the environment. Reich compared this investment plan to a business plan for a technology company: a corporation that wanted to be healthy three, five, 10, or 20 years from now had to invest in research and development and the skills of its employees to ensure its competitiveness down the road. Reich argued that the United States had to do the same thing to keep up: make sure that both current and future workers (today's schoolchildren) had skills and resources to compete with low wage foreign competition. But doing so would also involve a fight with Republicans who, after 12 years of driving up the deficit with tax cuts for the ultrarich and bloated defense spending, were now suddenly trying to control Democratic spending by raising the issue of the deficit again.

Looming over the whole debate was Federal Reserve Chairman Alan Greenspan. He was the one with the actual power to decide the benchmark short-term interest rates at the center of the dispute. Greenspan, an economic conservative originally appointed to his post by Ronald Reagan, desperately wanted to win the confidence of the Wall Street bond marketeers. These were the lenders who would see their profits decline if inflation went up, and whom Greenspan saw as central to the fiscal health of the economy. Although the Federal Reserve was supposed to act independently of the White House and Congress, Greenspan was a master of the Washington power game and knew how to exert his pull clandestinely. He was also a master of the "Art of the Possible" – sizing up those with whom he was dealing and figuring out how far he could push them. With Clinton, he knew he could push very far indeed.

His power to do so was tremendous. Essentially the whole goal of the Clinton administration economic policy was to reduce the deficit enough so that Greenspan would be willing to lower interest rates without raising inflation. If Greenspan thought the deficit was too high for Wall Street, he could keep interest rates high, putting a damper on the economy, or even raise them. He had done this to George Bush, Sr., who paid for it with a weak economy going into his 1992 election. In January, Greenspan held a confidential discussion with Treasury Secretary Lloyd Bentsen and dictated his goal for deficit reduction: $140 billion in 1997. The number was essentially arbitrary, but to some extent that didn't matter. If Clinton's deficit reduction proposal fell short of that mark, he risked angering Greenspan into keeping interest rates high – and making it harder for Americans to borrow money to start or expand new businesses, buy a house, or pay for college.[16] James Carville summed up the power dynamic when he said, "I used to think that if there was reincarnation, I wanted to come back as the president or the pope or as a .400 baseball hitter. But now I'd like to come back as the bond market. You can intimidate everybody." [17]

So Clinton had to make a decision – appease Greenspan and the bond markets or fulfill his campaign's progressive promises to middle class Americans. As the White House drew up its budget in a series of lengthy late-night meetings, they could see the impact of this big-picture choice on specific priorities: reduce the deficit or invest in creating the Internet? Reduce the deficit or provide out-of-work Americans job retraining? Reduce the deficit or protect the environment? Reduce the deficit or cut taxes on the middle class? There was no clear short-term political advantage to one or the other of these choices. On the one hand, Ross Perot remained a media darling and was continuing his anti-deficit crusade in appearances around the country. On the other hand, pollster Stanley Greenberg had found that voters considered Clinton's promises to create jobs, reform health care, and reform welfare all as more important than deficit reduction.[18]

Perhaps because of the competing pressures, Clinton kept putting off a decision. But when he decided, the decisions came down again and again on the side of Wall Street's deficit reduction plan and against fulfilling many of the campaign promises. Rather than cutting middle class taxes, Clinton eventually decided to include a small middle class tax increase in his plan – a proposal to tax energy (that was also constructed to help the environment by discouraging fossil fuel consumption). He also dropped his welfare reform plan, which would have required an additional $2 billion in spending to move people off welfare and into work. His plan also dramatically decreased his planned investments in improving America's education, infrastructure and economic stimulus. Even as he went ahead with it, the tilt towards Wall Street pained Clinton. In one meeting, he fumed at his advisers, "Where are all the Democrats? I hope you're all aware we're all Eisenhower Republicans, and we are fighting the Reagan Republicans. We stand for lower deficits and free trade and the bond markets. Isn't that great?"[19] Nevertheless, some important campaign promises did make the cut. The final Clinton proposal included a scaled-down economic stimulus plan of government spending to get the economy moving, the AmeriCorps volunteer service program, and the Earned Income Tax Credit (which provided important extra income for the working poor).

Now that Clinton had decided on his plan, he had to sell it to the American people and to the Democratic Congress. On February 15, he delivered an Oval Office address to the country in which he outlined his plan and followed it up two days later with a nationally televised address to a joint session of Congress. Polls indicated that the public responded positively to these speeches. He also got a lift in Congress. Most notably, conservative Democratic Senator David Boren, who held the swing vote on the Finance Committee that would have to pass Clinton's economic plan, pledged to "unreservedly" support it.

Still, passing the economic program would not be easy. Although his 83 seat majority gave him a good deal of flexibility, many liberal Democrats were reluctant to vote for the energy tax Clinton included, primarily out of fear that it would fall disproportionately on the poor and middle class. Oil state Democrats just didn't want to tax oil more. Clinton asked both groups to overlook their objections and go along with him to support the plan – and not deliver his Democratic presidency such a stinging rebuke so early in his term. Many congressmen were open to this appeal to partisan loyalty, but they remained worried that these politically tough votes could end up being pointless. They could bite the bullet, vote for a middle class tax increase, and then find out that the Senate had stripped it out of the bill anyway. Clinton promised that their votes wouldn't be in vain – that he wouldn't drop the tax in negotiations in the Senate – and sealed the deal. As a result, the House passed Clinton's budget 243-183 and passed the stimulus package 235-190.[20]

It was an important step forward, but Clinton still needed to pass the bill through the Senate. He got what seemed like a boost when Senate appropriations committee chairman Robert Byrd agreed to shepherd it through – and used his parliamentary expertise to prevent amendments from being offered. As wily as Byrd was, however, he couldn't prevent Republicans from blocking the package with the filibuster. And Bob Dole's 43 Republicans were united in their determination to stop Clinton's economic package cold and embarrass Clinton early in his term with a defeat. Byrd's maneuvers to cut off their ability to offer amendments solidified the Republican opposition. The Republicans needed only 40 votes to prevent Clinton's package from coming to a vote and as long as the moderates stuck with the right-wingers, they could stop Clinton's agenda. Suddenly, it looked like Bob Dole was in charge and not the big Democratic majorities in Congress. Of course, that was a double-edged sword for the Republicans. Their successful obstruction could play out in two ways – it could either make people see Clinton as ineffective and unable to get things done, or it could make the Republicans look like obstructionists willing to put politics before getting the country's economy moving again. It depended a lot on how much Clinton was willing to crusade against their intransigence.

To complicate matters, Senate Democrats grew disunited. Conservative senators David Boren of Oklahoma and John Breaux of Louisiana remained unenthusiastic about the energy tax and what they considered an excess of government spending in the economic plan. Meanwhile, Clinton's political standing was being battered because of declining poll numbers produced by the gays-in-the-military and appointments fiascoes. In turn, some of Clinton's prior congressional support grew wobbly. Most notably, Boren backed off his earlier pledge of unconditional support for Clinton's economic plan and repeatedly criticized it in public. Clinton would need both Boren and Breaux's votes to pass his economic plan through the finance committee, which was divided 13-11 between

Democrats and Republicans.

Clinton's advisers were split into two camps about a course of action – the policy professionals and more conservative members of his administration believed he needed to focus on paring back his proposals to appease Boren and Breaux – and possibly win over some Republican support. In contrast, Clinton's generally more progressive political advisers thought that Clinton needed to talk directly to the American people to rally their support and count on a "bankshot" effect – as public support increased, opposition from fence-sitters like Boren would crumble. Indeed, this strategy had worked in February when Clinton made his address to Congress about his economic plan and seen congressional support (including Boren's) solidify following a positive public reaction. But with a couple of exceptions, Clinton allowed himself to be sucked into the Capitol Hill horse-trading, essentially negotiating the exact size of his capitulation, and continued to spend hours and hours of his time negotiating with intransigent members of Congress instead of using that time to take his demand for a progressive economic program to the American people. Even the language he used when speaking to the press showed how much he'd allowed himself to get drawn into the muck: he repeatedly found himself talking about congressional process, not about the big picture of getting the American economy moving again.

Largely as a result of his inability to rally the American people anew behind his economic program, Clinton was unable to overcome the Republican filibuster of his economic stimulus package. Many Democrats, notably Robert Byrd, urged him to hang tough and rally the American people to pressure Republicans and recalcitrant Democrats to let Clinton do what he had been elected to do: stimulate the economy. Even if Clinton didn't focus his energy on passing the stimulus package through the Senate, he could just remain silent and see if Byrd and others could come up with the political support to pass it, or at least a modified version of it. They argued that it was critical that he not be seen capitulating once again.

But Clinton – and many of his political advisers – thought the focus on the stimulus package and the Republican filibuster was distracting attention from the upcoming battle over the federal budget, which not only couldn't be filibustered according to the rules of the Senate, but was also far more important to the economy (the budget included spending of about $1.14 trillion, the stimulus only about $32 billion). Clinton agreed and decided to throw in the towel on the stimulus package. On April 22, he had spokesman George Stephanopoulos issue a statement admitting defeat and blaming it on Republicans playing politics. The statement was accurate, but it didn't help Clinton with congressional Democrats or the media, who portrayed it as yet another capitulation. *The Washington Post* headline the next day read, "Stimulus Defeat Alarms Clinton Loyalists on Hill," and the article went on to quote an unnamed leading Democratic senator saying "In the Senate, patience is thin, credibility is a problem and enthusiasm is at its lowest since the start [of the Clinton administration.]"[21] Even though it was Republican intransigence that had most directly caused the defeat, Clinton caught the blame because it was he who had surrendered – giving up the opportunity to hang the albatross of the unpassed economic stimulus around the Republicans' necks. In a later analysis, Clinton pollster Stanley Greenberg would pinpoint the loss of the stimulus package as the point when "things came apart."[22] Clinton's approval rating dropped 15 points in a month to an abysmal 37 percent. Things weren't coming apart for Bob Dole – he was the big winner from the collapse of the stimulus package. Dole had taken on the Democratic Congress and a Democratic president and won. He now had the reputation of a lion killer – a reputation he would bring into the fight over the budget.

Despite this defeat, passage of Clinton's overall economic plan was still within reach through the budget. But the most significant obstacle was an increasing opposition in public opinion polls to all things Clinton. It was clear that Clinton needed to make some effort to rally the public behind the plan once again. On August 3, 1993, he delivered an Oval Office address to the nation about his economic policy. Much of the speech focused on clarifying that most of the new taxes asked for in the plan would come only from those making more than $200,000 a year. He also asked the public to "tell the people's representatives to get on with the people's business."[23] But the speech was blunted by his immersion in the details of the plan and because he declined to name names – not even singling out any senator, or even the Republicans in Congress. The speech failed to rally people behind an economic overhaul or to get the focus of blame for inaction off of Clinton. A CNN poll showed that only 33 percent of Americans wanted the President's economic plan to pass and even the president's own polling showed that fewer than 50 percent of the American people supported the plan.[24] It was far from the heady "Putting People First" days of the campaign less than a year earlier.

With his effort to garner public support an apparent failure, Clinton was left once again to the insider horse-trading game. So he had to deal with the motley assemblage of Democrats who held the swing margin in the Senate: a crew of oil industry lackeys (Breaux, Johnston, and Boren), eccentric former rivals of

Clinton (Nebraska Senator Bob Kerrey, who had run against Clinton in the primaries), conservatives (Nebraska's James Exon), and perfectionists (Wisconsin's Russ Feingold). Clinton's way of dealing with opponents was rarely to seek ways to punish them for opposition, but rather to win their support through a combination of charm, concessions, and pork. In pursuing this accommondationist strategy, Clinton forgot the lesson of his fellow (albeit semi-fictional) southern politician Willie Talos in Robert Penn Warren's *All the King's Men* (who was modeled after the real life Louisiana governor and senator Huey Long). When asked to go easy on a corrupt city politician looking to win a hospital construct contract, Talos bellows at his advisers, "I've bought too many sons of bitches already. Bust 'em and they'll stay busted, but buy 'em and you can't tell how long they'll stay bought."[25] By this point, senators knew Clinton was no Talos, and no Huey Long. So the demands for buy-offs kept coming.

The oil state senators wanted the energy tax that Clinton had promised to Democratic House members taken out. It was – and replaced with a tiny 4.3 cent gas tax that would insulate far more toxic fuels like crude oil and coal from taxation. To make up for lost revenue, the Senate cut $8 billion from Medicare, scaled back tax credits for the working poor, and reduced food stamp funding by $7 billion. But the concessions didn't get Clinton anything in return. Boren, who had pledged his unconditional support for Clinton's original economic plan, told the press he would vote against it anyway just days before the vote. Kerrey, who saw himself as above the run-of-the-mill pork trading for votes, wanted the administration to appoint a commission to look at the issue of reforming entitlement programs like Medicare and Social Security. After holding out until the day of the vote, he got it.

In the end, the Senate passed the pared-back version of the bill, with Vice President Al Gore casting the tie-breaking vote. Despite all the give-aways, the bill represented a genuine accomplishment: ultra-rich Americans were now paying a greater share of the tax burden; five million working poor would now see their taxes lowered through the Earned Income Tax Credit. 4.5 million children would get more food stamps. 6.5 million would get free immunizations.[26] It also meant that the deficit would decline, putting less of a financial burden on future generations. Clinton heralded the victory as "the sound of gridlock breaking… After a long season of denial and drift and decline, we are seizing control of our economic destiny."[27] While it's hard to separate out the effects of any one piece of legislation on the health of the overall economy, it's likely that the economic package did keep inflation down, allowed fairer distribution of wealth and kept the fundamentals of the economy sound – forming the basis for the enormous boom in economic growth of the 1990's.

Despite this major achievement, Clinton's capitulations, surrenders, and concessions had lasting negative political consequences for his presidency and for the country. Most immediately, it seriously damaged his credibility for subsequent battles. His abandonment of his pledge to fight for a broad-based energy tax hurt his credibility with House Democrats who had gone out on a limb for it – making them much less willing to either strike deals with him in the future, risk their political capital for him, or even identify themselves with him. It even made him appear weak with the man who had largely dictated the broad outlines of his economic package: for all of Greenspan's talk about the necessity of meeting the $140 billion goal to keep interest rates low, Greenspan went ahead over Clinton and Gore's objections and raised them twice just four months after Congress passed the deficit reduction package that had been tailored specifically to his demands.[xix]

Perhaps most importantly, it's likely that Clinton's original package of investments in better training for American workers, environmental protection, education, and infrastructural improvements would have had a similar, if not greater, positive effect on the economy because increased government spending would have stimulated the economy. Its long-term effects would have been even more positive: his job retraining programs and improved education would have given the American workforce a greater ability to withstand the global economic forces buffeting working class America in the 1990's and would have prevented or slowed the decline in real wages. Improved environmental protection, in addition to its ecological and health benefits, could have made America a more attractive place for companies looking to attract workers with a high quality of life.

This promise of investments in the economy – not a package of deficit reduction – was part of the reason progressive voters and organizations had backed him in 1992, and its absence in his final economic package was an early indication to progressives that Clinton had abandoned the priorities that had got him elected. Politically, a package of the kind he had originally envisioned would pay even greater dividends. It would have bolstered some of his core constitu-

---

[xix]Although Clinton and Gore urged Greenspan to keep the rates low, some of Clinton's more Wall Street-oriented economic advisers, notably Lloyd Bentsen, argued that an increase in interest rates in 1994 would mean that the Fed wouldn't have to raise them in 1995 when they could tamper economic growth going into the 1996 election (this proved to be the case: economic growth slowed in 1995 and then picked up again in 1996).

encies and shown others that he could stick to his guns when it mattered. But that would have required confronting, organizing, and movement-building, and none of these were Clinton's strengths.

Priorities

Despite his low standing in the polls and in the trust-o-meters of many Democrats in Congress, the immense power of the presidency gave Clinton numerous opportunities to rebuild his credibility, his movement, and his popularity. The biggest opportunity was the one he had put at the centerpiece of his presidential campaign: his plan to provide low-cost, universal health care to all Americans. It would be the kind of monumental achievement that would make all his past mistakes pale in comparison. It had been instrumental in Clinton's winning the support of middle class Americans feeling the pinch of rising health care costs and worried about losing health care if they lost their job. If he succeeded in passing health insurance, he had the opportunity to win back the enthusiastic allegiance of those same middle class Americans, many of whom had been turned off by the increasing Wall Street orientation of his economic package, his early capitulations on appointments, and the gays-in-the-military fiasco. He might even be able to win the allegiance of some captains of industry happy that Clinton's health care plan had relieved them of the high burden of health care costs – and the allegiance of industrial workers grateful that he'd saved their jobs. Most important politically, it would be a monumental achievement that had the potential to create a major new Democratic constituency in the same way that civil rights, Social Security and Medicare had under prior Democratic administrations.

But if Clinton failed to pass health care reform, it would jeopardize everything he had achieved in his economic plan. Health care costs were rising two to three times as fast as wages, meaning that much, if not all, of the economic growth generated by Clinton's economic plan would be eaten up by the rising cost of health care and health insurance. These rising costs would also put big, old-line industrial companies like Bethlehem Steel and General Motors on the brink of collapse because these companies remained responsible for providing health care for both their employees and their immense population of retirees.28 As a result, health care costs had the power to doom Clinton's political prospects – if high health care costs were preventing people from seeing more money in their pocket, and if big corporations were going out of business, it would spell trouble for the Democrats in 1994 and 1996.

But there was, as always, competition for the top spot on the national agenda. Vice President Al Gore had been pouring effort into his "Reinventing Government" project to downsize the federal workforce, reduce unnecessary regulations, and improve the government's service. Reinventing Government had the potential to produce $108 billion in savings for the federal government and make the government work significantly more efficiently. Perhaps most importantly, it was constructed to help restore Americans' faith in government. This could have political benefits for Democrats, who generally believe that government should play a relatively active role in society. But there were also major political risks to the project. Because it reduced the federal government workforce, it also reduced the size of one of the most reliable Democratic voter bases – federal workers. Indeed, at the end of the Clinton administration, the project boasted that it had cut 423,000 government jobs, reducing the size of the federal government to its lowest level since the Eisenhower administration.[29] It was as if Republicans had suddenly thrown one third of America's CEO's out of work in a bid to restore faith in the plutocracy. The reduction in government jobs was one reason why the number of Americans in unions declined so heavily during the Clinton administration.

The other big competitor for space on the agenda was the North American Free Trade Agreement. The first Bush administration had negotiated this agreement between the United States, Canada, and Mexico to reduce barriers to trade and investment between the three countries. That meant reducing or eliminating tariffs and providing guarantees to U.S. and Canadian investors that future Mexican governments would not nationalize any factories or other assets they constructed in Mexico. If the agreement went through, it could be a big boon for manufacturers. They could send relatively high-wage, unionized jobs to Mexico and take advantage of that country's cheap labor, weak labor unions, and lax environmental laws (DDT was still allowed in Mexico, for example) and still sell their products in the United States without having to pay high tariffs on those goods – significantly boosting their profit margins. The idea was that jobs lost in this process would be more than made up for by increased U.S. exports to Mexico, particularly of high-tech products like cars and computers.

It sounded great, but the idea was untested. It would be the first modern attempt to wholly integrate the economies of three countries with dramatically different levels of development, economic systems, legal and environmental standards. The European Union had successfully integrated highly developed economies like Germany with less developed ones like Ireland and Portugal, but there was a big difference: the European Union poured development aid into its less developed members and insisted that they adopt common budgetary, legal, and environmental standards – lifting the less developed countries up to the standards of everyone else. Nafta was an attempt to achieve economic integration on the cheap – free trade without any of the social investment Europe had made to ensure its success. Clinton had supported Nafta during the campaign, but had stipulated that his support was conditional on the negotiation of side-agreements to protect the environment and labor rights "so that we could both go up together instead of being dragged down." He never made it a centerpiece of his campaign, and so it would be comparatively easy to let it die without being accused of breaking a promise, blaming it on the lack of effective side agreements to blunt its negatives.[30]

If Reinventing Government had political risks, Nafta was as dicey as forming a union in Nogales. The majority of Democrats in Congress, including House Majority Leader Dick Gephardt and Whip David Bonior, opposed it. Ross Perot was touring the country with a new book, *Save Your Job, Save Our Country: Why NAFTA Must Be Stopped – Now!* saying that Americans would hear a "giant sucking sound" of American jobs going to Mexico if Nafta passed. The Sierra Club, Greenpeace, and other politically active grassroots environmental groups opposed the agreement out of concern that it would not only allow manufacturers to get out from under environmental protections by exporting manufacturing operations to Mexico, but would also force the United States and Canada to weaken their environmental laws, which corporations would now be able to challenge as "unfair barriers to trade."[xx]

Most of all, the American labor movement almost unanimously and vociferously opposed it. They were already seeing union jobs go overseas as manufacturers took advantage of low-wage labor and lax environmental restrictions abroad – Nafta would accelerate that trend. In his first meeting with Clinton's new Secretary of Labor Robert Reich, AFL-CIO President Lane Kirkland told Reich, a former Harvard professor, that he thought the agreement was "a fucking dis-as-ter. Even a Harvard professor ought to be able to understand that." Labor's leadership wanted to put their millions of dollars, hundreds of organizers,

---

[xx]Clinton and Gore tired to blunt the environmental groups' criticism by recruiting six corporate funded and less politically active groups, including the Natural Resources Defense Council, the Environmental Defense Fund, World Wildlife Fund to support it on the grounds that the Nafta rules would somehow boost efficiency (disappointed that Nafta didn't live up to its environmental promises, most of these groups opposed subsequent trade agreements).

and thousands of active members into Clinton's campaign for universal health care, but they told Clinton that if he went with Nafta first, they'd put all those resources into stopping Nafta instead. Although campaigning for Nafta would surely tamp labor's enthusiasm for Clinton, passing it could have one big benefit for Clinton's 1996 bid for re-election and the Democratic Party: it could win the Democrats greater financial support from big business. Clinton desperately wanted to even the balance between the Republicans and Democrats on getting contributions from big corporations – and passing Nafta could help him pick up some corporate dough for his campaign coffers. Finally, in the race for time on the schedule, Nafta had a deadline on its side: Congress had to approve it before the end of the year, or it would have to be renegotiated.

The dilemma for Clinton was very similar to the one he faced on the budget when he decided between two competing priorities: adhere to Wall Street's vision for the budget or the progressive vision he had campaigned on. Now, he could choose to prioritize corporate America's priority, Nafta, his Vice President's priority, Reinventing Government, or the progressive priority from his campaign: universal health care. In a series of late-night White House meetings in August, 1993, following the victory on their economic plan, Clinton's aides argued the various options. On the one hand, Gore pointed out that Clinton had earlier promised to roll out the Reinventing Government initiative in September. Hillary Clinton argued that health care had been put off long enough. In addition, Senate Democratic Leader George Mitchell counseled Hillary Clinton that delaying a serious health care push until 1994 would likely doom it. With little time before the midterm elections, the Republicans would be able to kill the bill through delaying tactics alone. Ira Magaziner, the Clintons' top health care adviser, echoed Mitchell's advice, as well as that given Clinton by James Carville, in a February memo to the president that said, "The more time we allow for the defenders of the status quo to organize, the more they will be able to marshal opposition to your plan and the better their chances of killing it." This was the critical moment – universal health care not only had strong public support, but strong political support as well. Fearful of being left out of the negotiating process, even potential health care reform opponents like the American Medical Association and Chamber of Commerce were coming forward and endorsing specific measures like universal coverage and requiring employers to cover their employees' health insurance (positions both organizations would later reverse when support for the Clinton health plan appeared to be collapsing.)[31] Meanwhile, George Stephanopoulos argued that pushing Nafta was extremely risky because not only would it divide the Democratic Party, but was the most likely of the three to fail in Congress, dealing a serious blow to Clinton's already diminished prestige.

Clinton's Chief Trade Representative Mickey Kantor offered Clinton a way out of the Nafta debacle: he said he could "blow up" the final negotiations with Mexico over the labor and environment side agreements, saying they weren't tough enough. That would allow Clinton to focus on health care and Reinventing Government. But Kantor also laid out a second option: keep his promise on Reinventing Government by rolling out that program for two weeks; then, make a major address to Congress to roll out health care, followed by two weeks of campaigning for that and then spend October and November in a full court press to pass Nafta. Kantor said that if Clinton succeeded in passing the treaty by bucking the labor and environmental movements and forging an alliance with Republicans, Clinton would show that he could transcend partisan differences, overcome internal opposition, and be a unifying leader.[32] Kantor's option appealed to Clinton's reluctance to exclude any option. Clinton went with Kantor and chose to give two weeks each to Reinventing Government and health care, and then make corporate America's priority his priority by putting his all into passing Nafta – putting health care off until 1994.

Clinton and Gore launched their Reinventing Government initiative on September 7, 1993 at a White House event where Gore displayed mountains of government regulation and said in his speech, "Mr. President, if you want to know why government doesn't work, look behind you."[33] They followed it up with two weeks of events to showcase government waste and solutions to it, including Gore's famous appearance on *David Letterman* where he smashed an ashtray into pieces to demonstrate the ridiculousness of overly specific government regulations that specified, for instance, the size of smashed ashtray shards. Reinventing Government received a good deal of bipartisan support and Congress ultimately endorsed many of its recommendations. But it had also eaten up valuable time on the agenda. And it wasn't the only thing creeping into the already packed White House schedule. In the middle of the Reinventing Government drive, Clinton hosted Israeli Prime Minister Yitzhak Rabin and Palestinian Liberation Organization Chairman Yasir Arafat at the White House to sign a peace agreement that was intended to end decades of armed struggle between Israel and the Arabs. Although the agreement had been negotiated by Norway, both the Israelis and the Palestinians wanted to sign it at the White House to show that it had the backing of the world superpower.

The very next day, Clinton hosted former Presidents Jimmy Carter, Gerald Ford, and George Bush at the White House to celebrate the signing of Nafta side-agreements on environment and labor. The agreements Clinton signed, however, were essentially window-dressing that didn't live up to the standards laid out in his campaign: although they set up commissions to monitor environmental and labor violations and recommend redress, the side-agreements included no enforceable provisions. During the next two weeks, Clinton conducted events on all three topics: health care, Nafta, Reinventing Government, and a variety of foreign policy matters. Finally, on September 22, health care got a brief time in the spotlight when Clinton rolled his plan out to the American people in a joint session of Congress.

But it was only temporary. The real priority for the fall was Nafta, and, as planned, health care was put on the back burner until 1994. Given the many obstacles to passing the agreement, Clinton knew he had to put his all into passing the trade agreement. First, he recruited Bill Daley, brother of Chicago Mayor Richard Daley, and son of the late Richard J. Daley to become the White House's "Nafta Czar." Not only did Daley come with the right political pedigree, but he also had strong connections with the labor movement, having just finished a stint as chief of the Amalgamated Bank, a bank partially owned by a Teamsters local. Clinton even took time out of his schedule to recruit former Chrysler chairman Lee Iacocca to be a new spokesman for USA*NAFTA, the corporate lobbying alliance directing the pro-Nafta effort of General Electric, American Express, Big Ag, the U.S. Chamber of Commerce, and others. To top off his involvement in the corporate lobbying effort, Clinton turned the White House South Lawn over to the pro-Nafta forces for "Products Day" to display everything from pancake syrup to aircraft engines which Nafta backers said could be exported to Mexico under the treaty.

These efforts helped, but the pro-Nafta team needed to seal the deal. Public opposition remained high, and passionate in some quarters. Increasingly, the media was giving a platform to a more diverse array of Nafta opponents, not just Ross Perot. Labor leaders and articulate congressmen like David Bonior were making the movement look less and less like a reaction against international engagement of any kind (which sometimes seemed like the just-under-the-surface attitude of Ross Perot and his supporters) and more and more like a sophisticated and appealing critique of Nafta's threats to jobs and the environment. Jack Quinn, Al Gore's chief of staff, came up with a solution – have Gore challenge Ross Perot to a debate. It was a potentially brilliant tactical stratagem. If Perot accepted (and it would be hard for him not to), it would ensure that the Nafta opposition would once again come to be identified with the eccentric Texas billionaire. Though he had proven an ability to attract a certain strain of ornery American, Perot could come off as a fanatic on television – and often an unprepared fanatic at that.

Gore banked on Perot being Perot and self-destructing. Meanwhile, Gore spent the week before the debate closeted with briefing books and rehearsed several times with Oklahoma Congressman Mike Synar played a camped up version of Perot, full of folksy, self-assured witticisms and outlandish claims. When the lights came on for an extraordinarily large audience of 16.3 million people, Gore was ready, and Perot was very demonstrably not. It was Gore who had prepared the folksy anecdotes about how the agreement would help working people and Perot who became exasperated and looked ridiculous – dealing a significant blow to the image of the entire anti-Nafta movement.

Gore's huge triumph over Perot gave the Nafta proponents some big momentum, but Clinton still had to contend with Democrats concerned about the export of jobs and pollution and isolationist Republicans who either wanted to protect domestic industries or who harbored suspicions that participating in international treaties would lead to a U.N. takeover of the corn silos of Idaho. Clinton continued to pour both his time and the full power of the presidency into winning. He and Gore made more than 200 calls to wavering members of Congress, and his cabinet made more than 900 calls.[34] The pork, private deals, and special favors shot out of the White House like so much spam-in-a-cannon to win the support of wavering Democrats. The White House wooed California Congressman Esteban Torres, a former auto worker and UAW member, by agreeing to his idea to set up a North American Development Bank to finance environmental and other projects in the border region. Clinton agreed to go duck hunting with Oklahoma's Bill Brewster in exchange for his vote.[35] He said he would speed up deportations of imprisoned illegal aliens to Mexico to win the votes of Californian Members of Congress; he made deals with individual members of Congress to devise special protections for wheat, tomatoes, cut flowers, citrus fruits, and wine; subsidize a shipyard in Representative Gerry Stubbs's district; and monitor broomcorn broom imports. As the deal-making progressed, many members of Congress who were intending to vote for Nafta anyway held off declaring their intention until Clinton cut them a special deal as well.

Clinton never fulfilled many of these promises and others: he told Members of Congress representing textile producing states that he would deliver a slower phase-out of quotas for textile imports from foreign countries, but then a month later agreed to the regular phase-out. He promised Texas Representative Bill Sarpalius a new plutonium research laboratory in his district at the Pantex Nuclear Weapons facility in Amarillo, Texas. Instead of building the new facility, the Clinton administration slashed jobs there.[xxi] These failures to deliver further damaged Clinton's credibility on Capitol Hill and cost him votes on trade and other issues in later fights.[36] Nevertheless, Clinton's efforts – and those of the well-financed corporate effort – beat out the labor unions, environmental groups, and Perotistas with room to spare. The House passed Nafta 234-200, with the support of 132 Republicans and 102 Democrats and the Senate followed three days later to pass it 61-38.

It was a huge victory for Clinton, for corporate America, and for the Republican congressional leadership, particularly Republican Whip Newt Gingrich. Clinton showed that he was strong enough and skilled enough to defy the Democratic majority in Congress, spurn the labor unions and environmental groups that had been instrumental to his victory in 1992, and forge a successful alliance with Republicans. In a remark relayed by journalist James MacArthur in his excellent 2000 book *The Selling of Free Trade*, American Express Chairman James Robinson summed up Clinton's political achievement. "He stood up against his two prime constituents, labor and the environment, to drive it home over their dead bodies." Robinson was right, and Clinton reaped some short-term benefits. Although Clinton was fighting his friends instead of his enemies, at least he was fighting. Following the victory, Clinton's approval ratings shot up to over 50 percent and stayed there until mid-1994 when his health care effort began to unravel. The success also likely helped Clinton attract corporate donations to the Democrats. Although it's hard to separate out the "Nafta effect" on the increase in corporate donations to the Democrats between 1992 and 1996, some of Nafta's biggest supporters dramatically boosted their contributions to Democrats between 1992 and 1996. James Robinson's American Express increased their contribution to Democrats from $1,950 in 1992 to $121,000 in 1996 (though it still gave Republicans more – $193,550), while General Electric departed from its usual practice and actually gave slightly more to Democrats than Republicans in 1996.[37]

But there were serious long-term consequences to leaving two of your best constituencies "dead." Clinton's Nafta fight had seriously damaged relations

---

[xxi]From a policy perspective, Clinton's reductions at the plants were justified: the site was a toxic waste nightmare, and its nuclear-weapons-building mission was becoming obsolete in the post-Cold War world.

with the Democratic leadership and labor unions whose support he would need to pass universal health care and turn out and motivate Democratic voters in the 1994 elections. And although Gore's debate with Perot helped clinch the legislative victory, Clinton's pro-Nafta campaign created a huge problem with die-hard Ross Perot voters. Many of these voters had as strong an affiliation with Perot as other voters did with the Republican or Democratic parties – as a result, when Clinton took on Perot, he was bound to pay a price with Perot's still-large following of less-educated, working class, primarily male voters who would form a big part of the swing vote in 1994 and 1996. Partly as a result, 68 percent of Perot voters went for Republican congressional candidates in 1994, whereas in 1992 they had given Republican congressional candidates just 53 percent of their vote.[38] In 1996, 1992 Perot voters again went Republican in the congressional elections by a 2-1 margin.

But the most lasting effect was in how Nafta and the other free trade policies pursued by Clinton transformed the American economy and the American political landscape. To put it in the simplest terms possible, Bill Clinton's Nafta put a lot of Democrats out of work. Between 1994 and 2002, the Department of Labor certified 524,094 workers for its NAFTA-Transitional Adjustment Assistance program, primarily in the heavily unionized manufacturing sector. The program provided up to 52 weeks of income support for workers who had lost (or were threatened with losing) their jobs to due to imports from Canada and Mexico or because their companies were relocating to one of those countries.[39] Because many laid-off workers either didn't participate in or were not eligible for the program, it's likely that this number significantly underestimates job losses due to Nafta.[xxii] Of course, these job losses might be worth it if Nafta created what its backers touted – in Clinton's words, "a million jobs in the first five years of its impact" and that those jobs paid better than the jobs that had been lost, or spurred economic development in Mexico in a way that reduced immigration or gave Mexico a greater ability to protect its environment.[40]

Unfortunately, not only did these benefits not materialize, but in almost

---

[xxii]Many workers, particularly non-unionized workers, may not have known about the program because there was no requirement to publicize the program to workers threatened with Nafta-related job loss. Many other laid-off workers may have moved to other, lower-paying jobs without going through retraining, rendering themselves ineligible for the program. At the same time, it is possible that some of those who received benefits never actually lost their jobs because the program allowed workers to receive benefits who are facing a legitimate threat of job loss. See Hufbauer, Gary Clyde and Ben Goodrich. "Lessons from NAFTA" *Free Trade Agreements.* Institute for International Economics. http://www.iie.com/publications/chapters_preview/375/02iie3616.pdf Finally, while the NAFTA-TAA program would cover workers in an aircraft engine plant that was moved to Mexico, it wouldn't cover the workers in parts-suppliers or restaurants, whose jobs also relied on the factory.

every category, there's strong evidence that Nafta's net effect was to put people out of work, pollute the air and water, and do nothing to stem the immigration tide from Mexico (some studies suggest it may even have increased immigration from Mexico by driving farmers off their land through dumping of low-priced American agricultural surplus on the Mexican market). An authoritative 2003 study by the Economic Policy Institute found that Nafta caused 879,000 more job losses than job gains.[41][xxiii] What's more, pollution in Mexico has dramatically increased, especially in the U.S. border zone. In part, it's because the increase in cross-border shipments has caused the use of those exhaust spewing diesel trucks to skyrocket, fouling the air.[xxiv] But at least as much pollution is due to a Mexican scam: in the lead-up to Nafta's passage, the Mexican government doubled its spending on environmental enforcement, in part to convince the U.S. Congress that it wouldn't just become a haven for American polluters. But since then, it's decreased environmental spending and enforcement by 45 percent.[42] Finally, because Nafta opened up Mexico to U.S. agricultural products, U.S. farmers dumped surplus products onto the Mexican market, putting pressure on many small Mexican farmers. To survive on lower profit margins, Mexican farmers have had to increase production; to do that, they've cut down tropical forests and other pristine lands to expand their crops.[43]

Despite the big negatives, some businesses have performed extremely well. Foreign investment in Mexico surged $124 billion between 1993 and 2002 and the (short-term) costs of producing many goods has declined as companies have taken advantage of cheap Mexican labor and lax environmental laws.[44] Partly as a result, companies like WalMart, Target, and Costco have been able to offer Mexican-made goods at low prices to consumers, helping boost profits. Nafta's defenders additionally point to the overall growth in the American and Mexican economies as evidence of Nafta's benefits, though even pro-Nafta economists admit that even under the most generous assumptions, Nafta accounts for less than 1 percent of the condition of the overall U.S. economy.[45]

Nevertheless, Nafta remains important in part because it paved the way for later trade agreements that had an even more profound impact on the U.S. economy. In the years following his Nafta win, Clinton won passage of permanent reductions in tariffs for China and global tariff reductions and investment

[xxiii]In 1997, the Clinton administration released a study saying that "NAFTA has boosted jobs associated with exports to Mexico between roughly 90,000 and 160,000," short of Clinton's prediction of 200,000 export (non-net) jobs in the first two years.

[xxiv]For a more comprehensive discussion of Nafta's environmental impact, see Scott Vaughn's 2004 article in *Environment:* "How Green is NAFTA? Measuring the impacts of agricultural trade," an analysis of just one part of Nafta's environmental impact.

guarantees through U.S. ratification of the World Trade Organization. Like Nafta, these agreements departed from the previous generation of trade agreements. Not only did they lower tariffs, but they allowed international trade bureaucrats to weaken domestic environmental, labor, and civil rights laws if these laws were deemed to be an "unfair barrier to trade." For instance, WTO courts forced the United States to change its clean air requirements for gasoline imports, and ruled that the United States had to allow importation of shrimp from India, Malaysia, Pakistan, and Thailand even though those countries caught shrimp in a way that killed endangered sea turtles.[46] Because the WTO and Nafta allow international bodies to force changes in U.S. domestic law, Clinton not only angered union members and environmentalists, but also inflamed paranoids who opposed any government efforts to relinquish sovereignty to international bodies.

Outmatched

Despite his higher approval numbers going into the new year, passing universal health care would still be a huge challenge: Although between 60 and 78 percent of Americans consistently said they favored a government guarantee of universal health coverage (depending on the poll), actually passing it through Congress would be hard.[47] FDR, Truman, Nixon, Ford, and Carter had all tried to pass universal health coverage with similarly high levels of public support and all had failed. They had succumbed to the entrenched power of the American Medical Association and the insurance industry, as well as major institutional barriers to change, such as the filibuster and the power of the different, often conservative, congressional committees.[48] What's more, Clinton had severely damaged his relations with America's labor movement. He knew he needed their enthusiastic support if he was going to have a chance of passing universal health care.[xxv] He moved quickly to repair relations with union leadership by inviting AFL-CIO President Lane Kirkland to sit by his wife in the gallery during his State of the Union speech. That helped, but it would be harder for Clinton to win back the hearts of the rank and file organizers and workers who had poured their hearts into the anti-Nafta campaign only to see Clinton team up with

---

[xxv]Many of the details in my discussion of President Clinton's effort to pass health care reform come from Haynes Johnson and David S. Broder's 1996 book *The System: The American Way of Politics at the Breaking Point*. The book provides extraordinarily detailed and entertaining first-hand reporting and analysis of the politics of Clinton's effort to reform health care. Those seeking a more academic analysis of the failure of the Clinton health care effort should read Sven Steinmo and J. Watts's classic article "It's the Institutions, Stupid!: Why the United States Can't Pass Comprehensive National Health Insurance," published in the *Journal of Health Politics, Policy, and Law* in 1996.

big business and anti-labor forces in the Republican Party to beat them. Labor had the grassroots network that could help provide counter-pressure when the HMOs, private hospitals, and the insurance industry squeezed Members of Congress to oppose health care for all Americans.

But getting their backing wouldn't be easy. Labor was so angry about Nafta that it had cut off its contributions to the DNC for six months. This dealt a crippling blow to the Clintons' efforts to raise the $10 million they thought they needed to finance an independent advertising and grassroots campaign in support of universal health care to counter the health care industry's growing political war chest. And despite everything the Clinton administration had done to help big corporations pass Nafta, big business made clear that their gratitude didn't extend to helping the DNC with the health care drive. Several big corporations who had been at the lead of the Nafta fight turned down DNC chief David Wilhelm when he asked for their contributions to fill the gap left by labor. Clinton tried to make amends with labor in ways both symbolic and substantive. Most importantly, the Clintons went along with labor demands that they not finance their plan by either taxing workers or increasing health care taxes on employers.

Clinton and his team may have been operating under the illusion that fighting labor and environmentalists on Nafta would yield permanent good feeling on the part of those corporations for Clinton policies. Unfortunately for them, corporations saw the Nafta fight for what it was: a fight in which they got lucky by having a Democratic president align with them and pass a treaty that they wouldn't have been able to do alone. But in politics, there are no permanent enemies and no permanent friends, and many of the pro-Nafta corporations now opened their wallets to the forces looking to defeat universal health care. While the Democrats were struggling to raise even this relatively modest $10 million, the corporate opponents of universal health care were building a budget estimated at between $100 million on the low end to $300 million on the high end. Not only were the insurance and HMO industries able to raise a lot of money, but they also assembled a powerful political coalition. Gratitude for Clinton's help in passing Nafta didn't stop corporate lobbies like the Business Roundtable and National Federation of Independent Business from putting their considerable heft into total opposition to Clinton's health care drive. The health care industry was also able to win the energetic backing of low-wage employers like Burger King and Pepsico, who didn't want to have to provide their employees health insurance. Health security opponents worked not just in Washington, but mobilized a grassroots operation around the country. The National Federation of Independent Businesses employed field organizers in key states; in Montana, they turned out more than 700 business people for town meetings aimed at getting Democratic Senator Max Baucus to oppose the Clinton plan. The insurance industry had its agents write letters to Members of Congress and represent their interests at community meetings.

The business coalition was able to draw on the resources of major non-business allies like evangelical minister Pat Robertson's Christian Coalition. Flush with donations from big corporations, the Christian Coalition happily poured its effort into making sure that social conservatives who might want health security as badly as other Americans lined up instead with the insurance industry to kill universal health care. They launched a huge grassroots operation and put their name on ads that falsely suggested that the Clinton health care plan would mean mandatory abortion.[49] Most famously, the anti-health security lobby used their huge financial resources to launch a highly effective ad campaign to raise doubts about and opposition to the Clinton plan. In the ads, two actors (Harry and Louise), sat around a kitchen table ostensibly reading about the Clinton health care plan. The insurance industry had learned that the greatest vulnerability of government health care was public mistrust of bureaucrats, and so they focused on that. "The government may force us to pick from a few health care plans designed by government bureaucrats," an announcer says in the ads. "Having choices we don't like is no choice at all," follows Louise.[50] Over the next several months, the insurance industry amplified the effect of the $10 million they spent on the ads. They played them primarily in the Washington, DC and New York media markets where journalists and opinion-makers would be more likely to see them. Their stratagem was a wild success – national and local news media replayed the ads on news shows all over the country, giving the insurance industry's arguments hundreds of millions of dollars in free coverage.

The business campaign was successful in part because Clinton's supporters were divided almost from the beginning. For years, labor unions and progressive policy organizations had built a movement in support of government-financed health care, usually referred to as "single-payer" health care because the government would be the sole financier of health care. At the time, Canada and most European countries had already employed the system for decades. Under the system, government would use general tax revenues to pay health providers directly for the services they provided at pre-approved rates. It was simple, low-cost, and was already a proven success, providing quality low-cost health care in most of the industrialized world and, in a slightly modified form, to America's elderly through the Medicare program. It also had the passionate support of progressive Americans.

Depending on how it was constructed, single-payer universal health care had the potential to garner the support of at least some segments of corporate America. Auto companies, airlines, and manufacturers were all seeing big reductions in profits because of the rapidly rising cost of health care. An estimated $1000 of the cost of the average American car went to pay workers' health care costs. In their initial discussions with the Clinton administration, these companies said they were open to supporting a Clinton health care plan if it reduced their responsibility for providing health care for their employees or dramatically lowered costs by cutting down on the immense corporate health care bureaucracy that wasted billions of dollars every year in unnecessary paperwork, redundant management structures, bloated executive salaries, and pure fraud. Nevertheless, none of the major companies ever gave any firm commitments to Clinton to back a single-payer package or indeed any other proposal for universal health care. When Clinton's plan collapsed, many of these companies paid the price in continued high health care costs – and some, like Bethlehem Steel, went out of business completely in the next few years. And those health care costs are responsible for a great deal of U.S. automakers' current financial woes.

Meanwhile, the private health care industry bitterly and clearly opposed single-payer health care. Although it would give Americans health security and dramatically reduce the growing burden of out-of-control health care costs, it would also put most HMOs and health insurance providers out of business. With their very existence at stake, it was likely that the health industry's survivalist opposition to reform would overwhelm whatever tepid support other elements of big business would give the pro-reform effort. And they weren't in the mood to propose compromises – they were making billions under the current system and wouldn't cut a deal unless they absolutely had to.

Wary of total war with the health care industry, the Clintons tried to plot a middle course that would achieve the goals of cost reductions and universal coverage but still keep the insurance industry in business. This not only meant that they would lose the enthusiastic support of the progressive alliance, but also that they would continue to allow corporate profit and inefficiency to be part of the nation's health care bill. They put their friend Ira Magaziner in charge of a Health Care Task Force to figure out the best solution. Magaziner reflected the policy-wonk side of the Clintons. He had begun his policy career as a sophomore at

Brown University, where he constructed a 400-page plan to totally overhaul the university's curriculum by eliminating course requirements, creating a new grading system, and giving students more flexibility. With the enthusiastic support of the 1960's student body, the faculty adopted his plan essentially unchanged, and it remains in effect today. Magaziner went on to use the model of creating a highly complex plan that dealt with all possible occurrences in a business consulting career and then in government. He came up with an 1100-page plan to transform Rhode Island's economy that was defeated 4-1 in a public referendum. He then proceeded to create complex blueprints to overhaul the Rhode Island health care system and create a national industrial training program – neither of which garnered the political support to succeed.

Undeterred by Magaziner's record of political failure, the Clintons allowed him to construct a massive, months-long effort to consider every possible option in the construction of a new health care system.[xxvi] Even Clinton's top health care staffers found the plan difficult to explain; Members of Congress experienced in health care did no better. Its complexity made it that much harder for the Clintons to win enthusiastic backing for it; if the wonks didn't get it, how could ordinary people, to say nothing of lazy reporters? Corporate lobbyists, labor unions, independent health care advocates, health care bureaucrats, and Members of Congress all wanted a piece of the Task Force. Magaziner and the Clintons attempted to do as much as possible to please them all while still achieving their goals of universal health coverage and cost reduction. But doing so took months and months and made the plan more and more complicated – severely damaging its political prospects. The longer they took to construct it, and while their allies were quibbling over the details, the more time their opponents had to build opposition. What the Clintons came up with in the end made no one truly happy: a highly complex system based on the principles of "pay or play." Companies would have a choice: either "play" by providing health care for their employees or "pay" into a national health care insurance fund for the uninsured. In addition, companies and workers would be able to form "health alliances" with each other

---

[xxvi]Ironically, Magaziner only started his work in seriousness after Clinton was foiled in an attempt to pass an earlier version of his universal health care package through the Senate as part of his overall economic package, which couldn't be filibustered because it was part of the budget. Senator Robert Byrd told Clinton he couldn't consent to consideration of such a complex topic as health care without treating it as a normal bill, subject to the Senate's prerogative of unlimited debate and the filibuster. Clinton accepted Byrd's verdict and didn't try to organize around him. It's possible that if Byrd had gone along with Clinton's attempt to pass a massive economic recovery-health care plan as part of the budget, Clinton could have passed both early in his term. It's also possible of course, that attempting to add health care onto the rest of the package would have cost votes that Clinton didn't have to spare (his economic package passed by only one vote in both the House and Senate).

to negotiate volume discounts with insurance companies. If these alliances failed to lower costs sufficiently, government limits on health care prices would kick in, guaranteeing cost savings.

Clinton gave the plan a second roll out in his 1994 speech to Congress, combining powerful personal stories about individuals without health insurance finding their life savings wiped out as a result of illness with convincing statistics about the breadth of the problem. Just as the Clintons were attempting to explain their package to the American people and to Congress, Clinton's fellow New Democrat, Tennessee Congressman Jim Cooper, ambushed him. Although Cooper was a liberal on many social issues, he saw the future of America in further loosening the reins on business and reductions in the government safety net. Early on in the health care fight, Cooper told journalists Haynes Johnson and David S. Broder, "Big government doesn't work. Great Society doesn't work. New Deal doesn't even work. We've got to have a new way for government to work cost-effectively." Cooper joined with Iowa Republican Fred Grandy and former Democratic Leadership Council Chairman John Breaux to introduce a bill that he called "Clinton lite."

If Clinton's bill was friendly to the health care industry, Cooper's bill groveled towards it. Although his bill sought some cost reductions by allowing workers and companies to join in Health Care Alliances that could seek volume discounts, his bill didn't require employers to provide health insurance for their employees, place any caps on prices, or guarantee universal coverage. Cooper's energetic efforts on behalf of the insurance and private health care industry was likely no coincidence – he was running for the Senate in Tennessee in 1994 and was raising hundreds of thousands of dollars from Tennessee's big hospital and insurance industry, notably the Frist family's HCA corporation, the largest private hospital chain in the country. Typical of New Democratic policies, Cooper's plan wasn't very popular either in the nation at large or in Congress. He introduced it with only 48 cosponsors, far fewer than the 95 that the single payer plan had and the 99 that Clinton's plan had. Despite its small chances of passing, the Cooper plan pulled the rug out from Clinton's plan just as it was getting off the ground. It stole the spotlight and, worse, made it look like even the Democrats were turning away from not just Clinton, but also the principle of universal coverage.

Health care reform supporters were furious at Cooper. Labor unions threatened to either sit out the November election or endorse Cooper's opponent, Republican Fred Thompson. An AFL-CIO rally in Memphis burned a copy of the "phony" Cooper-Grandy bill. In March, the United Paperworkers Interna-tional Union included the front page headline, "Jim Cooper, Grand-Standing on Health Care, Forgets His Constituents" and featured a story about a $30,000 Cooper fundraiser at the Nashville home of Clayton McWhorter, CEO of for-profit health chain Healthtrust, Inc. The war between labor and Cooper got so bad that Tennessee senator Jim Sasser, who was also facing re-election in 1994, demanded that the two sides work out their differences. Cooper agreed to scale back his criticism of Clinton, but then went back on his word. Hillary Clinton urged her White House colleagues to "kill" the Cooper bill before it got out of hand, but the Clintons never launched an all-out assault on Cooper – allow-ing him to keep pushing his bill. Cooper was convinced that the White House would ultimately bend and adopt his approach.

Just as Democratic and progressive support for the idea of health care reform was splintering, outright Republican and corporate opposition was crystalliz-ing. In the first of a series of memos he would distribute, on December 2, Dan Quayle's ex-Chief of Staff William Kristol circulated a political argument for total opposition to the Clinton plan to congressional Republicans. Kristol wrote that passing universal health care,

> will relegitimize middle-class dependence of 'security' on government
> spending and regulation. It will revive the reputation of the party that
> spends and regulates, the Democrats, as the generous protector of mid-
> dle-class interests. And it will at the same time strike a punishing blow
> against Republican claims to defend the middle class by restraining
> government... Any Republican urge to negotiate a 'least bad' compro-
> mise with the Democrats, and thereby gain momentary public credit
> for helping the president 'do something' about health care, should also
> be resisted... The plan should not be amended; it should be erased. Its
> rejection by Congress and the public would be a monumental setback
> for the president, and an uncontestable piece of evidence that Demo-
> cratic welfare-state liberalism remains firmly in retreat.[51]

It was the kind of confrontational, movement-building, hardball approach that the Clintons would never have touched, but Kristol's advice hit a chord with Republicans who sensed that Clinton was losing public and corporate support for the plan – and that he would be severely damaged by defeat. By late spring, right-wing Republicans were coalescing around this position. On May 31, six right-wing leaders including Phyllis Schlafly of the Eagle Forum and Republican strategist Richard Viguerie told Dole and Gingrich that any "willingness to compromise on behalf of big government" would make it "almost impossible" for them to get right-wing support in 1996. Gingrich endorsed the letter – putting at risk Dole's efforts to win right-wing support for his presidential bid if he backed efforts at compromise. Dole soon backed off and joined Gingrich and the other hard-core right-wingers working to kill any Clinton attempt at health care reform.

Meanwhile, Clinton's health care reform bill remain stalled in Congress. With "New Democrats" like Cooper rejecting Clinton's approach, and moderate Republicans heeding Kristol's advice to stick together and oppose any health care proposal, it was clear that it would be a challenge to pass a universal coverage bill that included a mandate that employers provide coverage through either the House or Senate. Nevertheless, on July 1, Clinton met with the Democratic leadership in Congress to discuss a way forward. Senate leader George Mitchell sought – and got – authority to pursue a compromise proposal with moderate Republicans like Rhode Island's John Chafee that would get 95 percent of the way to universal coverage. The pro-reform forces felt a new optimism that they would make major progress in providing health security to Americans. But then Clinton spoke to the National Governors' Association on July 19 and, in response to a question by conservative Nebraska governor Ben Nelson, announced that he could be satisfied by a "phased-in, deliberate" program that reached "somewhere in the ballpark" of 95 percent coverage.[52] Clinton's remarks were, of course, a total retreat from his January State of the Union pledge to veto any bill that didn't achieve universal coverage; more immediately, it took the wind out of Gephardt's and Mitchell's renewed efforts to convince Members of Congress to support one of the universal coverage bills and suddenly moved the terms of debate much closer to those set out by Cooper and the Republicans.

It was the beginning of the end for the 1994 health care campaign. Worst of all, the Democratic effort to reform health care didn't go down in a dramatic fight that Democrats could blame on Republican opposition and the filibuster; with Clinton's retreat from his advocacy of universal coverage, the lines between Democratic calls for health reform and Republican statements about it blurred. Soon, leaders on both sides of the aisle realized that they wouldn't be able to put together a plan that could pass Congress and they gave up, allowing Members of Congress to go home and campaign. Even though Republicans were largely responsible for the death of health care reform, even though health care costs continued to soar, and even though 37 million Americans remained without health insurance, William Kristol's prophecy came true: the Democrats took the blame.

The 1994 Elections

Despite the failure of health care, Clinton had still racked up an impressive record of legislative accomplishment: in addition to his economic program and Nafta, he signed the Family and Medical Leave Act, which protects workers from being laid off if they have to take a leave of absence from work because of pregnancy, sickness, or a family illness; his AmeriCorps National Service program would enable millions of Americans to earn money for school while serving their communities; his Goals 2000 education program; a huge expansion of Head Start, providing preschool for children of the poor; and expanded college student loans. He had also had the courage to take on the National Rifle Association and pass an assault weapons ban and a crime bill that put 100,000 more police on the street and funded important crime prevention programs that likely helped generate the massive reduction in crime rates during the 1990's.

Politically, however, he was suffering. His approval ratings remained stuck in the 40's. The Republicans had opposed and attacked him at almost every turn and blocked him at key points – notably on the economic stimulus package and health care – and got him to look weak by surrendering over and over on matters of principle. And they were able to lay out a positive and unified agenda in their Contract with America – a litany of right-wing policy initiatives that scored above 60 percent in the polls – things like making American laws apply to Congress and instituting a $500 per child tax credit, reductions in lawsuits, prohibiting Americans from serving under United Nations command, and their tough welfare program. Polls showed that most Americans didn't know what was in the Republican plan but the fact that they had a plan helped convince people that the Republicans were ready to govern and not just rabid extremists. Republicans also played aggressive ads that, for instance, morphed pictures of Democratic candidates into the unpopular Bill Clinton, helped them fuel right-wing anger and turn out their base in huge numbers on Election Day. In 1994, conservatives represented 37 percent of the electorate, a 7 percent jump from 1992. And despite all Clinton's efforts to raise corporate cash with his business friendly initiatives, corporate America in 1994 did what they'd always done and divided their money approximately equally between Democrats and Republicans in their direct campaign donations.[53] Of course, this doesn't count the hundreds of millions of dollars in off-the-books advertising and other Clinton-bashing efforts financed by the health insurance industry aimed at defeating Clinton's health care plan.

What's more, an overall healthy economy was leaving a lot of people behind – and those left behind were blaming the incumbent Democrats for the problems. Median income in inflation adjusted dollars had actually declined between 1989 and 1994.[54] Early Nafta-related job losses were already rippling through the manufacturing sector, creating anxiety about the greater changes to come. More Americans were working longer hours. People dissatisfied with the economy deserted the Democrats in droves – at an even higher rate than conservatives did. There was a whopping 36 percent shift against the Democrats among people who thought their personal financial situation had gotten worse, and large shifts against the Democrats among those who felt that the economy had deteriorated.[55] As political scientist Ruy Teixera pointed out in a 1995 *American Prospect* article,

> The Democrats keep getting hurt by declining living standards because the story the public believes about these long-term changes casts them as the villain. The dominant story among the general public is that the long-term decline in living standards has to do with wasteful government spending (especially on the poor, minorities, and immigrants), high taxes, inefficient and obtrusive public administration, selfish behavior by interest groups, and excessive social tolerance and loss of values... Because the thrust of current Democratic strategy, especially its "New Democrat" variant, implicitly accepts this dominant story, the Democrats start every election with two strikes against them.

With everyone, including a Democratic president, ganging up on Democratic ideals of activist government, Democrats were bound to get a bad name. Worse for the president, Democrats in Congress were running away from Clinton and the idea that government could do good in the face of Republican attacks. The New Democrats who ran away from Clinton generally fared worse than progressives who ran unashamed of what they had accomplished. Indeed, a 1996 statistical analysis by Professors Neil Wollman and Leonard Williams of Manchester College that got wide media attention found that more liberal candidates fared significantly better than moderates, with 95 percent of the most liberal House members winning election and only 74 percent of moderate incumbents winning election. This was true even when the authors corrected for the possibility that moderates came from marginal district. Even in marginal districts, 85 percent of liberals won re-election, while 43 percent of moderates did.[56]

Perhaps the best illustration of this phenomenon was the fate of Jim Cooper, who had done so much to undermine Clinton's chances of passing health care reform through his "Clinton lite" health care bill. His opponent Fred Thompson ran an ad in Tennesse saying, "Career politician Jim Cooper. No wonder they call him 'Clinton lite.'" In the words of Broder and Johnson, "Thompson effectively hung Cooper with a noose the young Democratic congressman had placed around his own neck."[57] The Tennessee election provides the best proof that running away from Democratic principles was dangerous: because both Tennessee Senate seats were up for grabs in 1994 because Al Gore had retired his seat to assume the Vice Presidency, the race affords a rare opportunity to compare the effectiveness of two different strategies in a similar political environment. Although Republicans won both seats in the Republican tidal wave, Cooper fared worse than his fellow Democrat Jim Sasser, who had been largely supportive of Clinton. Despite all the big money he raised, Cooper lost by 23 percentage points, whereas Sasser lost by (only) 14.5[8] In Oklahoma, DLC Chairman Dave McCurdy, who had refused to vote for Clinton's economic plan, failed in his effort to succeed David Boren – losing by 15 points to ultra right-winger Jim Inhofe.

In total, the Democrats lost eight Senate seats and 54 House seats, losing the majority in the House for the first time since 1954. Even Speaker of the House Tom Foley had been beaten. In his autobiography, *My Life*, Clinton offers his interpretation of the defeat:

> The Republicans were rewarded for two years of constant attacks on me and for their solidarity on the contract. The Democrats were punished for too much good government and too little good politics. I had contributed to the demise by allowing my first weeks to be defined by gays in the military; by failing to concentrate on the campaign until it was too late; and by trying to do too much too fast in a news climate in which my victories were minimized, my losses were magnified, and the overall impression was created that I was just another pro-tax, big-government liberal, not the New Democrat who had won the presi-

dency... Ironically, I had hurt the Democrats with both my victories and my defeats. The loss of health care and the passage of NAFTA demoralized many of our base voters and depressed our turnout. The victories on the economic plan with its tax increases on high-income Americans, the Brady bill, and the assault weapons ban inflamed the Republican base voters and increased their turnout.[59]

Clinton was arguing, essentially, that he had lost because he had exhausted his political capital pursuing a vital, but unpopular, agenda – putting too much time into acting as "legislator-in-chief" rather than leading with big ideas that could unite America as a nation. Most notable, perhaps, is the lack of hardly any contemplation of the idea that as president, he had at least some power to change the tone of the media coverage and Congress's response.

But then Clinton goes on to write favorably about Democrats like Senator Kent Conrad and Congressman Earl Pomeroy of North Dakota and Congressman Bart Stupak of Michigan who aggressively defended their votes and their records – and won. They did it by pointing out, and repeating, for instance, how many people in their districts got tax cuts from Clinton's economic plan instead of tax increases. But then Clinton turns around and says that he thinks he could have won by changing his stances on issues to be more conservative: dropping his fight for the assault weapons ban, his economic plan, and tax increases on the ultra-rich. Clinton took this ambiguity into the remainder of his presidency: whether to wage an aggressive and bold defense of activist government like Conrad, Pomeroy, and Stupak did, or to drop the progressive platform he had run on and move to the right.

The Era of Big Government is Over, The Era of King Poll Has Begun

The day after the election, Clinton signaled the new ambiguity at a nationally televised news conference. He touted his legislative achievements, but acknowledged that despite them, "not enough people have felt more prosperous and more secure, or believe we were meeting their desires for fundamental change in the role of government in their lives." He reached out to the Republicans and, in his first specific policy proposal, asked them to support the creation of the World Trade Organization, even though he had felt that his pursuit of Nafta had damaged him during the election. He also said he was willing to support some elements of the Contract with America and was open-minded about supporting measures like a $500 per child tax credit and the Republican version of welfare reform. But at the news conference, and later in his State of the Union speech at the beginning of January, Clinton signaled that there were areas on which he would fight: protecting women's right to choose, the environment, and key programs like AmeriCorps. Despite these assurances, the overall tone of both speeches was conciliatory – he talked much more about the elements of the Republican platform he agreed with than making any attempt to rally Democrats around a renewed fight against failed Republican economic and social policies that had already failed and that indeed had propelled him into office. His conciliatory tone also deepened Republican doubts about how hard and long he would fight even in those areas he said he would.

Over the next two years, Clinton would seek to pull off a political tight-rope act – mouth conservative principles and acquiesce to many Republican policies, but rally at key moments for popular progressive priorities like Medicare, Social Security, education, and the environment. It was a strategy to which Clinton gravitated naturally. To give the approach shape, Clinton turned to an adviser who had helped him in another time of political disaster. In 1980, as part of the Reagan sweep of America, Arkansas voters ousted Clinton from the governor's office, after installing him there just two years before. He went from being the youngest governor in the country to the youngest ex-governor in the country. To rehabilitate himself, he turned to New York political strategist Dick Morris. Morris succeeded, helping Clinton win back the governor's mansion during the Reagan recession of 1982 – and win re-election every time after that.

Now, Clinton turned to him again in his hour of defeat. But Morris had changed. He had begun working both sides of the aisle, and counted right-wing Republicans like Jesse Helms and Trent Lott among his clients. He had lost any discernible ideological or partisan agenda, but he had one core belief: that issues drive voters' choices in the ballot box; that voters choose candidates who agree with them most on the issues; and that the successful candidate will identify the most popular issues and run on them. He believed it so strongly that he even applied it to the smallest initiatives with the tiniest audiences, and insisted on testing every element of a policy by poll before rolling it out. Those that played well with the "swing vote", the 20 percent of the electorate that wasn't committed to either the Democrats or the Republicans would get aired; those that didn't, wouldn't.

For Morris and Clinton, that meant driving constantly to the political center where people in public opinion polls would respond. It meant looking for issues, no matter how small, that could get 60, 70, or 80 percent support in polls.

Unfortunately, few of these issues were the kind that inspired deep passion or that could build a movement. It just wasn't that likely that the V-chip – a card that could be put in televisions to allow parents to censor what their children watched, which Clinton included as the first policy proposal he mentioned in his 1996 State of the Union – would catch the imagination of a generation. It also imperiled the most important personal quality in presidents – strong leadership. Indeed, Clinton's "strong leadership" ratings were the lowest of any president in the history of the National Election Survey asking questions about it.

Because Clinton tried to avoid taking on the big fights and the big issues, it meant surrendering the agenda to the Republicans. Regardless of how valuable one thinks his policy proposals were, focusing on them meant less of an emphasis on basic Democratic values. The Republicans didn't share that shyness; as a result, they were able to do more to set the public agenda and create the rhetorical framework in which it was debated. At least initially, Clinton attempted the impossible task of avoiding conflict with them, under the theory that Americans would naturally, and permanently, gravitate towards the Republicans' right-wing ideology – and that the ones who fought the Republicans would feel the brunt of a right-wing electorate's wrath. It was the opposite of Paul Wellstone's "You've got to start a fight to win one" and it most certainly was a rejection of the idea that "It's hard for your opponent to say bad things about you when your fist is in his mouth."[60]

This aversion to conflict created a big vulnerability that would ultimately come back to haunt Clinton over and over again. Clinton's enemies saw his reluctance to join the battle, his willingness to surrender on matters of principle and it boosted their confidence. They saw that in many cases Clinton would eventually buckle under no matter what they were proposing if they kept attacking. As a result, they grew braver, pushed the envelope and succeeded in passing a great deal of transformative legislation that few could ever have imagined a Democratic president approving. Drunk on Clinton's early capitulations, the Republicans came to believe that he would buckle no matter what they proposed. But they forgot that the polls could go against them too and that polls would stiffen Clinton's spine like nothing else. When their proposals, their rhetoric, and most of all their behavior went too far and the polls turned against them, they found themselves facing not the conciliatory Clinton they'd gotten used to, but a new fighting Clinton who would hang tough until they – the Republicans – caved.

Accepting the Republican Frame

Newt Gingrich had promised during the 1994 election campaign to put his "Contract with America" up for a vote within the first 100 days of the Congress – and he intended to keep his word. He began the Congress with a 14-hour session – one of the longest in history – that passed sweeping changes in the way the House of Representatives was governed. The House passed bills to apply the laws of the United States to their own operations, required most committee meetings to be conducted in open, banned proxy voting, and instituted terms limits on committee chairmen and the Speaker of the House.[61] But that was only the symbolic beginning. Over the next several months Gingrich and his fellow Republicans pushed a barrage of legislation that threatened the basic safety net of social and environmental protections constructed since the New Deal.

They started with an effort to pass limits on what they called "unfunded mandates" – federal laws that included requirements for state government action. Environmental and welfare laws in particular relied on state governments to enforce and finance many of their basic requirements. Passage of the unfunded mandates bill would mean that the federal government would be required to spend far more money for states to meet their basic obligations to clean up their own messes and provide basic services for the poor among them. In practice, that meant that spending on environmental protection would decline dramatically. Many leading Republicans opposed America's basic environmental protection laws: the Clean Air Act, the Clean Water Act, the Endangered Species Act; more generally, they opposed government efforts to put limits on corporations – even polluting corporations – of any kind. But popular support for these basic environmental protections was too strong to permit even many of the more radical Republicans to unleash a direct assault. The unfunded mandates bill was a way to gut enforcement of these laws while making it seem like they were just looking to act fairly toward state governments. The greatest irony behind the bid to reduce unfunded mandates was that even before the Gingrich bill passed, the federal government delivered far more money to the states than it required them to spend in "unfunded mandates." As part of his strategy of acquiescence, Clinton proclaimed his support for a "reasonable" unfunded mandates bill in his January State of the Union address and both the House and Senate passed it by overwhelming margins a few days later – and he signed it.

The unfunded mandates bill was just one part of the Republicans' assault on the environment. They passed a bill to prohibit the Clinton administration from issuing any new protections at all in 1995, and a bill requiring environmental benefits to be weighed against economic costs (a difficult task unless one is comfortable putting monetary value on a healthy lung, the survival of an owl, or a clear blue sky). Despite the opposition of many of the remaining, largely Northeastern, Republican moderates, the bills passed because many of Clinton's fellow "New" southern Democrats went along. Clinton initially resisted advice from his EPA Chief, Carol Browner, to take a strong stand against these attacks – Clinton and his advisers believed that environmental regulations were a backburner issue that wouldn't capture the public's imagination. But when they hit the front pages of several national newspapers, Clinton changed his mind.[62] And so, on February 21, he denounced the Republican environmental rollbacks, telling a public meeting of federal workers that the proposal "sounds good but this stops in its track Federal action that protects the environment, protects consumers and protects workers… It would stop good regulations, bad regulations, in-between regulations – all regulations. No judgment."[63] But after a month of attacks from Gingrich and other Republicans accusing Clinton of defending the status quo, Clinton let Chief of Staff Leon Panetta signal the Republicans that despite his forceful denunciation, he was willing to sign the environmental rollbacks, with the exception of the regulatory moratorium.[64]

During the 1994 campaign, Republicans had successfully exploited many voters' anger about welfare by proposing a "get tough" program that would dramatically reduce government spending on single mothers with children. They called for denying welfare permanently to single unwed mothers under 18, denying aid to welfare recipients who had additional children, and a two-year lifetime deadline on the amount of time someone would be allowed to spend on welfare. When Gingrich introduced legislation to enact these principles, it quickly became apparent that the program was even tougher in some of its details. Although it included a five-year time limit rather than a two-year time limit, it also prohibited payments for children who had no identifiable father, holding children responsible for their unknown fathers' irresponsibility. The bill also included no funds for job training – breaking a key promise of both the Contract with America and Clinton's welfare proposal. Clinton vetoed the first two versions of the Republicans' welfare reform bills, but agreed to the third (as did most Democrats in the House and Senate) after Republicans modified some of its harsher elements – but retained elements like time limits. Clinton's decision infuriated many of the liberals in his administration and in the general public.

Clinton's friend and social policy adviser Peter Edelman, husband of Save the Children president Marian Wright Edelman, resigned in protest. Clinton tried to blunt the effect of the rollbacks on welfare benefits by establishing a "Welfare to Work Partnership" of corporations who would pledge to hire former welfare recipients.

Judged in terms of its own goals, the welfare bill was largely a success. By 2006, it had played a part in reducing welfare rolls 60 percent (though Clinton's expansion of the Earned Income Tax Credit for the working poor and the improved health of the economy in the Clinton years had more to do with it. But its impact on families has been more dubious.[65] On its most basic level, it forced mothers to hand their children over to professional child care workers while they worked generally low-income jobs, creating a potential ticking time bomb of young, poor children getting inadequate involvement from their parents. The consequences are already being seen in schools where less involved parents' children perform worse and encounter serious disciplinary problems. When these children get a little older, they are at much greater risk of joining gangs, dealing drugs, and becoming prostitutes. Economically, the reform hasn't been much better.

Those who got jobs through welfare-to-work requirements earn an average of $16,000 a year – not much for the average two-child family; but many of the half who didn't get jobs (and their children) live a much more precarious existence. While some have found alternate forms of sustenance by living with relatives or boyfriends, at least 1 million mothers and 2 million children have neither a job nor receive welfare benefits, often because they've run up against the time limits. Many of these mothers are relying on other federal benefits like food stamps to put food on the table; others have no discernible source of income.[66] Politically, it achieved an extremely important goal for Clinton, and potentially for Democrats as a whole. Because he signed the bill, Clinton basically took welfare off the table as an issue Republicans could use against him. Even by August, 1996, just a month after signing the bill, 47 percent of people in a national *Newsweek* survey said they favored the Democratic Party's approach to welfare, compare to only 35 percent who said they favored the Republican approach (other poll results in the same period found an almost identical advantage for Clinton over Dole), a huge lead for Democrats compared to surveys in the spring that had found the parties and the candidates about equal.[67] And it's stayed off the table. The mid-90's working and middle class anger at poor people doing nothing and getting paid for it is largely gone. There's little evidence about how the welfare changes have impacted the poor's political inclinations except that lower income Americans have voted increasingly Republican.

Within the first months, the House Republicans also passed laws to make it harder for people to hold corporations accountable when they were injured by them – a so-called "tort reform" bill. They proposed abolishing the Departments of Energy, Education, and Commerce, the Food and Drug Administration, and even entertained the idea of cutting off funding for public radio and television until public reaction against "killing Big Bird" got too much even for them. At the center of their agenda was a tax package that would deliver a $500 per child tax credit for couples earning up to $200,000 (but didn't extend this credit to families whose incomes were too low to pay direct income taxes), reduced capital gains taxes, eliminated the Alternative Minimum Tax that ensured that corporations that took advantage of tax loopholes still had to pay some tax, and repealed Clinton's 1993 effort to have the rich pay Social Security taxes at rates closer to those paid by the poor and middle class (who paid a much higher percentage of their income in Social Security taxes). Clinton had proposed a child tax credit as well, but only for families earning less than $75,000 and he didn't exclude lower income families from the tax credit.

The Republicans piled $16 billion of these cuts into one package – plus cuts to school lunch programs and Medicare and the "salvage rider" – a three-year suspension of the Endangered Species Act, the Clean Water Act, and other environmental laws in national forests to expedite logging in areas that had experienced forest fires (which are part of the natural forest life cycle). The White House leaked a threat to veto the package, but Clinton wanted to avoid having to issue his first veto and appear that he wasn't acting constructively. In an April 21 meeting, Clinton told his advisers that he wanted a more positive approach. "I'm the President; I have to lead; I can't be in the position of just attacking."[68] Nevertheless, the Republicans forced his hand by going ahead with their cuts – and he finally pledged to veto the package, saying that the Republican approach was the "wrong way" to cut spending; he demanded that the Republicans cut pork barrel projects for new courthouses and roads before dipping into funds for education and health care. Referring to the Republican proposal to suspend environmental laws, he said, "There's another thing which is in this bill which I really object to, which would basically direct us to make timber sales to large companies subsidized by the taxpayers, mostly in the Pacific Northwest - that will essentially throw out all of our environmental laws and the protections that we have that surround such timber sales."[69] On June 9, he made good on his pledge and vetoed the package.

But he continued negotiations with the Republicans and finally reached an agreement, signing the bill in July with relatively minor modifications. It still included most of the big cuts and much of the pork in the initial bill, but it had been salted with a relatively modest $700 million more for education, school-to-work transition programs, child care, and environmental enforcement. But despite all of Clinton's rhetoric denouncing the suspension of the Endangered Species Act, Clean Water Act, and other environmental laws in the national forests, and after receiving more than 50,000 calls and letters from environmentalists urging him not to, he signed the bill even though it still included that environmental attack, although the suspension had been shortened to two years. In response, Sierra Club executive director (and formerly strong Clinton supporter) Carl Pope wrote to his membership that "At the time of his original veto, Clinton declared that 'suspending all the environmental laws of the country for three years is not the appropriate way' to log the nation's forests. Somehow suspending all the environmental laws for two years was acceptable."[70] Things got worse once the impact of the timber salvage rider went into effect: timber companies successfully argued in court they should be allowed not just to log burned forests, but also healthy, green, rare, old-growth forests – and immediately started clear-cutting forests across the West. They often cut right up to the edge of streams that had previously been protected by The Endangered Species Act because they contained runs of endangered salmon and trout and put a significant dent in the 5 percent of America's original pristine forests that still remained. Clinton later called agreeing to the bill a mistake, and Gore said it was "the biggest mistake" of the Clinton-Gore administration's first term. [71] Despite their contrition, many environmentalists would never forgive Clinton (or Gore) for acceding to this environmental rollback.

Among the Republican pledges in the Contract with America was a constitutional amendment requiring the government to balance its budget. At the time, the federal government was running a deficit of about $160 billion a year, significantly below the $200-$300 billion figures of the Reagan/Bush administrations. The GOP put passage of the popular amendment at the center of their plan – in part in an effort to capture Perot voters who were thought to share their candidate's intense concern about fiscal policy and America's indebtedness. But balancing the budget, especially when the Republicans were cutting taxes, would cut into the revenue available for any kind of government spending. That meant, less than a year after the collapse of Clinton's effort to give all Americans health care, that programs like Medicare and Social Security would have to be cut, as well environmental protection, food aid to families, student loans, and others to make the numbers add up. Making the drastic cuts immediately was something even the Republicans weren't able to stomach politically, but they were pushing as hard as they could to get the budget balanced as quickly as possible.

To fulfill his goal of offering a constructive approach, Clinton weighed sending a second budget proposal to Congress, this one that included a balanced budget in 10 years, slower than the Republicans' proposed seven years – and one that put more of an emphasis on cutting corporate welfare and did more to protect education. Democratic leaders urged him not to do it out of fear that offering his budget would undermine their increasingly successful attacks on the draconian cutbacks in the Republican budget; if both sides were going to cut Medicare and education, it would be harder for voters to tell the difference. The normally subdued Senate leader Tom Daschle went so far as to tell Clinton that he felt more strongly about Clinton not offering a budget than any other matter he had discussed with him.[72]

But Clinton decided he had to go ahead anyway and had Al Gore ask television network executives for time to explain the new budget to the nation before he even let Democratic leaders Gephardt or Daschle know about his decision to reject their advice. In part, Clinton saw offering his own new plan as a way of taking away the deficit reduction issue from the Republicans – and prevent them from sticking him with the label "tax and spend Democrat." But there would be major political drawbacks, all coming at the expense of the Democratic base and Democrats in Congress, as well as Clinton's credibility. The cuts he proposed to Medicare came just months after he had made appearances on behalf of Democratic candidates around the country in which he argued that voters should elect Democrats because the Republicans would cut Medicare. He was also giving the elderly less of a reason to stick with the Democrats. What's more, he never proposed cutting the deficit as much as Republicans; as a result, true deficit hawks were more likely to stick with the Republicans: Dole won 52 percent of voters who said the deficit was the most important policy issue in their voting decision, compared to just 27 percent for Clinton.[73]

In words he would perhaps regret later, Clinton said, "It took decades to run up this deficit. It's going to take a decade to wipe it out. Now, mind you, we could do it in seven years, as Congressional leaders propose. But the pain we'd inflict on our elderly, our students, and our economy just isn't worth it."[74] His proposal made congressional Democrats look ridiculous. They'd been spending months attacking Republicans for their proposed cutbacks. Now, here was the leader of their own party proposing many of the very same cutbacks. As a result, in the wake of Clinton's speech, it wasn't just Republicans attacking Clinton's proposal. Senior Democrat David Obey, Ranking Member of the powerful House Appropriations Committee told *The New York Times* in widely repeated remarks, "I think most of us learned some time ago that if you don't like the President's position on a particular issue, you simply need to wait a few weeks. If you can follow this White House on the budget, you are a whole lot smarter than I am."[75] It seemed as if Clinton almost preferred fighting a war on two fronts – one with right-wing Republicans and one with congressional Democrats, who felt betrayed.

Republicans were ecstatic that Clinton had accepted their framework and had cut the knees from under the congressional Democrats. A Republican adviser told *The Washington Times,* "The more divided the Democrats are, the better it is for us. Call it the divide-and-conquer strategy." Gingrich himself signaled the upcoming GOP strategy to hang tough with Clinton until they extracted more concessions by telling the press after emerging from a closed door Republican planning meeting, "You can't assume anything with Clinton. Just because he doesn't propose something, it doesn't mean he won't accept it in the end."[76] Feeling their oats, Republicans went ahead and packed some of their most extreme proposals into both the budget and a series of appropriations bill: proposals to slash funding almost in half for environmental enforcement, a prohibition on wetlands protection, prohibitions on non-profit groups like universities and churches that receive government grants from speaking out on public affairs issues (a ban that Republicans refused to extend to government contractors), and vast cuts to PBS, NPR, the National Endowment for the Arts and the National Endowment for the Humanities, and a ban on new protections against repetitive stress injuries. They also put a huge tax cut, primarily for the rich, in the bill – just as they were cutting spending on the middle and working classes.

This gave congressional Democrats a huge opportunity to say that Republicans were slashing environmental protection and education just to pay for tax cuts for the rich. It was an effective line, and Democrats used it over and over again. But then on October 17, Clinton told a roomful of wealthy donors at a fundraiser in Houston that "Probably people in this room are still mad at me – at that budget, because you think I raised your taxes too much. But it might surprise you to know that I think I raised them too much too."[77] Democrats who had cast tough votes for his budget were livid – some of them may have even paid for their votes with their seats. New York Democratic Senator Daniel Patrick Moynihan said, "It just knocked us over when we saw that report this morning. He keeps conceding these things. He doesn't understand that he's conceding the principles." The Republicans gleefully jumped on the remarks. Dole and Gingrich held a joint news conference in which Dole declared that, "I think he's just now discovered that this big, big, big tax increase didn't just hit the rich," while Gingrich said, "When you have a President of the United States who is capable of making up whatever fantasies fit his current position, I don't know how as a serious person you can do anything."[78]

Clinton was forced to respond by issuing a statement saying he had "no regrets" about his economic plan. In part to make it up to Democrats, he held a news conference that opened by pledging to veto the Republican plan to slash Medicare and give $425 billion in tax cuts, primarily to the rich. But then, at the end of the conference, he added, "I think there's a way for me to meet their stated objectives, which is a balanced budget in seven years, with a family tax cut, and I think they want a capital gains tax cut, and extending the Medicare Trust Fund to 2006, and for them to meet our stated goals…"[79] It was classic Clinton – unable or unwilling to make a fight with Republicans the centerpiece of his image even when he was attempting to stand strong against them, he offered a premature concession – a budget in seven years that accepted their broad terms of engagement and moved the fight to the details – whether to cut Medicare by $270 billion or $124 billion. It was a major announcement that would define the terms of the final agreement between the Democrats and Republicans.

It was yet another sign to Republicans that there was no limit to Clinton's flexibility. But just as he was moving toward the Republicans, Clinton was also solidifying a bottom line. He was pushed to do so by his advisers, who had even been shielding him from direct negotiations with Republicans out of fear that Clinton couldn't resist making too many concessions in direct negotiations. He was willing to heed their advice, in part, because on November 8 Colin Powell announced that he wouldn't run for president as a centrist Republican candidate, meaning Clinton could worry less about the defection of independents. On Morris's advice, Clinton had also launched a $40 million national advertising campaign attacking Republicans for their proposed cuts and asserting that Clinton was "doing what's moral, good and right by our elderly."[80] What's more, the polls were turning against the Republican proposals and their authors. An October 26 *New York Times* poll showed that only 27 percent of people polled preferred a balanced budget to cuts in Medicare, with 67 percent choosing to maintain Medicare spending at the same level (a position considerably more hard line than that Clinton had adopted). 40 percent of people said Clinton was doing enough to cooperate with Republicans, while only 29 percent said the same of the Republicans and significantly more people approved of Clinton than either Gingrich or Dole.[81]

It's important to understand these poll numbers in the context of just how extreme the Republican proposals were. Gingrich and Dole were pushing pretty radical changes in the fabric of American social safety net. On October 24, in remarks republished by Democrats in advertisements, Gingrich told insurance giant Blue Cross/Blue Shield that Medicare should be left to "wither on the vine;" the same day Dole bragged to the American Conservative Union that he had voted against the creation of Medicare in 1965 "because we knew it wouldn't work." They were also pushing pretty extreme cutbacks on environmental protection (like allowing oil drilling in Alaska's Arctic National Wildlife Refuge) and cutting taxes for the wealthy. With strong public support for protecting Medicare and other government programs and Republicans repeatedly shooting themselves in the foot, Clinton dug in for the first time. In a private meeting with Dole and Gingrich at the end of October, Clinton signaled his new attitude, "If you want somebody to sign your budget, you're going to have to elect Bob Dole to sit behind that desk, because I'm not going to do it."[82] He repeated similar pledges to veto the Republican plan in public.

Despite their plummeting public support, Republicans were committed to altering the balance of power in America by gutting the social safety net and giving corporations even more power – and they passed their budget complete with increases in Medicare premiums, attacks on the environment, and drops in education funding even if they had to defy the polls to do it. If Clinton didn't sign the package, it would mean much of the federal government would shut down – meaning workers couldn't process applications for government service like passports, Social Security and Veterans' benefits, national parks would close, and 800,000 "non-essential" federal employees would be temporarily out of work. Nevertheless, Clinton followed through on his threats and vetoed the Republican package on November 13. The next day, he told the country that "If America has to close down access to education, to a clean environment, to affordable health care, to keep our government open, then the price is too high."[83] And he reiterated his willingness to sign the seven-year budget package he had previously denounced as too harsh as long as Republicans scaled back cuts on Medicare, health care for the poor, education, and the environment. So while he had momentarily stood up, he had only stood up after the Republicans had already won most of what they wanted. Clinton had drawn a line in the sand, but the line was awful close to the core Democratic and New Deal fabric of government and society. Republicans would have been wise to take what Clinton was offering, which was almost everything they had asked for. But they had gotten used to total conquest, and had seen Clinton retreat from other lines in the sand as well.

Even though polls showed continued backing for Clinton and declining support for Republicans, Gingrich kept pursuing more. However, Gingrich damaged his own efforts by blaming the extreme quality of the Republican package on being forced to exit Air Force One by the back stairs when he came back from Israeli Prime Minister Yitzhak Rabin's funeral a week earlier. "I think that's why, by the way, that you ended up with us sending down a tougher continuing resolution....This is petty, but I think it's human," Gingrich admitted to a breakfast of reporters, in widely relayed remarks.[84] Clinton came up with a masterful response, managing to avoid a smile while he said, "I can tell you this – if it would get the government open, I'd be glad to tell him I'm sorry."[85] He appeared even more reasonable, while Gingrich appeared that he was willing to make all Americans pay for a perceived personal slight. With Republicans seeming increasingly cruel and petty, Dole saw the writing on the wall and decided it was time to cut a deal. Congress passed legislation to keep the government open. It was unclear which side had blinked, but Republicans got the blame. Congressional Democrats were happy that Clinton had stood up to Republicans, and for one of the first times since Republicans took office, Clinton and congressional Democrats presented a united front.

But the fight wasn't yet over. Extremist Republicans engineered passage of another budget that fell short of Clinton's minimum standards, thinking that while he might take a strong stand once, he wouldn't stomach shutting down the government again. But with the polls, and even Dick Morris telling him not to give in, Clinton vetoed the budget again. As a result, most of the government shut down once again. Extremist elements in the House Republican caucus wanted to keep up the fight, but the political support just wasn't there. Dole was growing increasingly concerned about how negative public perception of Republicans in the budget fight was impacting his presidential chances. He led Senate Republicans to break with their House colleagues and pledge to vote with Democrats to keep the government open. The pressure eventually got to be too much even for Gingrich, who had to put down a revolt among Republican freshmen to get them to allow the government to re-open. Even though they got almost everything they wanted, the extremity of the Republican proposals and their insistence on holding the government hostage to get *everything* they wanted made them the political, though not the substantive, losers. A December 24 analysis by *Washington Post* reporter Thomas Edsall entitled "Confrontation Is the Key To Clinton's Popularity; Adviser Morris's Strategy Proves Inconsistent" summed up the year's political dynamic. It noted that Clinton's approval ratings remained stuck in the 40's until he took on Republicans in the fall – providing evidence that the conciliatory part of the Clinton-Morris triangulation strategy wasn't working.[xxvii][86] Clinton himself took note of the article and passed it onto adviser George Stephanopolous.[87]

Nevertheless, Clinton remained committed to Morris's strategy and in his 1996 State of the Union speech at the end of January unveiled the platform he would ride to re-election. Clinton began by taking credit for the accelerating economic boom – the rising stock market, 8 million new jobs, lower interest rates, declining crime, and lower teen pregnancy. He also put traditionally peripheral ideas like the V-Chip, a plea to tobacco companies to stop marketing cigarettes to children, and an endorsement of school uniforms at the center of his platform (all these ideas had scored the best in Morris's polling). But the speech would be remembered most for the ultimate accomodationist statement. The president who proposed government-guaranteed universal health care, had staked his political future on a defense of New Deal and Great Society programs like Medicare and Social Security, and had just won a huge political victory defending those priorities now gave his opponents a rhetorical victory that they had no rights to. "The era of big government is over," he told Congress and the nation. To be sure, Clinton followed the statement with a declaration that, "We cannot go back to the time when our citizens were left to fend for themselves. Instead, we must go forward as one America, one nation working together to meet the challenges we face together."[88] But the declaration of big government's demise – which Clinton repeated at the end of his speech – was seen as a philosophical repudiation of himself, his record, his party, and most of all the progressive philosophy. And while it put him at the center of the philosophical debate over the role of government raging in Washington, it also moved that center squarely in the Republican direction – and once again cut the knees out from under congressional Democrats who were planning on running for re-election on a defense of those very big

---

[xxvii]The article noted that the poll numbers were an only partial repudiation of Morris's strategy – although Morris was reluctant to fight Republicans on all fronts or to push hard for the social safety net, Morris did believe that Clinton should develop certain bottom lines and fight like hell for them.

government programs that Clinton was at least rhetorically rejecting.

The repudiation of big government did, however, help Clinton squash Dole's effort to paint him with the epithet "liberal." Fortunately for Clinton, Dole had little else to fall back on. Although many voters continued to feel economic anxiety as a result of Nafta, manufacturing losses, and reductions in the government safety net, overall consumer confidence remained relatively high.[89] Unemployment had dropped to 5.4 percent and the economy was growing at a relatively healthy 3.7 percent.[90] Per-capita household income was growing – and had been growing at over 4 percent a year.[91] As far as most Americans were concerned, Clinton had also conducted non-economic foreign policy in a responsible fashion. He had won a war of nerves with North Korea by persuading them (with the help of Jimmy Carter, the threat of air strikes and an additional 50,000 U.S. troops in South Korea) to abandon their attempts to develop nuclear weapons in exchange for nuclear technology, food aid, and normalization of diplomatic relations.[xxviii] He had ordered an invasion of Haiti to restore that country's democratically elected government, only to find it unnecessary when Carter, Colin Powell, and Senator Sam Nunn won the agreement of the military junta that had taken over the country to restore control to the democratic government. He had given support to a relatively popular (though ultimately failed) peace plan between Israel and the Palestinians. He had brought Serb dictator Slobodan Milosevic to the negotiation table and won a peace agreement for Bosnia (which didn't stop Milosevic from later launching a genocide in Kosovo). To be sure, he had done nothing to stop genocide in Rwanda, but this was far from a top tier issue for most Americans.

At least as importantly, Clinton was blessed with a weak opponent. Dole was making his fourth run for national office; he had been in the U.S. Senate for so long that he'd become a creature of it – unable to resist arcane references to legislative procedure in public speeches (a trap that even Washington neophyte Clinton had fallen into during his first two years in office). He was also a creature of the World War II generation and draped his overwrought rhetoric in a dream of restoring America to the virtues of his youth, saying in his convention speech,

---

[xxviii]The United States didn't keep up its end of the bargain – diplomatic recognition never materialized and the United States, South Korea, and Japan never delivered the light-water nuclear reactors they had promised to North Korea. The North Koreans damaged their prospects for getting the light water reactors by landing spy submarines in South Korea in 1996. After a series of broken promises on both sides, the North Koreans restarted their development of nuclear technology in the late 1990's. However, most experts believe that they didn't actually develop plutonium until President Bush refused to either negotiate or threaten them with military attack, at which point North Korea expelled international inspectors and publicly proclaimed its intent to develop nuclear weapons.

"Let me be the bridge to an America that only the unknowing call myth. Let me be the bridge to a time of tranquility, faith, and confidence in action. And to those who say it was never so, that America has not been better, I say, you're wrong, and I know, because I was there. And I have seen it. And I remember." While it may indeed have been a time of tranquility, faith, and confidence, it was also, more concretely, a time of racial segregation, economic hardship, and war that not all Americans were sure they wanted to return to. Dole's idolization of America's past allowed Clinton to take a none-too-subtle swipe at Dole in his Democratic convention speech: "But with all respect, we do not need to build a bridge to the past. We need to build a bridge to the future."[92] He made the line the theme of his fall campaign. Clinton also artfully transformed the Dole-Kemp campaign into the Dole-Gingrich campaign, successfully tying the marginally popular and respected Dole to the decidedly unpopular Gingrich. Clinton's admen became expert at finding bits of footage of Gingrich ranting about weakening the social safety net or attacking public education while Dole lurked in the background.

With all these advantages, Clinton had the kind of edge that only Richard Nixon in 1972 and Ronald Reagan in 1984 had had in history of post-War politics.[xxix] With so much going in his favor, he could have asked for just about any policy mandate he wanted, as well as a mandate for progressive candidates at the congressional level. But Clinton remained so afraid that the American people were so inherently and irretrievably opposed to a progressive agenda, especially after the 1994 Republican takeover, that he stuck with what he thought was the more cautious course of only attacking Republican excesses and putting forth a small-scale agenda for his second term. He also decided to wear a suit without any coattails – at the same time that he attacked the Dole-Gingrich Congress, he decided against running a coordinated campaign with the Democrats in Congress actually fighting Dole-Gingrich in the trenches. His positive agenda consisted mainly of ideas like a $1500 a year college tax credit, expanded health benefits for the unemployed, and a promise to send AmeriCorps volunteers to teach kids to read – rather than the congressional Democrats' broad promise to defend and expand the social safety net. Indeed, the Clinton campaign made a conscious decision to try and separate Clinton from the rest of the Democratic Party; Clinton's centrist pollster Mark Penn even argued that "we have nothing to gain by identification with the Democratic Party. We are seen by the voters

---

[xxix]Most notably, these advantages allowed Clinton to overcome one usually very significant deficit in comparison with Dole. 37 percent of voters gave Dole higher marks on morality, which usually played an important role in determining vote choice.

more favorably – more fiscally responsible, more values-oriented, more compassionate, more of everything – than the party as a whole. We don't want this convention to be about the party. We want it to be about Bill Clinton."[93]

Unlike Clinton, the Democrats running for Congress were not usually blessed with opponents as relatively weak as Dole. In competitive districts, they were usually the ones running against Republican incumbents – with all the fundraising power that incumbency brought. Indeed, despite all of Clinton's efforts to curry favor with Democratic contributors (including possible abuses like rewarding big donors with presidential face time and overnight stays in the Lincoln Bedroom), Republican candidates (including Dole) outraised the Democrats 56 percent to 43 percent – a huge 10 point shift away from the Democrats since 1992.[94] This shift wasn't just due to big business's increasing enthusiasm for the Republicans. It also happened because Republican grassroots donors were more enthusiastic about their party and its aggressive pursuit of a conservative agenda than progressive grassroots Democrats, disappointed in Clinton's constant policy moves to the right, were about their party. This lack of enthusiasm showed in overall depressed voter turnout numbers in 1996 – only 49 percent of people turned out, the lowest in any post-war election. In part, this was because Clinton (and the Republicans) spent almost all of their money and time on a TV air war, rather than investing major resources in building a grassroots, people-based campaign that could help turn out voters on Election Day.

Nevertheless, Clinton out-debated, out-campaigned, and out-did Dole by every measure – and won by a healthy 8.5 point margin. He fell short of the 50 percent majority he had hoped for, winning just over 49 percent of the vote (Perot took 8 percent), but racked up a big electoral college win. But his victory hardly helped his party. The strategy of triangulation bore its bitter fruit for congressional Democrats. Without Clinton's help, congressional Democrats had to fight not only well-financed Republican opponents but also the implicit criticism of their progressive agenda contained in Clinton's oft-repeated repudiation of big government. They also had to contend with unenthusiastic progressives who were put off by Clinton's repeated capitulations and embrace of corporate policies – and who often didn't take the time to see the difference between Clinton and the Democratic congressional candidate in their district or state. As a result, Republicans retained their Congressional majorities for the first time since 1928 (though Democrats did pick up two seats in the House of Representatives, and actually received more popular votes in House races; they lost two seats in the Senate).

Clinton did help achieve one very important lasting gain for Democrats in his 1996 presidential campaign. He was able to take advantage of the rising tide of progressive political opinion in California, the country's biggest electoral college prize, by making dozens of visits to the state since he took office. As a result of his attention – as well as California's rising working class Latino population and increasing social liberalism – Clinton was not only able to beat Dole by 13 points, but also solidified the state's Democratic leanings enough to make it difficult to imagine this onetime Republican stronghold choosing a Republican presidential candidate or a Republican legislature anytime in the near future. Unfortunately for California Democrats, in 1998 Clinton also helped saddle them with a cautious Clintonian Democrat in the governor's office – Grey Davis. Davis was more Clintonian than Clinton. He took Clinton's centrism, inattention to progressive movement-building, and most of all focus on raising big bucks from big business, to possibly illegal extremes. He even set up a "pay to play" system of state contracting that infuriated Californians of all political stripes, making him look corrupt and not just over-eager to please. Furthermore, Davis lacked the charm that, along with weak opponents, had repeatedly helped Clinton overcome a disastrously misguided political strategy. It was no surprise, then, when spurned progressives showed up in very low numbers during California's 2003 recall election, helping put Arnold Schwarzenegger in the governor's office.

Surrendering the Agenda

Ultimately, it wasn't just congressional Democrats (or the American people) who would reap the bitter fruit of the 1996 Republican victories in Congress. Continued right-wing Republican domination of Congress following the 1996 elections meant that Republicans retained the power to sustain their ongoing personal attack on the Clintons – backed up by both their subpoena power and their Constitutional power to impeach the president. Beyond all policy considerations, this was the one big political drawback to leaving congressional Democrats to fend for themselves in the 1996 elections – without congressional Democrats in power, Republicans retained subpoena power and Clinton would face the threat of continued investigations that sought, above all else, to take the focus of the American people off the Republicans' attempts to demolish the social and environmental safety net.

But Clinton didn't believe Republicans would keep up the attacks into his second term. When Clinton was recruiting a new chief of staff to replace Leon Panetta – who had to be dragged, kicking and screaming, to accept both Dick Morris personally and Morris's strategy of triangulation – Clinton tried to get moderate, mild-mannered former Deputy Chief of Staff and wealthy business-man Erskine Bowles to come back to Washington to take the top job. Clinton believed Bowles's soft manners would make it easier for him to reach out to Republicans. But Bowles refused, telling Clinton that the second term would be characterized by continued Republican scandal-mongering and partisan war-fare; the reserved Bowles told Clinton "I don't do scandals." Clinton remained insistent, telling Bowles that he thought that the Republicans had basically given up on pursuing scandals and that he needed someone in the Chief of Staff role who could effectively reach out to Republicans on common legislative initiatives. Bowles accepted – but only after he had won a commitment from Clinton that he wouldn't have to defend Clinton against mudslinging.

Clinton's choice of the confrontation-averse Bowles represented the triumph of hope over experience – especially since he was at the very time carrying on an affair with former White House intern Monica Lewinsky, whom he later acknowledged he always knew wouldn't be able to resist telling people about the affair.[xxx] From the moment he started campaigning for president, indeed from the time he entered politics 20 years earlier in Arkansas, his uncompromising right-wing foes had unleashed personal attack after personal attack against him, Hillary, and anyone else in his circle they could lay their hands on. But Clin-ton, like many other non-confrontational politicians, could never seem to step out of his own head and his own situation and understand that just because he wouldn't launch a vicious personal attack against an opponent, that meant that his opponents wouldn't either. As a result, Clinton always seemed caught a bit off guard when Republicans played dirty and hit him below the belt – no matter how many times it happened.

And hitting below the belt was the main way Republicans went after Clin-ton. Particularly when they began to realize that Americans wouldn't necessarily side with their ultra right-wing crusades against government, they began to sling even more mud. It started with their efforts to make an issue out of Whitewater, the Clintons' 30 year-old land deal. And continued when they tried to transform

---

[xxx]In his deposition about Lewinsky on August 17, 1998, Clinton told prosecutors from Starr's office, "I formed an opinion early in 1996, once I got into this unfortunate and wrong conduct that when I stopped it, which I knew I'd have to do, that she would talk about it. But I knew the minute there was no longer any contact, she would talk about this. She would have to. She couldn't help it. It was, it was just part of her psyche."

Clinton friend Vince Foster's suicide into a grand (though undefined) conspiracy. It evolved into their effort to convince America that Bill Clinton had somehow sexually harassed Paula Jones during a brief encounter in the 1970's. When they couldn't find enough mud, they just concocted it from innuendo, unreliable or bribed sources, and sheer hatred.

At the beginning of his administration, the Clintons had responded to the scandals in a largely open and conciliatory way, hoping that full disclosure and honesty would tame the scandal monster. In an attempt to clear the air of scandal surrounding the White House, Clinton agreed to ask Attorney General Janet Reno to appoint a special counsel who would investigate the Whitewater allegations independent of normal Justice Department supervision. He also agreed to release the vast majority of documents regarding Whitewater to the press and testified about the different scandals at the White House. Hillary Clinton testified before Congress about Whitewater and held an hour-long, full-scale press conference in which she answered questions from reporters about Whitewater.[95] Most dangerously of all for Clinton, he signed the Independent Counsel statute in 1994, which ultimately led to the appointment of arch-Republican Kenneth Starr as the prosecutor investigating any and all Clinton scandals, a choice Clinton would come to regret. Even though Starr was mired in conflicts of interest (he had advised Paula Jones's lawyers on legal strategy, had repeatedly spoken out publicly and privately against Clinton, and continued to work for a million dollars a year at corporate lobbying firm Kirkland & Ellis even after taking the prosecutor post), Clinton gave him a free pass. "I'll cooperate with whoever's picked," he told the press after Starr's name was floated.

Gradually, however, as the independent counsel inquiry became more aggressive as Starr became more single-mindedly zealous, the Clintons were forced into attack mode. In a way, Starr's aggression was a huge gift to Clinton. Clinton feared confrontation, but did very well in the polls when forced into it. Starr took a number of actions that provoked Clinton and turned the American people and even the media against him. He forced Hillary Clinton to testify to the grand jury at the federal courthouse rather than at the White House, going so far as to compel her to do a perp walk through an assembled throng of reporters. He demanded that White House aide Jane Sheburne do a closet-by-closet search of the Clintons' private living quarters at the White House, in a vain quest for some lost Whitewater documents. He even coerced Clinton's personal valets and Secret Service agents to testify, creating a dangerous precedent that might prompt future presidents to avoid their security detail when discussing sensitive matters.

Most damagingly, Starr routinely violated federal grand jury secrecy rules which required that testimony delivered in a grand jury hearing be kept secret. Starr and his deputies regularly leaked secret testimony that would be damaging to Clinton to reporters.

In response, the Clintons employed aggressive, media-savvy lawyer Bob Bennett to complement their legal team. Bennett helped make sure that Clinton's opponents got as good as they gave in the media. Bennett and other Clinton staffers appeared frequently on talk shows to criticize Starr's conduct. The Clintons themselves worked to persuade the country that Ken Starr's office was merely a political campaign posing as a judicial entity – and that its sole purpose was to destroy Clinton's presidency. When PBS News anchor Jim Lehrer asked Clinton if he thought that Starr's prosecution was a personal and political vendetta rather than a legitimate judicial proceeding, Clinton responded, "Isn't it obvious?"[96]

Despite all the Washington maneuvering, Whitewater and the other Clinton scandals didn't make too much of an imprint on the national consciousness until the Lewinsky sex scandal emerged. When it did, it threatened the very existence of Clinton's presidency – but because it forced Clinton into the confrontational posture in which he thrived, was in many ways a major political boost to his presidency.

When Clinton appeared before Judge Susan Weber Wright in a room at the Skadden Arps law firm in Washington, DC to testify in the Paula Jones sexual harassment case, he was presented with a definition of sexual relations that, after being narrowed by the judge, read, "For the purposes of this deposition, a person engages in 'sexual relations' when the person knowingly engages in or causes – contact with the genitalia, anus, groin, breast, inner thigh, or buttocks of any person with an intent to arouse or gratify the sexual desire of any person." During the course of the inquiry, Jones's lawyer asked Clinton if according to the definition of sexual relations, "Did you have an extramarital sexual affair with Monica Lewinsky?" Clinton responded, "No…I have never had sexual relations with Monica Lewinsky. I've never had an affair with her."[97] Clinton's answer was, at a minimum, untruthful – and would provide the basis for the later Republican efforts to impeach him. Meanwhile, the *Drudge Report,* a right-wing internet news site of only intermittent accuracy, was publishing a constant stream of information about the Lewinsky-Clinton relationship supplied by Lewinsky "friend" Linda Tripp. The reports set off a public firestorm as the alleged details of the affair made their way into the mainstream press. To decide what to do,

Clinton called Morris and told him he'd "slipped up" with Lewinsky and asked what he should do. The pair agreed that Morris should conduct a poll to see what response would fly with the American people. Morris's pollsters asked respondents to assume that Clinton had indeed had an affair with Lewinsky, had lied about it, and had asked Lewinsky to lie about it as well. The results showed that only 47 percent of people would want him out of office if that was the case. Morris interpreted (or misinterpreted) these results as showing that voters weren't ready for a confession. "Well, we just have to win then," Clinton said, and embarked on a strategy of deceiving the American people rather than coming clean right away.[98]

A few days later, on January 26, Clinton wagged his finger at the White House press corps and said "I did not have sexual relations with that woman, Miss Lewinsky. I never told anybody to lie, not a single time, ever." The next day, Hillary Clinton went on the Today show to tell the nation that Clinton had denied the allegations and decried the vast right-wing conspiracy that was attacking them. The White House communications team joined the attack. Clinton was taking on his enemies, who seemed like they were casting sleazy accusations at him, and the American people rallied to his side. Rather than being damaged by the accusations, his approval rating surged 18 percent almost overnight to 73 percent – the highest level of his presidency. He was confronting (and being confronted) and the American people loved it. From that moment on, with just a handful of exceptions, his rating would stay above 60 percent for the rest of his term.

Meanwhile, the Starr prosecutors were in a bind. They were unable to reach a deal with Lewinsky under which she'd get immunity in exchange for her testimony about her affair with Clinton – and wouldn't strike a deal for another six months. Until they did, they had little ammunition to either tarnish Clinton in public or build a stronger case for impeachment. All the most salacious details of the Clinton-Lewinsky relationship had already been leaked to the press – including the fact that Lewinsky might have physical proof of their relationship in the form of a Navy blue Gap dress stained with Clinton's semen. The constant drip of information about the affair – much of it coming from Lewinsky's outlandish lawyer William Ginsburg – gradually convinced most Americans that Clinton had indeed had an affair, but they didn't seem to want to kick him out of office for it. In part, it's because Clinton didn't let the simmering scandal distract him excessively from governing. He delivered a well-received State of the Union address, traveled on a first-ever presidential tour of Africa, oversaw the signing of Northern Ireland peace accords, and implemented a patients' bill of rights for federal health care plans, all while under the cloud of the Lewinsky scandal. On April 1, 1998 Clinton got another boost when Judge Susan Weber Wright granted summary judgement to Clinton in the Jones sexual harassment case.

But then on July 28, Starr finally reached an immunity agreement with Lewinsky, and she agreed to testify about her affair with Clinton. On the one hand, this was a major betrayal of Clinton by Lewinsky – she could have decided, as others in the Whitewater investigation did, to refuse to testify and so prevent Clinton from having to risk his presidency. Doing so would have put her at risk of a perjury conviction because of her false affidavit, but she also could have avoided the Starr inquiry's lurid inquiries into her private life and their subsequent airing to the world. But Monica Lewinsky wasn't constituted to put anyone – even a president she admired and had loved – before herself and never seriously considered putting Clinton's presidency before her own freedom. And she seemed to enjoy at least some of the round the clock media coverage of her personal life – even agreeing to a risqué Herb Ritts *Vanity Fair* photo shoot on the beach in Malibu.

Perhaps Lewinsky's willingness to betray Clinton was just another instance of Clinton's failure to inspire great feelings of loyalty. He drove Lewinsky crazy by resisting finishing sex acts, conjuring up an explanation that "they didn't count" if they didn't finish. It was a failure to commit, even to a sex act, that wounded Lewinsky's pride. From a political perspective, Clinton's minimally ambitious second term made it less likely that the liberals in Lewinsky's circle would advise sacrificing herself to save such a small-bore presidency. It was a personal manifestation of Clinton's great political weakness – that he inspired neither love nor fear. He inspired little love because of his unwillingness to take on and fight for big changes that would, win or lose, warm the hearts of his supporters. And he inspired little fear because of his own fear of playing hardball and because of his repeated capitulations in the face of stiff (or sometimes not so stiff) opposition. Lewinsky's deal was reported in the press on July 28 – making it clear that Clinton would likely be caught in a lie, especially after Starr's office demanded that Clinton submit a blood sample – suggesting strongly that the persistent rumors that Lewinsky had kept a dress stained with Clinton's semen were true. In this context, Clinton agreed to provide videotaped testimony to the grand jury at the White House on August 17.

In his testimony, Clinton admitted to his affair with Lewinsky, but denied all the other charges that Starr was pushing in media leaks and would later push in his report to Congress. He denied encouraging either Lewinsky or Betty Currie to lie to the grand jury. He denied that he had helped get Lewinsky a job through his friend Vernon Jordan in exchange for Lewinsky's silence, and said he didn't try to retrieve gifts he had given Lewinsky to avoid having to give them to the Jones lawyers (the Jones lawyers had subpoenaed any gifts he had given to Lewinsky). That night, Clinton read a statement to the nation in which he not only expressed contrition for misleading the country, but also attacked Starr's invasion of his privacy and how Starr's investigation was distracting the country's attention from more important matters.

> I answered their questions truthfully, including questions about my private life, questions no American citizen would ever want to answer. Still, I must take complete responsibility for all my actions, both public and private...But I told the grand jury today and I say to you now that at no time did I ask anyone to lie, to hide or destroy evidence or to take any other unlawful action. In addition, I had real and serious concerns about an independent counsel investigation that began with private business dealings 20 years ago, dealings, I might add, about which an independent federal agency found no evidence of any wrongdoing by me or my wife over two years ago.

> The independent counsel investigation moved on to my staff and friends, then into my private life. And now the investigation itself is under investigation. This has gone on too long, cost too much and hurt too many innocent people. Now, this matter is between me, the two people I love most – my wife and our daughter – and our God. It is time to stop the pursuit of personal destruction and the prying into private lives and get on with our national life.[99]

Clinton had been confrontational – and the media was determined to pummel him for it. From their perspective, he should have been at a minimum purely contrite. If he was largely in the right, why had they focused all the attention on his misdeeds? All the national media immediately unleashed a deluge of criticism, blasting Clinton for being insufficiently apologetic and attacking Starr's investigation when he should have just been apologizing. On ABC News, correspondent Sam Donaldson led off his network's coverage of the speech by saying Clinton "didn't come clean tonight with the country," setting a tone for many other curious journalists who criticized Clinton for not providing details about his relationship with Lewinsky. Even George Stephanopoulos, Clinton's former senior adviser who was now working at ABC News, criticized the speech for not being "as contrite as necessary" and dismissed Clinton's claim that his affair with Lewinsky was a private matter.[100] Only NBC got it right, by turning its cameras for reaction not to journalists, but to 15 Americans from different parties who had watched the speech together; following the speech, only one out of the 15 said they wanted Clinton impeached.[101]

Similarly, polls showed that despite the media lashing, the American people didn't seem to want the gory details of Clinton's sex life – and responded overwhelmingly positively to Clinton's speech. The night of the speech, *Nightline* released a quickie poll, whose results were echoed by later polls. 61 percent of people continued to say they approved of the job President Clinton was doing. And though 52 percent of people said they thought that Clinton had obstructed justice, 69 percent of people thought Ken Starr should end his investigation, and only 28 percent said Clinton should resign.[102] The poll results showed that Americans were responding positively when Clinton took the fight to the American people – even when the Republican attack machine and much of the media was aligned against him, and even when he had admitted to a bald-faced deception of the American people. Meanwhile, approval of the Starr investigation remained extremely low – getting between 19 and 44 percent support, depending on the poll.[103] Clinton was confronting and winning, despite the media crusade against him.

Typically, Clinton's public support didn't stop the Republicans. Starr went ahead (with the help of future Bush circuit court appointee Brett Kavanaugh) to write a 452 page report full of pornographic detail about Clinton and Lewinsky's relationship – all ejaculation, cigars, and genitalia. Not only did the report violate any reasonable standard of good taste or legal discretion, it also violated Justice Department norms by deliberately excluding exculpatory evidence. Starr sent the report to Congress with a conclusion that "There is Substantial and Credible Information that President Clinton Committed Acts that May Constitute Grounds for an Impeachment," citing 11 different acts that Starr said could be impeachable offenses, including perjury, obstruction of justice, and suborning perjury. Despite Starr's recommendation, the evidence was thin. Although Clinton had given a dishonest answer in his deposition to the Jones case, it would be difficult to prove that his legalistic responses about an extramarital sexual affair actually met the high standard usually required in perjury prosecutions. What's more, neither Lewinsky, Vernon Jordan, nor Betty Currie said that Clinton had encouraged them to lie, giving Starr precious few grounds to accuse Clinton of obstruction of justice. Congress voted almost immediately to release the Starr report to the public, without even reviewing it (Starr hadn't warned them that a great deal of the material was extremely graphic).

By this point, congressional Democrats were threatening to abandon Clinton, despite his continued high standing in the polls. Many of them, like Clinton's own White House staff, felt that Clinton had betrayed them personally by urging them to deny the allegations against him over the past six months and making them look like fools or liars now. On August 25, House Democratic Leader Richard Gephardt said that both Clinton's conduct and his comments on the affair were "wrong and reprehensible," spoke extensively about his role as a "potential grand juror" in an impeachment proceeding, and said that if Clinton was removed from office, "we'll get through this."[104] Days later, Joe Lieberman delivered a pious speech on the floor of the Senate denouncing Clinton's behavior.

Congressional Democrats' and the media's obsessions with the Clinton scandals and their willingness to discuss impeaching Clinton for transgressions related to his private life didn't play well with grassroots progressives. They continued to see the Starr inquiry and the impeachment effort as yet another attempt to undermine democracy and distract the public from the Republican attacks on civil rights, the environment, and economic fairness. With passions running high, the environment was ripe for something to mobilize them. As a result, when software millionaires Wes Boyd and Joan Blades sent an email to 500 friends asking them to sign a petition urging Congress to "immediately censure President Clinton and move on to pressing issues facing the country," the email went viral. Within a week, more than 100,000 people had signed the petition; within a month, more than 300,000. The organization that would come to be known as MoveOn.org was born. MoveOn would go onto to become one of the country's most powerful and innovative progressive organizations – with its membership growing to more than 3 million by 2005 and raising more than $40 million in the 2004 election cycle.[105] Because of this and other efforts, it ended up being the very progressives that Clinton had betrayed throughout his term who became some of his most ardent, though temporary, backers in the impeachment battle. In contrast, it was Clinton's fellow centrists in the Senate who were quickest to abandon him.

But MoveOn's future mobilization of progressives was at this point just a California dream. August remained the moment of greatest peril for the Clinton presidency. The media resumed its feverish coverage of the Lewinsky affair. Record numbers of reporters from all over the world descended on Washington. The right-wing continued to whip up anger from its hard core supporters, generating millions of calls into congressional offices and talk radio shows. Senate

Democratic Leader Tom Daschle counted seven Democrats who were contemplating bailing on the president and coming out in favor of impeachment – Robert Byrd, Florida's Bob Graham, California's Dianne Feinstein, Nevada's Harry Reid, Russ Feingold of Wisconsin, Fritz Hollings of South Carolina, and Joseph Biden of Delaware. In an attempt to shore up Clinton's support in his caucus, Daschle invited Erskine Bowles (who had told Clinton "I don't do scandals") and Deputy Chief of Staff John Podesta to the Democratic senators' Tuesday lunch. Joe Biden expressed his preference that Clinton resign to help Democrats in the fall elections. North Dakota's Kent Conrad told Podesta, "You're about three days away from having a senior delegation of Democratic senators going to the White House to ask for the president's resignation." Having just faced the onslaught, Bowles was true to his word that "I don't do scandals". He told press secretary Mike McCurry to leak news that he would leave at the end of that session of Congress, saying, "I just want you to know that I'm not going up and doing any more defense of the president on the Hill."[106] Suddenly Clinton saw how his abandonment of congressional Democrats was coming back to haunt him. "For six years I have not been out there with the Congress; maybe I should have," he told his advisers.[107]

With grassroots Democrats disillusioned with their own party leaders and congressional Democrats infighting over how to proceed, Republicans were relishing the prospect of making major pick-ups during the mid-term elections, and even convinced many members of the punditocracy that they were within striking range of picking up a filibuster-proof 60-seat majority in the Senate. But Clinton's approval ratings remained above 60 percent, and as Election Day got closer, the polls started showing many more voters planning on choosing Democrats in the ballot box than the Republicans had confidently predicted. Feeling the heat, the National Republican Congressional Committee spent $10 million on three ads starting in the last week of the race that urged voters not to "reward Bill Clinton" for his lies and "make the Democrats more powerful."

One ad entitled "What did you tell your kids?" went for the jugular:

> Woman 1: What did you tell your kids?
> Woman 2: I didn't know what to say.
> Woman 1: It's wrong. For seven months he lied to us.
> Woman 2: But aren't there other things to do?
> Woman 1: And say it's OK to lie? Besides, the Republicans are doing
> them. They cut taxes, they helped balance the budget, and they're put-

ting people on welfare back to work. And now they have a plan to save
Social Security.

Woman 2: But the Democrats say ...

Woman 1: ... The truth is the Democrats gave us higher taxes and more
government.

(Fade to black and the words, "Republicans. The balanced leadership
we need.")

Woman 2: Now, there's a difference that really matters.

Woman 1: Republicans are the balance we need.[108]

Democrats countered with ads describing Republicans as "so intent on attacking the president they've forgotten about us."[109] The tracking and exit polls conducted after the release of these advertisements don't provide conclusive evidence about whether the focus on the Clinton scandal helped or hurt the Republicans, but Republican plans to impeach the President did help mobilize base supporters on both sides.

On Election Day, Republicans fell short of the lofty media expectations they had helped generate, giving Democrats the appearance of a major victory. Democrats stopped Republicans from picking up any seats in the Senate and actually picked up five seats in the House. Most notably, voters in New York and North Carolina ousted the Republican Senate leaders of the Clinton scandal crusade – Al D'Amato and Lauch Faircloth (while Republicans picked up formerly Democratic seats elsewhere). Even though Republicans retained control of Congress, the election results were widely interpreted as a rebuke of Republican obsession with Clinton's sex life and their plans to impeach him.

With this setback behind them, Republicans figured they had already paid the price for impeachment at the polls; if they pressed ahead with impeachment immediately after the election, voters would have forgotten it by the time 2000 rolled around (they were largely correct in this assessment). Outside of all political motives, many Republicans remained consumed by their hatred of Clinton. But it quickly became apparent that hatred might have been clouding their judgment. Newt Gingrich announced his resignation in the wake of the Republican losses, perhaps afraid that his own three year extra-marital affair with a House staffer 23 years his junior would become public.[110] His replacement, Louisiana's Bob Livingston, was set to seize the reins of power when he admitted to the world that he had "on occasion strayed" from his marriage after four women told *Hustler* publisher Larry Flynt that they'd had affairs with Livingston, in response to Flynt's offer to pay $1 million for stories about federal officials' extramarital canoodling. The media soon reported that Henry Hyde, who chaired the House committee in charge of the Congressional impeachment effort, had fathered an illegitimate child. Flynt also published allegations by anti-choice House Republican Bob Barr's former wife Gail that he had not only had an affair, but had also paid for his wife to have an abortion. But the Republicans were nothing if not dogged. Despite growing disgust with the inquiry, the Republicans shepherded the impeachment charges through committee on a party-line vote and then passed them on the House floor by narrow margins, with just five Republicans and five Democrats defecting from their party's positions. Now, it would be up to the Senate to decide Clinton's fate in the constitutionally mandated trial.

By this point, Clinton had ceased to play much of a public or private role in defending himself. He said that there was little he could do and it was now up to Congress, the American people, and God. But the Republican presentation of evidence at the Senate trial didn't go well – they had little evidence to prove Clinton's crimes or to prove that his crimes deserved removal from office; furthermore, Clinton's approval ratings remained sky high, making it that much more politically difficult for members of Congress to vote to remove him. In the midst of it, Clinton also delivered a well-received State of the Union speech. It quickly became clear that no Democrat would support impeachment, and many Republicans were threatening to vote against impeachment as well. The House Republicans became concerned that if less than a majority of senators voted to impeach Clinton, they'd wind up looking ridiculous for having tied up the country for so long with Bill Clinton's sex life. So they ginned up right-wing activists to put pressure on Republican senators threatening to bail on impeachment and even threatened to put up primary opponents to senators who voted to keep Clinton in office – and were able to get more support as a result. In the end, the Senate voted to acquit Clinton 45-55 on the charge of perjury. On the second count, they voted to acquit 50-50 (two thirds were needed to remove Clinton from office). Clinton held all the Democrats in both votes, got 10 Republicans on the first perjury count, and five on the second. He was acquitted.

Ever the conciliator, Clinton went to the Rose Garden after the vote to tell the American people, once again, "how profoundly sorry I am for what I said and did to trigger these events and the great burden they have imposed on the Congress and the American people." He then took a single question from the press corps: "In your heart, sir, can you forgive and forget?" "I believe any person who asks for forgiveness has to be prepared to give it," Clinton responded, an extraordinary gesture considering the events of the previous year. The statement signaled that Clinton wouldn't press his political advantage and hold Republicans accountable for hijacking the national agenda. By taking responsibility, Clinton also undermined the ability of other Democrats to keep the issue alive – if Clinton said the whole thing was his fault, it legitimized the whole Starr inquiry and undermined all of Clinton's previous attacks on Starr and the Republican Congress. It also sandbagged his staff, who had spent years executing Clinton's strategy of going on the attack against his pursuers, making their attacks look craven and unfounded (though by this point in his administration, they should have expected that Clinton wouldn't exactly repay their loyalty in rhetorical full). More importantly, it was a rebuke to all the progressives who had passionately defended Clinton to their friends – leaving them feeling less than exuberant about Clinton and the Democratic Party even after they had invested so much energy in protecting him over the last year.

After the Lewinsky scandal passed, Clinton did return to working on his agenda. Until the last moment, he continued to pursue a Middle East peace deal, a worthy venture that ultimately failed due to Arafat's unwillingness to compromise. He continued working to raise money from big dollar contributors for the Democratic Party, providing some important help for Al Gore's 2000 presidential bid. He fulfilled George Bush, Sr.'s pledge to protect Kosovo's Albanian ethnic group from an attempted massacre by Serb dictator Slobodan Milosevic by launching a bombing campaign to drive out the Serbs. On the domestic front, he achieved some important successes in realizing some of the "smaller" ideas he had advocated in the 1996 election: expanding after school child care, reached an agreement with handgun manufacturer Smith & Wesson to add safety features to some handguns, and announced new worker safety protections.

He used his executive authority to create five new national monuments: the Giant Sequoia National Monument in California to protect the largest trees on Earth, as well as the Canyons of the Ancients National Monument in southwest Colorado, the Cascade-Siskiyou National Monument in southern Oregon, the Hanford Reach National Monument in south central Washington, and the Ironwood Forest National Monument in southern Arizona. Following the 2000 election, in response to more than 1.6 million public comments over three years, Clinton signed an executive order to protect 60 million acres of America's last remaining pristine forests (known as roadless areas) – one of the biggest conservation acts by a president in history. Unfortunately, George W. Bush immediately set to work to undermine this policy and ultimately reversed it, putting the fate of these forests in jeopardy. Of course, Clinton intended his most important legacy to be Al Gore, whom he hoped would continue his policies and perpetuate his political legacy. But the Lewinsky scandal lessened the help Clinton could give Gore. At the very least, rightly or wrongly, the scandal made Gore's advisers wary of giving Bill Clinton a big role in the campaign. They worried, like Clinton himself had in 1998, that Clinton's presence on the campaign trail would do more to rile up cultural conservatives than it would help with blacks, among whom he remained extremely popular, and among voters who would respond to his record of economic prosperity.[111] Similar to the situation in 2000, all of Clinton and Gore's efforts to raise big money from big corporations (and pass corporate friendly policies) didn't pay off – Bush outraised Gore $190 million to $130 million – a huge financial disadvantage for Gore to overcome.

At least as importantly, Gore had to wrestle with Clinton's legacy of distancing himself from and betraying progressives on a whole range of issues. As a result, Gore had to spend a great deal of effort in his campaign working to prove to labor unions, environmentalists, and progressive activists that he would be more of a champion for them. Largely for this reason, he adopted the "people versus the powerful" slogan aimed at appealing to progressives eager for a dose of populism in their presidential candidate. Gore's efforts certainly helped – by September, 2000 he had vastly improved his popularity among progressives. But this improvement wasn't enough – no matter how much he did, a certain type of idealistic or angry progressive would never believe that Gore, who had enthusiastically stood by Clinton throughout Clinton's many betrayals, would be any different. Clinton had blurred the lines between Democrats and Republicans so much that many progressives felt that Clinton's anointed successor just wouldn't be different enough from Bush-Cheney to make a difference – and ended up casting just enough votes for Ralph Nader to swing the election away from Gore in both New Hampshire and Florida. Clinton remained on the sidelines of the Florida recount in 2000, limiting himself to issuing bland statements about the importance of an orderly transition of government.[xxxi] When George W. Bush took office in January, he completed the Republican takeover of power begun in the third year of Clinton's administration; this was as much Clinton's legacy as any other.

[xxxi]Ironically, Jeffrey Toobin reports in *Too Close to Call* that Clinton privately urged Gore's team to adopt a much more confrontational attitude: calling protesters into the streets, suing the Republicans right and left, and arguing repeatedly that Republicans had stolen the election, which was rightfully Gore's. Clinton's public statements reflected none of this confrontational style however.

Clinton Has Left the Building

When Clinton left Washington, there was no one left behind with the power to protect not only the great Democratic achievements of the 20th century government such as Social Security, Medicare, and environmental laws, but even many elements of his own far more centrist legacy. Because Clinton had defined success largely in terms of his own personal popularity and achievement rather than in terms of the strength of a movement, there was precious little to fall back on when he was gone. Rather than the huge Democratic majorities when Clinton took office, Republicans now controlled both Houses of Congress and ran a far tighter, more loyal operation than the Democrats ever did. In the 2000, 2002, and 2004 elections, a whole generation of Democratic strategists trained on the Clinton model of cautious centrism showed that model woefully unable to compete with a Republican Party that had smoothed over its Gingrichian rhetorical excesses and had bolstered its own considerable movement-building. To be sure, there was a fat Rolodex of corporate donors over at the DNC, but Democrats were never able to bring their fundraising up to its pre-Clinton balance with the Republicans. The national progressive movement, such as it was, no longer existed in any organized fashion. Smarting from years of Clinton's betrayals and capitulations, many leaders of progressive organizations steered their organizations away from working through the Democratic Party or even the broader progressive movement and continued to concentrate on their own issues, rendering the Democratic Party unable to compete with the unified corporate-fundamentalist nexus on the Republican side.

Outside the beltway, the condition of the Democratic Party and the progressive movement was, if anything, worse. For instance, the percentage of workers in a union had dropped more than 14 percent during Clinton's time in office.[112] There were few people who felt passionately connected to the Democratic Party – it took at least two years of Bush's administration before many Democrats could see past the betrayals and capitulations of the Clinton years and started to put some energy into strengthening the Democrats to do battle in 2004 (this coincided with progressives and Democrats beginning to see the compromises of the Clinton years through rose-colored glasses once they compared them with the outright hostility of the Bush administration). And despite all the demonstrable and sometimes ridiculous excesses of Republican leadership, the Democratic lead over Republicans in party affiliation didn't change at all during Clinton's term in office, if anything declining slightly.[113]

Because of the lack of effective Democratic opposition, within a few years Bush had dismantled Clinton's protections of 60 million acres of roadless forests, had scarred the West with an unprecedented bonanza of logging, coal mining and oil drilling, and had weakened the many core clean air and water protections. Many Democrats didn't even protest when Bush undid much of Clinton's positive fiscal legacy by slashing taxes for the super rich and increasing the tax burden on the working poor. And there was little that the spiritually and infrastructurally eviscerated Democratic Party could or would do to stop Bush from destroying the new international era of good feeling that Clinton had won in much of the world through his engaged, multi-lateral foreign policy.

The saddest thing about this legacy is that it was so avoidable. Even the simplest measure of Clinton's political success (and one Clinton tracked very closely) – his approval ratings – show a familiar pattern: confront the Republicans and argue passionately for a progressive America and see your popularity and power skyrocket. Clinton could have seen this from his aggressive 1992 campaign, his 1995-1996 budget showdown with the Republicans, and his take-no-prisoners effort to save his presidency from the Republican impeachment campaign. Instead, Clinton frequently squandered the increased popularity and power he got from these confrontations and retreated into the accommodation and capitulation that hurt him over and over again – as it did in the appointments and gays in the military fiasco, in health care, and the initial caution of his second term. And when he did retreat he often also lost not only general support or progressive support, but also the policy battles that would shape America politically and practically for generations to come. That is the fruit of Clinton's politics of fear.

MOVEON.ORG
THE COURAGE OF CROWDS

How do you become the Google of politics? How does a single email spawn one of the country's most powerful political movements? What has transformed MoveOn.org, within a few short years, from accidental Internet sensation into a powerhouse capable of marshaling tens of thousands of volunteers, millions of dollars, and the votes of senators and congressmen – all with a few clicks of a mouse? To put it crudely, they gave the people what they wanted. At a time when the Democratic Party was characterized by weakness, doubt, and above all fear, MoveOn channeled the frustration of millions of grassroots progressives to demand a more courageous Democratic Party. And the people responded first with their forward buttons, then with their wallets, and finally with their time and energy. They provided the cash to fund immense advertising campaigns and the enthusiasm that has allowed MoveOn to field a grassroots political operation that can compete with all the traditional heavies of progressive America: the labor unions, the environmental and civil rights groups, and even the Democratic Party itself. They have won legislative campaigns, helped win back Congress, and most importantly, changed the practice of politics in America. In short, MoveOn's awesome success and continuing exponential growth are proof that the hunger for courageous progressive politics is so great that those who practice it will be richly rewarded.

In that way, this chapter is a little different. The others chronicle how courageous progressive leadership can succeed. This chapter isn't about the power of courageous leadership. It's about the power of courageous followership. It's not so much about how MoveOn bravely stood up for its beliefs when the chips were down (though at key times it did); it's about how its members rallied to the banner of courage – supplying the money, energy, and support without which politicians increasingly couldn't compete.

If you're looking for a nuts and bolts guide to Internet politics, look elsewhere.[xxxii] While MoveOn's pioneering use of the web for politics has certainly facilitated its growth, almost all of what it has achieved was possible in the era of snail mail and telephones too. The Populist movement of the late 1800's and the Vietnam-era Peace movement both grew at a lightning pace in response to a great need for political courage that the politicians of the era weren't meeting. The absence of the Internet didn't really slow them down (nor, in the case of the Populists, did the absence of telephones, radio, television, or automobiles).

[xxxii]Two good places to start: MoveOn alumnus Zach Exley's blog www.zachexley.com and Internet advocacy consulting firm M + R Strategic Services (www.mrss.com).

What has made MoveOn so attractive and sustained it over time is less its use of email and more the content of its emails. MoveOn is the political manifestation of the phenomenon described in *The Wisdom of Crowds*, a 2004 book by economist James Surowiecki. In it, Surowiecki discusses how large groups of people acting independently will usually make superior choices than a few experts in a room. Alas, wisdom too rarely plays a significant role in political choices. But courage can. Crowds of progressives consistently vote with their keyboards, their dollars, and their hours to support confrontational campaigns and courageous candidates. In part, it's because it's far harder for corporate lobbies or their Democratic insider friends to seduce crowds into the Politics of Fear. It's more difficult to persuade a crowd to "tone it down" in the service of some insider political scheme of dubious provenance than to squeeze some Washington lobbyist with whom you can trade favors. It's impossible to threaten a crowd with the loss of inside access when that crowd doesn't have any insider access; if you're selling political snake oil, the crowd won't buy it. If they want bravery, you better give it – or risk their wrath.

But when MoveOn was conceived, just having a crowd was a far off California dream. If you had walked into the King Tsin Chinese restaurant in Berkeley, California in early September, 1998, you could be excused for not knowing that the middle aged couple talking quietly at their table were in the process of hatching a movement that would, within a few short years, transform the Democratic Party, upend American politics, and revolutionize global civic engagement. Seated at the table were Wes Boyd and his wife Joan Blades – looking like any other unassuming Silicon Valley tech millionaires celebrating their good fortune with some Kong Pao Tofu.

But on the inside they were seething. Boyd, in particular, was feeling the incredulous rage that was at that moment uniting millions of Americans: how could congressional Republicans sidetrack the country for months and months over Bill Clinton's blow job? And the way they did it! Digging through his private life and exposing every pornographic morsel they could dig up or concoct. "It violated my sense of fairness that someone's private life would be so exposed," Boyd said.[1] Boyd was also feeling, perhaps more intensely than most, the anguish of the inactive: he was at once drawn in and repulsed by the media's saturation coverage of Clinton's private life. But, like most, he didn't feel that there was anything he could do about it: he had no outlet for his welling frustration. And so as the congressional hearings deteriorated into a torrent of stained dresses, amateur eavesdropping, and personal vendetta, he stopped sleeping, tormented by anxious nightmares about the Republican persecution. But as they dined, Boyd and Blades happened to hear the conversations going on around them in the restaurant. They were surprised to hear diners at other tables talking impeachment. This being Berkeley, Boyd and Blades weren't the only ones among the diners who thought the Republicans' jihad an abomination.

It got Boyd and Blades thinking: there are all these people out there who hate what the Republicans are doing, but no real way for them to affect the process. What could we do? Boyd and Blades actually had some resources at their disposal. They'd built a successful computer business and had recently sold it for millions of dollars. They suddenly had a lot of time on their hands. Most importantly, they had a flair for divining what could make an idea go viral. Their computer business hadn't been about just building a faster microchip. They'd made their first big breakthrough with the "Flying Toasters" screensaver, which went from zany concept to ubiquitous computer screen feature in just a few short years. Fresh from that success, they'd published the highly addictive "You Don't Know Jack!" CD-ROM trivia game – another surprise hit that became popular even though it consisted largely of a virtual game show host splurting out creative put-downs at players when they got a question wrong.

Ugly, But Simple

Boyd and Blades's techie background helped them understand the burgeoning potential of the Internet. And so they didn't go home and just send a big contribution to the Democratic Senatorial Campaign Committee or write a letter to the editor. They went home, called a programmer friend for help, and made a website (plunking down $89.95 to get the whole thing going). This being the mid-1990's, it wasn't pretty. Set on a black background, it haphazardly combined fonts, capital letters, colors, bold, and italic. It was ugly, but it was simple. No pictures and no "frames" – those windows within windows that took forever to load in that long ago era of slow dial-up connections. It was made with the average 1998 user of the Internet in mind. Even simpler was its message: "The Congress must immediately **Censure** President Clinton and *Move On* to pressing issues facing the country." Then there was a space for people to fill in their names and email addresses, and make a short comment. At the bottom, there was a promise that the petitions would be delivered to President Clinton and members of Congress.

When it was ready, Blades and Boyd sent out an email to few dozen friends asking them to fill their names into the petition. Pretty soon, the email had been forwarded – and forwarded and forwarded and forwarded. More than 300 people signed it within the first 24 hours. It quickly reached beyond family and friends. 48 hours after the initial email, 1506 people had signed. By the end of the week, it was up to 100,000. Less than a month after Boyd and Blades had clicked "send" it reached 250,000 signatures and became the largest website petition ever. It was clear that Boyd and Blades had channeled an enormous national frustration and, crucially, given people a way to act on their frustration. It wasn't just Berkeley where people were outraged by what the Republicans were doing. "I felt real frustrated that I couldn't do anything, and this came along," said Jerry Gallagher, a 56-year-old family therapist from Allentown, Pennsylvania, who was one of the early signers.[2]

To be sure, MoveOn's innovative use of the Internet to facilitate participation in politics played a big role in the organization's explosive growth. But it also reflected a political reality of the Clinton years: progressives were increasingly furious at Republicans and frustrated that Democrats in Congress were afraid to stand up to them. All that frustration that MoveOn successfully channeled came not only from a sense that individuals couldn't do anything to stop the Republican impeachment, but also from a sense that *nobody was* doing anything to stop it. At the time Boyd and Blades sent out their email, after all, it really looked like Democrats might let Republicans get away with their impeachment scheme. This was the time when Connecticut Senator Joseph Lieberman was slamming Clinton's contention that "even presidents have private lives;" when only 63 Democrats in the House of Representatives voted to keep the details of Ken Starr's raunchy (and often untrue) report about Clinton private; and when Democratic leaders Gephardt and Daschle were known to be considering going to the White House to tell Clinton he had to resign. If Democrats didn't have the courage to confront the Republicans, the petition signers were saying, then we'll force them to! "The Democrats seemed to have absolutely no backbone in the face of the Republican brouhaha – the witch hunt," petition signer number 99, Creed Erickson, a software engineer in Silicon Valley told me. "I thought they should have been standing up and saying we have more important things to do."[3]

Despite the blockbuster start, political observers started asking questions that bedevil Internet politics to this day. Would all that online activity translate into real political action? Petition signatures, whether electronic or written, usually make little difference in congressional decisions. If all MoveOn could deliver was a bunch of names on a page, it really wouldn't be doing much to influence politics in America. But MoveOn didn't just have names on a page. It had a database of people passionate enough about politics and angry enough at Republicans to take action. So far, the only action they'd taken was sending an email, but that didn't mean that was all they *would* do. Boyd and Blades were keenly aware that online action alone wasn't likely to change many votes. And so almost immediately they began working to get people to take action offline. On October 1, they started asking people who had signed the petition to call their representatives' congressional offices to urge them to vote against impeachment – resulting in a flood of calls. By October 20, 3000 of the petition signers had offered to help the campaign by volunteering and doing something more than just calling or emailing. Boyd and Blades came up with the idea of having those volunteers organize meetings with their own members of Congress to deliver the petition signatures from their own districts. To Boyd and Blades, this seemed like a common sense way to allow MoveOn members to demands that their congressmen find the courage to stand up to the far right impeachment crusade.

But giving volunteers such control was actually quite radical for its time: most Washington organizations (and their professional consultants) had for a long time been moving away from authentic grassroots action. The biggest reason was the increasingly intense media scrutiny on all things political. Allowing activists at the local level control over events could be risky, the thinking went. If one of them was off message or did something outlandish and the media heard about it, they'd cover that and not the substance of what the group was trying to communicate. Conventional wisdom was that it was better to keep politics in the hands of the careful professionals (who were, not so coincidentally, the ones creating that conventional wisdom and cashing the checks it brought in). That was the nearly unanimous message Beltway consultants delivered to Boyd and Blades when they sought advice from people more experienced in politics than they were. "You must be crazy," the consultants told them.[4]

But MoveOn decided to go ahead. "We thought, these are smart people, sensible and grounded people – we can trust them," Boyd said about the members.5 So they set up ground rules for the meetings – and then let their members (what they called anyone who'd signed the petition) loose. It was the first in many steps that devolved a great deal of the power to shape the organization to its members; given that power, members would consistently demand a more courageous approach from Democratic politicians. Within a week, the members had set up 219 meetings across the country. By and large, Boyd and Blades's gamble paid off. Although a few media stories about the events featured only the most dredlocked or off-message activist from an event, in general the media played it straight. They told a story that even the most polished of professional lobbyists couldn't have provided: that ordinary Americans were demanding that their leaders find the courage to stand up to the Republican extremists pushing the impeachment crusade.

It was an even more powerful message for members of Congress impressed to see groups of constituents who in most cases had never met each other before, seemingly spontaneously showing up at their offices to state their case. In the conservative suburbs of Atlanta, a group of MoveOn volunteers met with an aide to right-wing congressman John Linder. Although the aide didn't express support for censuring President Clinton, "he listened attentively while we read, and when he saw the number "540," [representing the number of his constituents who'd signed the petition from his district] I think I saw a look of real concern cross his face," wrote volunteer leader Rachel Robinson. Another meeting helped convince Republican congressman Peter King to oppose impeachment. "The attendees and Rep. King's director were all impressed with the power of the Internet to create this coalition of people who had never met each other before this meeting," the meeting report read.

By the time the meetings had concluded, the 1998 elections were just days away. If voters were really upset enough about the impeachment charade, they could oust the people pushing it. For MoveOn, it was time to see if their Internet-based politics of courage could actually sway votes. The day before the election, they sent out two emails: one letting people know that they could take off work to vote and another humorous get-out-the-vote message, which they designed to get people to forward onto their friends. This kind of thing is standard practice now, even on city council elections, but at the time, it was novel – and people responded enthusiastically. Through a post-election survey, MoveOn estimated that each recipient forwarded the email to an average of 13 friends and that more than 4 million people saw the emails. Those were real numbers: although four million people getting a message once wasn't likely to alone significantly sway a national election in a country of 280 million people, it was still a lot of people – and it had been done at essentially no cost. What's more, people were receiving the message from trusted messengers: someone who at least knew them well enough to forward on an email. To reach the same number of people through far more impersonal means like television advertising, direct mail, or old-fashioned door knocking would have cost about $1 million or tens of thousands of man hours. If nothing else, MoveOn was demonstrating that tapping people's passion for progressive politics on the Internet could provide a far more efficient way of communicating a message than anything that had been tried before.

Courage and Cash

The 1998 elections did see some pick-ups for impeachment opponents: Democrats gained five seats in the House. Because the party that held the White House had historically done poorly in congressional elections in the sixth year of a president's term, the media treated the results as a clear repudiation of Republican plans to impeach Clinton. Although post-election data on that point are inconclusive, it was taken at MoveOn headquarters (Boyd and Blades's Berkeley bungalow) as further evidence that Americans backed their mission – and emboldened them to continue their work. As Republicans pressed on with impeachment despite the election results, more and more people signed the petition and got involved as volunteers. But what next?

MoveOn had shown that the Internet was a very easy way to tap into progressive frustration to generate petition signatures, phone calls, and even volunteer hours. But while that was all nice, it wasn't part of the vocabulary of your average television age politician. Cold, hard cash was a different matter. But would all those people who'd clicked their mouse a few times be willing to dig into their pockets to back up their sentiments with money? It was time to test the hypothesis. A couple of emails later, MoveOn had picked up pledges from its members for $13 million in contributions to candidates for the 2000 elections and pledges to dedicate 800,000 hours towards electing "candidates who courageously address key national issues, who reject the politics of division and personal destruction, and who respect the voice of ordinary citizens." In its own earnest way, MoveOn was promising revenge – and showing that it had the resources to back it up.

But there were greater forces at play than even $13 million and hundreds of thousands of volunteer hours could counter. Republicans eager to keep control of the national agenda away from Clinton went ahead and impeached him anyway. Of course, MoveOn's work may have helped keep Democrats in line so that only five House Democrats defected and voted for impeachment and no Democratic senators voted to actually remove Clinton from office (the polls showing overwhelming opposition to impeachment certainly helped too). The failure of the impeachment drive was a great victory for MoveOn – but also a moment of great peril for the young organization. MoveOn's *raison d'être* had ceased to exist. Sure – lots of people had pledged to get involved in the 2000 election, but that was two long years away, and nobody knew whether or not people who had gotten involved through the Internet would stay focused for that long. MoveOn had taken to describing its work as a "flash" campaign – and the implication was that it could be gone in a flash too.

What could the organization do next to keep the phenomenon going? To figure it out, MoveOn pioneered another new way to use the Internet for politics – soliciting the involvement of its members in its decisions. After the Senate vote, MoveOn sent an email to its supporters asking again for volunteers, but this time asking also for "Your ideas for the future of MoveOn.org" with a little web form where people could contribute their thoughts. Of course, this was hardly the first time a political organization had asked for feedback. But there was something about MoveOn's earnest tone and the personal nature of its emails that made it seem that MoveOn's leadership would really listen. The desire to offer ideas eventually grew so strong that MoveOn set up a separate website, ActionForum. com, that allowed people to propose and debate ideas for the organization. It allowed users to rank and comment on different submissions, so that the most popular quickly rose to the top – so staff and members alike could get a sense of any developing consensus among contributors. It was in many ways a precursor of the political blog and the "smart mob" craze. And MoveOn's leadership did listen; even when participation grew to levels so large that it was impossible for Boyd and Blades themselves to read every comment, they hired someone to send weekly summaries to all MoveOn's staff so they could get the membership's best ideas and a sense of their evolving concerns and passions.

The Great dot org Bust of 2000?

The forum generated a lot of ideas, but without some big mobilizing force capturing America's imagination, it was hard to translate them into action. But then, on April 20, 1999, teenagers, Eric Harris and Dylan Klebold, walked into their high school in Littleton, Colorado, armed to the teeth with pipe bombs, Molotov cocktails, sawed off shotguns, 9 millimeter semi-automatic rifles, and a Tec9 handgun – and killed 12 students and a teacher. The national media, relatively dormant since the end of the impeachment debacle, revved up its coverage to levels that exceeded even the Clinton-Lewinsky debacle.6 Much of the coverage focused on the grisly details of the shootings and the lives cut short by the rampage, but the incident also sparked a national debate about gun control. As with the Clinton-Lewinsky scandal, America was riveted and sickened all at once. It was a perfect MoveOn moment.

And so Boyd and Blades hit their keyboard, and tapped out a simple message asking people to let their leaders know that Congress should take action to prevent future Columbines. "It is time for government to accept its proper role in regulating firearms," read the new petition. Things had been going so well, it seemed like it was bound to work. But the petition was a flop, at least in comparison to the blockbuster success of the anti-impeachment email. Only 70,000 people signed it. Over the next couple of years, the organization tried to identify other MoveOn moments that would provide the right zeitgeist for another email to go viral and build the organization further. They sent out emails in response to the war in Kosovo, the 2000 election debacle, Bush's effort to repeal the estate tax, the McCain-Lieberman campaign finance reform effort, and the California energy crisis. None of it worked. Not only did none of the campaigns achieve its goals, none of them got the kind of response to keep MoveOn's "membership" constant, much less grow. Soon, their list started shrinking. One of the challenges of Internet organizing is that email lists deteriorate quickly. People churn through email accounts with great frequency as they change jobs or switch email providers. As a result, if you're not growing on the Web, you're dying on the Web. MoveOn increasingly looked like it might end up being the dot org version of the dot com bust – lots of buzz, little bite, and no staying power.

There was a reason why these campaigns fared so poorly compared to the original MoveOn drive: they weren't very confrontational. Boyd and Blades had always thought of themselves as political moderates and saw their effort to stop impeachment as an essentially centrist position. They'd even set up a short-lived "Republican Move On" for the few thousand petition signers who identified as Republicans. Boyd was even nervous about working with already established progressive group like People for the American Way. "Wes didn't want to have MoveOn considered liberal," said Mike Lux, a Washington-based adviser to MoveOn who is close with Boyd and Blades. "He wanted to be the radical center, no-nonsense people getting things done." But that wasn't how MoveOn's membership saw it. They saw the anti-impeachment petition for what it was: an aggressive challenge to Republican excess at a time when not many Democrats had the courage to confront the Republicans. And so the signers brought with them a gusto for confrontation that wasn't necessarily embraced by MoveOn's founders. So when MoveOn started sending out vague or tepid emails, progressives didn't sign and didn't forward it on. MoveOn was no longer channeling their anger or serving their hunger for courageous politics. Pretty soon, MoveOn's membership dropped to about half of what it had been at its peak.

Wide-Eyed Washington

Although MoveOn's overall membership was withering, their initial success with the anti-impeachment petition and fundraising efforts continued to pay some dividends – though not quite as much as they had initially envisioned. They ended up actually raising only $2 million of the $13 million their members had pledged. Nevertheless, they were still breaking all prior records for online fundraising – and making a difference in some key cash-starved campaigns. "Jesus Christ, we've never seen anything like this," an official with Mel Carnahan's Missouri Senate campaign told Lux when MoveOn supporters sent $125,000 into the campaign coffers almost overnight.

Beltway fundraisers' eyes widened when they realized that this new Internet thing could be an important cash cow. Pretty soon, everyone from Al Gore to Dan Quayle to the RNC began accepting credit card donations on the Internet. Although MoveOn's fundraising success was making a splash in the Beltway, the overall picture was not so rosy. The biggest failure was that none of the incumbent Republican proponents of impeachment they'd targeted in the 2000 congressional elections were defeated; indeed, most of them won by comfortable margins despite all of MoveOn's activity. Neither Boyd, Blades, nor MoveOn's membership had gotten into politics to demonstrate the fundraising power of the Internet to finance operatives; they'd gotten involved to stop the impeachment. They'd stayed involved to elect people who would never even think of sidetracking American public life for a small-minded political vendetta.

Getting Out or Stepping Up

Now that venture had failed, Boyd and Blades seriously contemplated moving on themselves to their next venture –developing the next computer game blockbuster, a happy early retirement, or something cool they hadn't even thought of. "We only saw our mission as to follow through on our initial commitment with the [impeachment] petition until the 2000 election," Boyd told me. "One reason was that we thought we didn't have to make a longer commitment was that we thought people would say 'Gee, this is obviously a good way to do stuff and in three months everyone would be doing it." But that didn't happen. Although politicians had begun accepting credit card contributions on the Internet and posting information about themselves on their websites, they were using the web almost exclusively as a fundraising tool (and as a place to post their news releases). In their excitement at MoveOn's fundraising successes, these Beltway consultants had ignored the courageous politics that made the MoveOn membership respond to their occasional appeals for money. It was proof that MoveOn's initial success came less because it was using the Internet for politics, and more because it was using the Internet for courageous, progressive politics.

The fact that the Democrats hadn't really learned MoveOn's lesson indicated to Boyd and Blades that MoveOn still had work to do. But so did the new post-2000 election political environment. They were hearing with increasing urgency from MoveOn's remaining members on the Action Forum that the organization was filling a vital niche. "I want to urge Move On to join the emerging effort to block the Ashcroft nomination as part of a broad effort in the coming years to defend social equality, the rights of women and minorities and the Bill of Rights," wrote member Dick Flacks in one of the most highly ranked entries on the Action Forum.[7] Whether it was stopping Ashcroft, reforming American elections after the 2000 break-down, or protecting the Arctic National Wildlife Refuge, the members weighing in on the Action Forum were clear: they needed MoveOn to help fight President Bush.

Indeed, it was Bush's actions that helped prompt Boyd to return MoveOn to its roots as a more explicitly progressive organization. When Bush pulled out of international efforts to stop global warming, started shifting the tax burden to the poor and middle class, and slashing funding for health care, he polarized America, including Wes Boyd. "Wes realized that the country was moving far to the right," Lux said. "What he thought of as moderate was now left. He became more comfortable being a progressive movement leader." Pretty soon, MoveOn's emails started getting back a little of their old edge – and then some. "The Cheney team has a three point energy plan: rape, burn and pillage," read their May, 2001 email responding to the Bush/Cheney energy task force. "Rape the environment. Burn fossil fuels 'til we choke. Pillage the consumer's pocket book. This is lunacy. Join us in calling for a sensible plan." Now MoveOn had all the ingredients that had made its first petition such a success: a hot issue, an opportunity to do something about it, and now, the kind of direct confrontational language that resonated with progressives furious about Republican abuses and frustrated with Washington Democrats' timidity. By September 10, 2001, they had started, slowly, growing again.

And then came September 11th. The attacks were horrific and shocking and awful. And they had a lot of ingredients of a MoveOn Moment: saturation media coverage, drama, and life or death ramifications. But the organization's proper response to the attacks was less clear. The United States had previously dealt with terrorist threats with a combination of police work and limited military strikes. Whatever the United States had done in the past hadn't prevented this one. And so when, in the days after the attacks, it became clear that Bush and leaders of both parties were contemplating a more robust military response to the terrorist attacks, people of all political leanings backed Bush's plan to go to war.

But that didn't stop MoveOn. The newly radicalized Boyd and Blades were viscerally worried that Bush would respond to the attacks in a way that would unnecessarily provoke an unending cycle of death and hatred. "It's a frightening thing to find out there are nations of people that think we're evil," Blades told the Knight-Ridder news service after the attacks. "We don't want to support that imagery; we want to turn it around."[8] And so they sent out an email to their supporters urging that the United States not "disregard the lives of others" in responding to the attacks. "If we retaliate by bombing Kabul and kill people oppressed by the Taliban dictatorship who have no part in deciding whether terrorists are harbored, we become like the terrorists we oppose," the petition went on. Though the peace message may have been outside the mainstream of American debate at the time, it resonated powerfully with the anti-Bush pacifist element of the population. It was a relatively small group, even tiny as a percentage of the overall population. But it was committed. And it was hungry for exactly what MoveOn was offering: a way to communicate their deeply felt longing for peace at a time when almost no one, Democrat or Republican, ultra-progressive or DLC centrist, seemed to be on their side.

Meanwhile, far off in another quadrant of cyberspace, 20 year-old Eli Pariser was working as the resident web geek at a small non-profit organization in Boston when the September 11th attacks happened. "I considered the possibility that out of this tragedy might come more tragedy—that in addition to the lives of the victims of September 11th, the United States might kill many others," Pariser would later say about his thoughts at the time. "I didn't really have it thought out – I just figured I knew how to make websites, and so I made one."[9] He too wrote up a petition that called on the United States and NATO to exercise "moderation and restraint" in response to the attacks and demanded that any response ensure that innocent civilians wouldn't suffer. Then he sent it to 30 friends. On September 18, Pariser woke up, rolled out of bed, and checked his email – and found thousands and thousands of messages in his inbox. Then his phone started ringing: his server was crashing. A BBC reporter called and asked, "What's up with this website and who are you?"[10] Within three weeks, the petition had more than 500,000 signatures – one of the largest in history.

Pariser's email had hit the same peacenik chord that MoveOn's petition had, but for whatever reason his email resonated far more than MoveOn's. Pariser seemed to have found the mobilization mojo that MoveOn had lost and was only slowly regaining. As a result, Pariser almost immediately got the attention of MoveOn's new executive director, Peter Schurman, who suggested a collaboration. MoveOn had what Pariser didn't – lots of technical and financial resources. And Pariser had what MoveOn had, in some measure lost: the magic that made an email go viral. They started working closely together; within a few months, Pariser had become a formal employee. He brought his now-giant email list with him, giving MoveOn the shot in the arm it needed to start growing again.

MoveOn had come very far since the early days when Boyd was afraid of being affiliated with mainstream liberal stalwarts like People for the American Way. It was now willing to stake out a position on the fringe of public opinion – and was reaping the benefits. It showed there was a market for political courage even at a time when almost all politicians were focused on building unity. The comments on the special Action Forum set up by MoveOn and 9-11 Peace show the attitudes that were fueling the positive response MoveOn's pacifist noises. All of the top ranked entries called for a peaceful response to 9/11. "Bomb Afghanistan with butter, with rice, bread, clothing and medicine," wrote Kent Madin of Bozeman, Montana in a message that got the support of 89 percent of the action forum's readers. "It will cost less than conventional arms, poses no threat of US casualties and just might get the Afghan populace thinking that the Taliban leaders don't have the answers."[11] This viewpoint may have represented a small minority, but it was a minority looking for someone to aggressively oppose war at a time when almost no one else was.

Of course, the flip side of being on the fringe is that while you may garner the enthusiastic support of a minority, you risk becoming irrelevant to main-stream politics. Indeed, it was about this time that some Democratic politicians lost their original euphoria about MoveOn and became more reluctant to be publicly associated with it. You also risk being wrong. The September 11th attacks were only one step in Al Qaeda's fanatical, genocidal war against all those who strayed from its particular violent Islamist vision: whether it was the United States government, Jews, Shiite Muslims, moderate Sunnis, citizens of London, Madrid, and Bali, or even the black Muslim tribes of the Darfur region of the Sudan. In the weeks after September 11th, their irredentism became crystal clear to even many of the most hard core war skeptics when the Taliban refused Bush (and the world's) reasonable ultimatum that the Taliban surrender Osama bin Laden and other al Qaeda leadership and shut down terrorist training camps in the country. It was a path that would have averted war and it was a path that the Taliban refused. Before, calls for moderation in response to terrorism seemed a bit fringy, though well-intentioned. Now they seemed ridiculous.

And so MoveOn – and Pariser – found a delicate balance. While they never explicitly endorsed U.S. military action against Afghanistan, they also never condemned it. The decision was politically astute. It allowed them to continue to draw the anti-war, anti-Bush constituency that had allowed them to grow so quickly, but without losing too much of their potential appeal to mainstream America. In the coming months, they continued with the same strategy: writing hard-hitting emails on hot issues that would appeal to their anti-Bush constituency but without ever taking positions so extreme that they would come to regret them later. They asked their members to stand up against the Bush administration's attacks on civil liberties like secret wiretapping and suspending *habeas corpus*. They demanded a thorough investigation of the Enron scandal. They asked Congress to end tax breaks to "war profiteers" like Halliburton.[xxxiii]

[xxxiii]That issue-to-issue jumpiness was and is a MoveOn trademark: It's not some political version of Attention Deficit Disorder. Instead, it's a calculated way to fuel the organization's growth. Through extensive testing, MoveOn discovered that it would get better response if it emailed about topics that were already on people's minds. As soon as a major event hit the headlines, MoveOn would jump on it right away. Although this has become somewhat more common now, in 2001, it was cutting-edge. Single issue groups and political campaigns were starting to invest major resources in their email and Internet activism programs, but it was relatively rare for them to get the kind of exponential growth that MoveOn had attained. Single issue groups were hobbled by their focus on *their one issue*. Unless it was in the news, the audience for an email about it just wouldn't be that great. Same for political campaigns: they continued to be hobbled by a tendency to use their email lists almost exclusively to ask for money, rather than trying to build the list through edgy petitions that were way more likely to be forwarded on than a request for money (never mind offering opportunities for supporters to provide real feedback). It was their combination of courage and cutting edge that set MoveOn apart from other attempts to use the Internet for politics.
I discovered this phenomenon in late 2002 when I was working for a political action committee

With their new more confrontational tone, and rising progressive anger at Bush's attempts to take advantage of the September 11th attacks to push his right-wing domestic agenda, the MoveOn membership grew substantially. But its explosion into the progressive powerhouse it is today had to wait for Bush's next move: his drive towards the Iraq War. When Bush started ratcheting up the White House war machine in August of 2002, MoveOn almost instantly swung into action. Naturally, it started by asking its members to sign a petition against the Iraq war. Suddenly, it seemed that MoveOn had its old mojo back as tens of thousands started signing on. Soon MoveOn's membership had surpassed what it was at the height of its original anti-impeachment campaign.

One reason MoveOn got such a big response was that a critical gap existed between strong anti-war feeling among progressive Americans and the lack of strong opposition to the war among Washington Democrats. At this point, even most of those representatives and senators who would later oppose the war were hedging their bets, urging caution and calling on Bush to make his case for removing Saddam Hussein to Congress. There was some good reason for their caution: in August Saddam Hussein was still refusing to admit United Nations weapons inspectors to Iraq and was rattling his rhetorical sabers – giving credibility to the claims that he was thumbing his nose at the international community and concealing weapons of mass destruction. Even Paul Wellstone wouldn't come out against military action for more than a month. But Americans at the grassroots, and not just progressives, were more suspicious. Lots of them just didn't trust George Bush; others agreed with Republican House Majority Leader Dick Armey that America should let Hussein "rant and rave all he wants and let that be a matter between he and his own country. As long as he behaves himself within his own borders, we should not be addressing any attack or resources against him."12 The country was ripe for an anti-war movement – and the Democrats weren't stepping up to lead it. "The Democratic Party failed to provide leadership at a critical time," MoveOn's Washington Director Tom Matzzie said. "Millions

---

focused on electing politicians who would champion wilderness protection. We were just launching our revamped website and wanted to find out how we could grow our email list to become an Internet eco-juggernaut. So we sat down in a meeting in San Francisco with MoveOn Executive Director Peter Schurman and asked, "How can we become the next MoveOn?" "You can't," came the response. Schurman told us that our exclusive focus on a single issue meant that it would be hard to get the kind of dramatic responses in the long periods between when our issue would be at the forefront of the national agenda. When I moved to a more general interest environmental organization a few months later and was put in charge of Internet organizing, I took his wisdom to heart – and tried to prioritize hotness over all other factors when deciding what email to send. It worked well – and pretty soon I was sending out emails that broke my organization's records for activist response.

of Americans created an underground economy for a new type of organization. It's like blue jeans in the Soviet Union."[13]

That underground demand for courage in confronting Bush meant that as the rush to war developed, MoveOn was suddenly able to raise the kind of big money it had talked about in 1999, but had never really delivered. For the 2002 elections, MoveOn endorsed candidates who had opposed the war with Iraq and let its members decide how much to give each candidate. If a member felt more passion for one candidate than another, he could divvy his dollars accordingly. In just a few weeks, MoveOn raised more than $170,000 each for Washington state congressmen Jay Inslee and Rick Larsen, and a whopping $670,000 for Paul Wellstone.

The depth of feeling about the coming war surprised even the usually optimistic MoveOn staff. When MoveOn sent out an email asking its members to together contribute $40,000 to publish a full page advertisement opposing the war in *The New York Times*, the MoveOn membership sent back $370,000. One donor was David Musgrove of Melbourne, Florida. Musgrove had never been involved in politics before but he was growingly suspicious of the rush to war and frustrated that Washington Democrats were doing little to stop it. And so Musgrove hit the Internet – and came upon MoveOn's website. "I was disgusted with both parties," Musgrove said. "The Democrats had the election coming up and they were sticking their finger in the wind and following it. If you want real change you've got to change the wind. MoveOn was changing the direction of the wind. That's what attracted me to them."[14] With the money flowing in and new activists like Musgrove joining, they could do a lot more than send petitions, arrange some congressional meetings, and run some newspaper ads. It was time for television! Wes Boyd contacted well known progressive adman Bill Zimmerman and ordered up "the next daisy ad," a reference to Lyndon Johnson's famous 1964 ad featuring a little girl plucking the petals of a daisy as the background announcer counted down to nuclear Armageddon. He got exactly that: an updated version of the daisy ad that said that an Iraq war could spread to other countries and allow terrorists to get their hands on nuclear weapons.

MoveOn stepped it up on the grassroots level too, joining with the anti-war umbrella organization United for Peace and Justice to organize nationwide (and planetwide) protests for February 15, 2003. More than 400,000 people turned out to the main event in New York City; up to 10 million turned out around the globe. MoveOn, in concert with a few close allies around the world, followed those events with more than 6,000 vigils around the world just three days before the war. The sight of thousands of regular Americans respectfully protesting the war transmitted an image that was peaceful, non-disruptive, and powerful. No one had ever marshaled such a large global event so quickly.

"I've Only Known Him Over Email"

Why was MoveOn so successful in getting millions of Americans to shake off not just their apathy, but also the seeming hopelessness of the situation? After all, Bush was suggesting that God was telling him to invade Iraq; and had dismissed the massive February 15 protests as a "focus group" – one to which he wouldn't listen.[15] It was not, to say the least, particularly likely that he was going to suddenly call off the war because a bunch of liberals were holding candles. And it wasn't like Democrats were suddenly reconsidering their support for the war as it grew in popularity as the invasion date approached. To be sure, MoveOn was channeling anti-war America's anger. But there were other groups doing that too and doing it with far more vitriol: many of the anti-war groups didn't stop at vigils and protests or polite condemnations of the rush to war; they committed acts of civil disobedience, briefly shut down San Francisco and Washington, DC, and denounced Bush, Cheney, Halliburton, and everyone else involved in the war in a fury that MoveOn's earnest tone couldn't compete with in volume. How was MoveOn able to create and sustain the possibility of hope, where it seemed like none existed?

MoveOn had finally hit upon the perfect combination of controlled rage and earnestness. They seemed angry, but not crazy. The personal one-to-one timbre of the emails created a sense that Peter Schurman, Eli Pariser, and the rest of the MoveOn email writers were regular people asking each person individually to take action – and not impersonally sending out blast emails. This sensation is so intense that whenever I've seen MoveOn leaders speak in public, at least one MoveOn member has always spontaneously said something to me along the lines of what my cousin said to me at a New York City event we both attended where Eli Pariser was speaking. "It's so great to finally see Eli in person," she said. "I've only known him through email until now," as if Eli was personally emailing my cousin – not my cousin and 3.2 million other people at the same time. "Well, I guess he's emailing lots of other people too, but it *feels* like he's emailing me." That personal connection immunized MoveOn, at least with its base, against Republican charges that MoveOn was some kind of front for some of the ultra-left, Communist-affiliated organizations that were also playing a prominent role in the anti-war movement.

Many Democratic politicians were more difficult to persuade. Most Democrats looked at opposition to the war as a major liability. The Democratic congressional campaign committees were officially advising candidates to support the war, and putting pressure on them to do so.[16] "In the early days, there was pure joy," MoveOn adviser Lux said. Candidates thought the money MoveOn was giving "was like manna from heaven. But then they got more nervous. They still wanted the money, but they were asking – were they wacky lefty freaks?"

The fact that lots of Democrats were asking this question could be problematic for MoveOn as it contemplated what to do next, including focusing its energies on the 2004 elections. Some observers speculated that MoveOn's opposition to the war could marginalize it from the mainstream of Democratic Party debate. But the summer of 2003 showed that MoveOn was a mighty force that had broad appeal within the Party – and could be ignored in national Democratic politics only at a candidate's peril. By this point, MoveOn had 1.4 million members, had raised $6.5 million for candidates alone (and millions for its own programs as well), and had proven that it could get hundreds of thousands of people to give money, attend an event, or call their member of Congress with just a few taps of a keyboard.[17] It was riding the growing tide of progressive opposition to the war in Iraq. And it had perfected its tone so that it was finding success recruiting new members on other hot, and even some not-so-hot issues: the environment, stopping television and radio corporate conglomeration, and getting Senate Democrats to sink at least some of Bush's most extreme judicial nominees. These issues were all compelling, but even by the summer of 2003, almost everything – even the Iraq War – was being eclipsed by the 2004 presidential election even though it was still 18 months away.

"Trust the Members"

Obsession with the election was so strong that from mid-2003 onward, it was like a constant background hum of MoveOn Moments – media coverage was intense, and progressive passions were more intense. MoveOn capitalized on the climate – and then some, creating an almost totally new phenomenon in national politics that would fuel its continued exponential growth and pioneer a path that many candidates would follow in the years to come. What characterized MoveOn's election campaign more than anything else was its participatory nature. MoveOn staff make "Trust the Members" their mantra; while they admit that they don't perfectly follow that philosophy at all times, they often tap all their members' energy, ideas, and resources in a way that gives those members far more leverage than more top-down groups do. As a result, they're more likely to execute their campaigns with their membership's needs and desires in mind, and so more likely to find success.

Nowhere was that more true than in MoveOn's June, 2003 Democratic presidential online primary. Usually, national political organizations make their endorsements by having a political committee interview prospective candidates and review their records. It's a top down approach, but one that allows politically knowledgeable insiders to weigh candidates' histories and their likelihood of victory to make decisions in the best interests of the organization. MoveOn decided to try a radical departure: let members decide for themselves which candidate best represented them. And so it invited its members to vote in an "online primary." "Ordinary people, at the grassroots, often stand back until a lot of this is decided – and it's doesn't make a lot of sense," Wes Boyd told *The Washington Post* to explain why MoveOn had chosen to give its members a greater voice in the primaries. "Why not play as much as the folks who attend the rubber chicken dinners play?"18 It represented enormous faith that even though its members didn't necessarily have access to all the inside dope on the different candidates, together they would do the right thing. And it immediately drew the eager attention of the candidates – especially since MoveOn promised to ask all the participants in its primary to contribute money and time to whichever candidate they supported, even if that person didn't end up winning. That was irresistible to the cash, volunteer, and buzz-hungry Democrats. All except pro-war Joe Lieberman (who, reasonably, didn't think he'd find much support from MoveOn's members) filled out MoveOn's questionnaire. The different campaigns even started doing MoveOn's recruitment for them: several candidates sent out emails to their own lists asking supporters to both register as MoveOn members and vote for them in the online primary.

The results impressed MoveOn staff and professional pundits alike. 317,647 MoveOn members voted, more than had participated in the 2000 Iowa and New Hampshire caucuses and primaries combined. Howard Dean won the overwhelming plurality of the ballots with 44 percent, Dennis Kucinich came in second with 24 percent, and John Kerry drew 16 percent. More than 54,000 volunteered for their favorite candidates and 49,000 pledged a combined $1.75 million.19 The results also showed that political courage could pay political dividends. At this point in the campaign, Howard Dean was perceived (rightly or wrongly) as the most progressive serious candidate because of his early opposition to the Iraq war and the grassroots feel of his campaign; second place contender Dennis Kucinich, who was considered more of a fringe candidate, nevertheless placed because of his even more confrontational stances toward Bush. They'd been challenging Bush when few others had the gumption to do it. It's debatable whether MoveOn's crowds were *wise* to make the choices they did – it's unlikely that Dean or Kucinich would have performed as well as Kerry did against Bush, but it was certain that MoveOn's crowds were richly rewarding those candidates who were perceived as being the most courageous in standing up to Bush and the Washington political consensus on Iraq and other issues.

The Internet had played a part in making this outpouring of progressive support for courageous candidates possible, but MoveOn's main innovation was the participatory nature of its endorsement process, not the technology used to facilitate it. While the Internet certainly made voting faster and easier, a telephone, snail mail, or even in-person balloting system would have gotten the job done too. MoveOn next took campaign participation to another level – allowing voters into what had always been considered the ultimate reserve of the political professional – the campaign ad. An entire industry of consultants, producers, and technicians existed to create and place television ads. They were generally the highest paid people in politics, with the top consultants taking 7 percent of total ad spending. They prided themselves on their skills. Some produced anodyne hackery, others evocative artistry, but they were all united by the idea that theirs was a field for professionals, not political novices. MoveOn wouldn't exactly turn the idea on its head, but it did show that unpaid amateurs could do as good a job as some of the best pros; what's more, they demonstrated that allowing ordinary people to be involved in high politics decisions like which ad worked best not only produced effective material, but also gave ordinary people a sense of investment in the ads – inspiring them to open their pockets to put their choices on the air.

In early December, MoveOn emailed its membership to announce its "Bush in 30 Seconds" contest: it invited members to produce 30-second political ads that would be voted on by the rest of the membership and then judged by a panel of celebrities that included filmmaker Michael Moore, rock star Moby, comedian Jack Black, and political consultant James Carville. MoveOn's new "cultural director," musician Laura Dawn, brought in the judges not just for their celebrity, but also because MoveOn didn't have total trust in its own "Trust the Members" mantra. The leadership was worried that the membership might pick an ad inappropriate for broadcast, and they wanted a safety valve. But the event ended up both reaffirming MoveOn's "trust your members" mantra and highlighting the dangers of MoveOn's participatory brand of politics. 1500 people submitted ads – some looked professionally done, others had what might be generously described as an "indie" feel to them, and a few were totally hilarious (like the "If Bush Were Your Roommate" spot in which the George W. Bush character occupies another roommate's room and accuses his roommate of "liberal bias" when asked to do his own dishes). The far-and-away top choice of MoveOn's members was Charlie Fisher's "Child's Play" ad. It had high production values and showed little kids doing adult menial labor like loading garbage trucks, working as maids, and repairing tires. In the middle of the ad, the message "Guess who's going to pay off President Bush's $1 trillion deficit?" appeared. When the judges cast their votes, it was by far their top choice as well – proving that crowds not only would respond to political courage, but also political art.

The other ads, whether funny, poignant, or funky, were almost all harsh attacks on Bush. Two were so virulent that they gave Republicans an excuse to attack MoveOn. Two submitted ads appeared to compare Bush to Hitler. Neither of the ads got much support from the 110,000 MoveOn members who voted in the competition. As a result, MoveOn pulled them from their website in December, 2004. But a Republican researcher found them by playing through all 1500 ads and posted the ones that mentioned Hitler on the GOP website. A few days later, RNC chairman Ed Gillespie called the ads "the worst and most vile form of political hate speech" and the GOP convinced Jewish groups to pile on. The founder of the Simon Wiesenthal Center, Rabbi Marvin Heir, even told the Washington Post that the ads "defamed the Holocaust."[20] Although MoveOn quickly apologized for the ads (and most Jewish organizations accepted the apologies), the Bush campaign didn't let them die – even featuring them in a heavily promoted web ad during the 2004 campaign. Although the flap was hardly the biggest issue in the 2004 campaign, the Republicans attacks did have their intended effect. They created a perception among both the media and even Democratic Jews that MoveOn was so extreme that it would endorse the most intemperate Bush-bashing. The "Bush in 30 Seconds" contest pioneered a new form of participatory advertising that would later become widespread even in corporate Super Bowl ads. But, like the Wellstone memorial rally, it highlighted the dangers of unfiltered grassroots campaigning in an era of intense media scrutiny.

Picking a Fight

Although its faithful were still loyal (if not more so because of the unjustified attack on the organization), MoveOn's image had taken a hit. But the group still had a confrontational move up its sleeve that could regain it some of the sympathy it had lost because of the Republican attacks. MoveOn knew that CBS had a policy against accepting advertisements that dealt with controversial political issues. Most political organizations accepted that ban to avoid battles with Big Media out of fear that the old saw, "Never pick a fight with someone who buys ink by the barrel" remained true in the era of bandwidth and browsers. But MoveOn went ahead and raised $1.5 million to air the ad.

When CBS rejected it (even though the network was planning on running a Bush administration ad promoting its new Medicare plan), MoveOn milked the rejection for all it was worth. It ran advertisements in major newspapers criticizing the company and asking its members to flood CBS offices with telephone calls. Their willingness to take on Big Media paid big dividends: news shows covering the controversy aired the ad hundreds of times for free. Kathleen Hall Jamieson, dean of the Annenberg School of Communication and one of the nation's top experts on political communication, told Newsweek that the ad "has achieved the most air time with the least dollars expended of any ad in the history of the republic." 20 members of Congress wrote a letter to CBS President Leslie Moonves accusing the network of limiting "the debate to ads that are not critical of the political staus quo and…of the President and the Republican-controlled Congress." [21] Even Fox News's Bill O'Reilly rallied to MoveOn's side, played the commercial for free on his show, and told his viewers that "I was surprised that CBS turned this down. It's not offensive, makes a legitimate point politically."[22] It was proof that confrontation generates coverage, and can even generate sympathy (MoveOn would go on to use this tactic by launching a more or less permanent war against Fox News.)

Testing the Limits

Spending big dollars advertising 12 months before the election was another controversial element of MoveOn's strategy for the 2004 elections. Campaigns traditionally horded their money until the few months before Election Day when polls said that people other than Beltway insiders were actually tuned into politics. But MoveOn adman Bill Zimmerman sensed that 2004 wasn't like other years: given how high passions were running about the Iraq war and George Bush himself, people were paying attention earlier. What's more, the Bush campaign was amassing an immense war chest, which it could use against whichever Democratic nominee emerged from the primaries – in all likelihood broke and bruised from the months of intra-party squabbling. And so MoveOn prepared to step into the breach.

Over the next few months, MoveOn tested the limits of its membership. It asked them to contribute an initial $10 million to fund anti-Bush ads that would help counter the expected Bush onslaught. It asked, and asked, and asked, and received, and received, and received. In between, it kept its email list primed with hard-hitting email campaigns like "If Bush won't repudiate torture, we must" following the Abu Ghraib scandal, "Fire Rumsfeld," and "Teachers = Terrorists?" (after Bush's education secretary called the National Education Association, the country's largest teachers' union, a "terrorist organization"). They also sponsored movie events like screenings of "Outfoxed" (Robert Greenwald's exposé about Fox News) and Farenheit 9/11. MoveOn aggressively took advantage of the loopholes created in the McCain-Feingold campaign finance legislation, which allowed the MoveOn Voter Fund to accept donations of any size from political donors. Soon, progressive zillionaires like currency trader George Soros and Progressive Insurance founder Peter Lewis were funneling millions of dollars to MoveOn to supplement their grassroots support.

MoveOn's high profile – and major ad spending – quickly attracted the attention of the Republican attack machine. "MoveOn.org is a huge threat and has hurt the president," Ken Mehlman said in a closed-door speech to the U.S. Chamber of Commerce.[23] In the same way that Republicans attempted to damage John Kerry's credibility with the Swift Boat attacks, the GOP also wanted to blunt the effectiveness of MoveOn's ad campaign by undermining their credibility. And so MoveOn became a popular Republican bogeyman. At every opportunity, Republicans brought up and replayed the Hitler ads, giving them millions of times more exposure than if they had been allowed to die when MoveOn pulled them from its site. And most of all, they somewhat inaccurately charged that MoveOn had opposed the invasion of Afghanistan. "If MoveOn had its way," said Bush spokesman Terry Holt in a typical attack, "the United States would not be fighting a global war on terror, and Saddam Hussein would still be the brutal dictator in charge of Iraq."[24] In most cases, MoveOn didn't give an inch, and indeed remained at the vanguard of progressive criticism of the Iraq war and Bush's foreign policy mistakes.

But it didn't mean they never gave in. Republicans fixated on George Soros, the currency trader who had previously been known primarily for his anti-Communist, pro-democracy work in Eastern Europe during the Cold War. That didn't give him any protection from Republican attacks for the millions he was donating to MoveOn and other organizations to beat Bush. The RNC took to calling Soros the "Daddy Warbucks of drug legalization" because he had separately funded groups supporting marijuana decriminalization. More explicitly right-wing news outlets went further – the NewsMax website said Soros "hates America," and described him as "somewhat loony," while Tony Blankley called Soros a "robber baron" and "pirate capitalist" on Fox News.[25] Although the attacks didn't resonate much with the American public – Soros had only tiny name recognition – they were effective in causing MoveOn, Soros, and other big donors to change course. In the wake of the attacks, MoveOn and Soros decided that big donors like Soros would from then on channel their money towards the Media Fund and America Coming Together, less controversial Democratic groups that were spending big on the 2004 elections, leaving MoveOn to focus on small donations up to $5000 in value. The change didn't phase the Republicans, who didn't much care whether Soros was giving $25,000 or $25 million – they kept trying to associate Soros with MoveOn well after the 2004 election had concluded and Soros had gone on to other causes and organizations. For all the hype, the conservative activist Grover Norquist would later call Soros's spending "goofy. The guy is worth, what, seven billion dollars, and he tried to buy the Presidency on the cheap. He should have been in for two and a half billion dollars, for crying out loud. Twenty-seven million dollars-that should have been ante money. What were they thinking?"[26]

From Wes Boyd's post-flap perspective, the decision to focus on grassroots donors has been a blessing. "You know the amount of energy goes into big donor fundraising. Leaders have to be out fundraising all the time and can't work on their program," Boyd said. "It's just not us. We're very satisfied just going with the $25 donors, God bless them." In addition to the time savings, the exclusive focus on grassroots donors means that MoveOn staff aren't orienting their campaigns to the demands of big donors, who may have their own agendas. If you "Follow the money," it leads right to MoveOn's grassroots donors and their demands for a courageous Democratic Party.

MoveOn takes the same attitude when it comes to its relations with politicians in Washington. Many more traditional organizations are seduced by access. They fall into the trap of judging their success or lack thereof not by how close they are to achieving their goals of peace, justice, or a living planet, but by how close they can get to leading politicians. As a result, they're often hesitant to criticize too harshly for fear of losing that access. It makes them vulnerable to having their agendas coopted by those with the power to give – or withhold – face time. At the very least, they often get sucked into the language and attitudes of the Beltway, making it harder for them to understand the hearts and minds of their grassroots supporters (if they have any). In contrast, MoveOn aggressively avoids spending too much time with politicians to avoid this very trap. Its Washington director, Tom Matzzie, is nominally in charge of interacting with congressional representatives, but only actually lobbies once or twice a month. Democratic leaders "don't completely understand how to interact with us," Matzzie told me. "They can't get us in a room and convince us that their path is the right one. It doesn't matter if I'm convinced. Our membership just won't respond if I'm selling snake oil."

Matzzie, like other MoveOn staff and members, has to be pressed very hard to talk about *his* role in helping MoveOn succeed – the staff like to keep the focus on the members. And the members often downplay their role and achievements and give credit to the staff. MoveOn members on staff are powerful, but individually they are humble. They control vast budgets and armies of volunteers, but do it with an (occasionally self-conscious) understatement. They do it from their bedrooms, with their dogs, wearing their pajamas. They're a lot less likely to name-drop than their Democratic insider peers and they're a lot less self-important, but they're a lot more *real*-important.

Nevertheless, while there are major advantages to this purposeful outsider status and humility, it can have its drawbacks too. MoveOn is occasionally caught unaware when Democrats make decisions. Furthermore, despite its grassroots clout, the organization is only rarely asked to contribute its ideas when Democrats develop policy. Because MoveOn isn't very visible on Capitol Hill (where personal presence usually counts for a lot), even many senators and representatives who have received significant financial and volunteer contributions from MoveOn are unaware of how much they benefit from the organization. For example, in the final days of the 2006 campaign, Democratic Leader Harry Reid (who *is* keenly aware of MoveOn's power) called MoveOn and asked if they could raise some quick money for Jon Tester in the ultra-tight Montana Senate race. Tester's campaign was nearly broke, and his Republican opponent Conrad Burns was surging. Matzzie emailed just a portion of the MoveOn membership asking for $150,000. Within 24 hours, they'd raised more than $240,000 – a lifeline for the tapped out Tester campaign. But when I asked a top Tester campaign official to comment on what MoveOn had done, he was completely unaware of it and had to go check with the campaign's finance team to confirm it. Needless to say, Tester is unlikely to give special weight to MoveOn's opinions as he decides how to vote.

Despite these drawbacks, MoveOn's outsider strategy means that MoveOn brings something unique to the national progressive movement – almost complete immunity to being co-opted. Other organizations may find themselves making agonizing trade-offs between doing what's right on a particular bill or amendment or preserving an important relationship with a key senator. MoveOn almost never find itself in that conundrum. So it can let its members decide what the best course of action is – and let the inside deals be damned. In a Democratic Party dominated by the Politics of Fear, having at least one major group free from distorted considerations of political expedience is a major asset for the movement as a whole.

Of course, MoveOn was able to resist the temptations of insider access because it didn't need it – it had a passionately committed membership that was looking for results, and didn't mind if that meant defying insider Democratic wisdom. But even in 2004, there were limits to the reach of that membership. Although it was over 1.7 million members strong, the membership was disproportionately concentrated in the big cities on the east and west coasts. That was fine for raising money and holding vigils and generating petition signatures, but MoveOn leaders recognized that in 2004 they needed to do more than generate those kind of one-off actions in the blue states if they were really going to influence the outcome of the presidential race. But how to do it? Thus far, MoveOn had relied almost exclusively on email and a bit of media coverage to spread the word about the organization. MoveOn leaders knew they needed to do more, but it would be difficult to do it with its staff of four.

Baking Back the White House

To get the job done, MoveOn called in brothers Adam and Justin Ruben, two hot-shot grassroots organizers who not only had the on-the-ground experience MoveOn was looking for, but a healthy heaping of technological savvy as well.[xxxiv] Adam quickly proved the new team's mettle by coming up with the idea of holding the biggest bake sale ever to "Bake Back the White House." MoveOn members would hold bake sales all over the country to "raise dough" for MoveOn's 2004 election efforts (Brownie, $1. Cookies, $2. Defeating George Bush… Priceless). The idea was that the events would also highlight the difference between Bush's reliance on big corporate donors and MoveOn's new independence from progressive high rollers. MoveOn members held more than 1000 bake sales. I happened to be on the Boston Common on the day of the bake sales, and was surprised to see three distinct MoveOn bake sales in different sections of the park. In New York, Moby turned his chic-chic vegan bakery Teany over to MoveOn and invited celebrity friends like Al Franken, Janeane Garofalo, and Al Sharpton to man the booths and sell lots of butterless cupcakes to help set the Guinness World Record for biggest bake sale ever. In the event, Guinness declined to name an all-time bake sale champion, but they did raise about $700,000 – representing an amazing number of grassroots sugar rushes.

With this gooey coup under their belt, the Ruben brothers set to their real task – constructing the kind of sophisticated mass field operation that would allow MoveOn to go beyond its usual simple tactics and get people to organize their communities. The organization quickly hired dozens of top-flight organizers and sent them to swing states to start building MoveOn's presence in those communities where the 2004 election would be decided. They quickly found that having people on the ground dramatically boosted the numbers of MoveOn members involved in these key communities that would decide the 2004 election. Soon hundreds of people were showing up at MoveOn events put on by these new organizers. But 15 organizers, effective though they might be, just weren't enough to actually move a national election. And so MoveOn decided to "go big" and get their members behind hiring 500 paid field organizers. For an organization that until a few months before had only four paid staff members, it was something radically new.

Because of its tiny (though talented) core staff, Ruben and the other MoveOn staff didn't feel that they had the ability to set up the infrastructure to recruit and manage 500 new staff members. So Adam turned to Douglas H. Phelps, his former boss at U.S. PIRG, who had recently launched a for-profit political consulting firm, Grassroots Campaigns. But 500 organizers, and the Internet age infrastructure to go with them, required a lot of money. So Eli Pariser

---

[xxxiv]Like Adam and Justin, I am a graduate of Green Corps; I'm friendly with both of them and have worked with each of them on several organizing projects.

sent an email to the MoveOn membership asking for $5 million to finance the program – and saying that MoveOn would only implement the program if members gave the first $1 million in the 48 hours after they received the email. "We can't do this without you," the email said, and it was right. Because MoveOn had by and large given up on a big donor strategy, it really did need its members to pitch in to make the field program happen.

In the event, MoveOn members turned out to be so passionate about beating George Bush – and about getting MoveOn organizers into the communities that could swing the election – that they wildly exceeded MoveOn's expectations, contributing $1.6 million in the allotted 48 hours. MoveOn had the grassroots green light it needed. All those confrontational emails, standing up to the Republicans in the face of skepticism from Washington Democrats was paying off in financing for a field program that would compete in its impact with all the established Big Feet of Democratic field operations: environmental groups, labor unions, and even the Kerry campaign itself. And so they swung into action – within eight weeks, they had secured office space, set up phones and broadband Internet access, and deployed hundreds of organizers across the country.

The ability to go from a four person to staff to 500 in a matter of months was testament to MoveOn's astounding nimbleness. But the operation also showed that setting up a lasting on-the-ground field operation had a great deal more challenges involved than setting up simultaneous movie nights across the country. For one thing, MoveOn (like many other Democratic campaigns) started their field campaign very, very late. In many places, organizers only got on the ground with five weeks left before Election Day – not much time to build a cohesive team, and definitely not much time to work out the kinks in the system. And were there kinks! MoveOn had decided to build a great deal of its election infrastructure from scratch – creating enormous technological problems. Though the MoveOn team was humble and adaptable enough to recognize and solve them, the campaign was slowed by technological snafus, exhausted staffers, and volunteers confused by the constant change.

Despite all the growing pains, however, the basics of the MoveOn system were sound. MoveOn had come up with a neighbor-to-neighbor recruitment system that mimicked with shoe leather the connections its members had previously forged via the web. The idea was based on research conducted by Yale political science professor Alan Gerber that showed that neighbor-to-neighbor, face-to-face voter turnout operations were the most effective at turning unlikely voters out to the polls. Organizers called MoveOn members and active Democrats and asked them to come into the central county MoveOn office for an "emergency" meeting. Then, they were asked to pledge to become precinct leaders and identify 150 Kerry voters in their neighborhoods through a door-knocking drive and turn at least 90 of them out to the polls. It was intense and moved beyond the usually earnest tone of MoveOn's emails – with organizers singling out potential volunteers in front of the crowd and asking them to commit to giving their all for the effort. It was high-confrontation politics at the most personal level, and it worked. Thousands of volunteers signed the contracts MoveOn gave them promising to work dozens of hours for Kerry's election. While not every volunteer hit their goals, the project as a whole exceeded them – turning out significantly more than the 440,000 voters for which MoveOn had initially aimed, according to MoveOn's own post-election analysis.

Although the MoveOn operation (and the broader Democratic turnout machine) was good, the Bush team was better. The Bush campaign didn't just rely on neighbors going to neighbors but aggressively tapped existing social networks in ways that MoveOn didn't and couldn't. They focused less on having a geographical neighbor, who might be a stranger, knock on someone's door and persuade that person to vote and more on figuring out who were the influential people in a voter's life and getting those influentials to persuade voters to turn out for Bush. While MoveOn and the Democrats were getting usually unknown neighbors to bother people at dinner with a knock on the door, the Bush campaign was figuring out how to reach its voters through their pastor, their boss, or even their friendly neighborhood real estate agent (the Bush campaign discovered that real estate agents are among the best connected people in most communities, and that they lean Republican). Ironically, this kind of networking was how MoveOn had built its email list, but the Republicans were doing a way better job of taking it offline.

It was a total mismatch. Of course, the problem wasn't so much MoveOn's. The organization specialized in giving people with limited time, little experience, but a lot of passion the ability to make a difference quickly and easily. Building a sophisticated, organization by organization, political operation wasn't what MoveOn at this point was set up to do. But that didn't make the Republican advantage any less. Bush combined that on-the-ground advantage with an extraordinarily tough and effective media operation that held nothing back in its attacks on Kerry.

In response, MoveOn tapped its membership's desire for a courageous politics of confrontation to defend Kerry more aggressively than Kerry was necessarily willing to defend himself. When Kerry made the understandable initial decision to avoid commenting on the Swift Boat veterans' slanders against his military record so as not to give those accusations more attention than they deserved, MoveOn was ready to fight back for him. They ran a hard-hitting ad attacking George Bush's own sketchy military record. By breaking the silence on Bush's own military record, and showing that doing so wasn't poisonous, MoveOn created space for the Kerry campaign to shine the spotlight on Bush's alleged desertion during Vietnam.

Although the individual ads MoveOn produced were often eye-catching, persuasive, and sometimes hard-hitting, they had some serious drawbacks: most importantly, it's impossible to define a common message among them. The problem wasn't so much that MoveOn's ad operation didn't have the ability to come up with a unifying theme, but that the Kerry campaign itself campaign didn't have one. And the outside groups like MoveOn that were advertising in the 2004 election wanted to amplify their own message by tying it into the Kerry campaign message. But the Kerry campaign's ads were all over the map – now focusing on health care, now on Iraq, now responding to the latest untrue Bush attack, now promising to support the troops. Bush's message, in contrast, was far clearer: his ads portrayed him as, as the line went, "a steady leader in times of change" who would fight hard for what he believed was right and defend America; his ads painted Kerry, in contrast, as a vacillating weak leader unsuited to the challenges of the post-September 11th world. So while MoveOn made some important tactical ad innovations in 2004, the quality of the Bush ads and the consistency of their message made them more effective as a whole.

In the end though, despite the defeat, the 2004 elections provided the genesis for MoveOn's future growth and successes. It started in the days after the election when MoveOn asked members across the country to let them know via email or in meetings with their local organizers what they wanted the organization to focus on next. I attended one of these meetings as a MoveOn organizer in Fort Lauderdale, Florida. Although the diverse faces were all fairly forlorn, the volunteers' words were filled with an invigorating hope and optimism. Although some members who had put their all into the election were depressed, the more common reaction was the one expressed by a volunteer in an email to MoveOn staff just after the election. "In light of what happened yesterday, my friend and I have decided to get personally involved," Chris wrote. "He wants to run for Congress in 2006, and I'm his campaign manager at this point. Do you know of a good information source for how we handle the legalities of forming a campaign, opening bank accounts, registering with the FEC, etc?"[27] In addition to the desire to keep fighting, the most common sentiment was a desire to stay connected with other MoveOn members over the long run – and not just let the progressive political communities MoveOn forged in the 2004 campaign die.

Unfortunately, MoveOn was not entirely equipped to make that happen immediately. Those 500 organizers who had provided much of the glue for the communities were only on contract until Election Day – after that, they went back to their regular jobs and lives. As a result, in many places, MoveOn lost a lot of the energy and activity that drove its election operation. MoveOn was in many ways repeating what had been the bane of Democratic political organizing for a long time: throw a lot of resources into building up a campaign and infrastructure from scratch and then let it die after the election.

Local Courage

But the connections they had built were, in many places, too strong to die just because the paid staff was gone. More importantly, the need for MoveOn's courageous politics was as strong as ever. Not only did the national Democrats need significant bucking up in the wake of the presidential and congressional losses, there was just as much need for courage at the local level too, where local Democrats were often just as enslaved to the Politics of Fear as their Washington counterparts. In Boulder, Colorado, dozens of members showed up at a post-election MoveOn house party to discuss MoveOn's agenda for the next two years. They saw that MoveOn didn't yet have a specific plan mapped out for post-election work, so they went ahead and gathered everyone's phone and email addresses and started working on local issues, like ensuring that elections were safe and secure (Boulder County had had major problems on Election Day 2004 and was one of the last counties in the country to report its results). Pretty soon, they'd gone beyond trying to convince county officials to install safer voting machines, and used their experience working with MoveOn during the 2004 election to run a successful campaign to elect a new County Clerk – the person who actually had the power to enforce more secure voting procedures. In North Carolina, MoveOn member Diane Frederick went to a MoveOn-sponsored rally featuring Cindy Sheehan, the mother of a soldier who had died in Iraq. She had become something of a national sensation by camping out the previous summer outside President Bush's ranch in Crawford, Texas to protest the war. After talking with some of the other attendees, they realized there was a need to continue

MoveOn-style activity – not just working on the Iraq war and other national issues, but also on the state and local level as well. And so they got together and started using some of the skills they'd learned in MoveOn to get North Carolina Democrats to be more courageous – and saw almost immediate results. They flooded North Carolina legislators with calls and emails urging them to raise the minimum wage and within months had convinced the legislature and governor to pass a $1 increase. "Many of the legislators have served for 15 years and they told us they're not used to having people use the Internet to get the grassroots to call them," Frederick said. "They were shocked and overwhelmed and got the message."[28]

With efforts like these taking off across the country, and MoveOn members begging for things they could do to take on President Bush and the Republicans, the brothers Ruben decided to take the field program they'd begun in the few months before the 2004 election to the next level of progressive movement-building. No longer would MoveOn members be able to participate only in MoveOn's courageous stances with emails, contributions, and a few one-time-only real world actions. They were going to build lasting community-by-community organizations that would provide some organizing depth to complement the Internet's breadth. Pretty soon, MoveOn had established hundreds of lasting neighborhood "councils" where members would meet regularly, build relationships, and increase their collective political skills and contacts. It could set the stage for the kind of long-term involvement that had thus far eluded MoveOn: in all my research, it was extremely rare to meet anyone who had stayed involved with the organization for more than two years. Some people dropped out because they'd lost interest, or lost hope that political activism could make a real difference. Many others, who'd had their first taste of politics through MoveOn, realized after a while that MoveOn, as currently constituted, represented just a starting point for politics – that there were much more sophisticated and effective ways to influence politics than just sending a few emails, going to a couple of spontaneously-organized events, or sending in a credit card contribution. MoveOn was, in the words of Washington Director Tom Matzzie, "a gateway drug to politics."

As MoveOn was deepening its field presence, it was also expanding into new territories. When a giant tsunami rocked South Asia in 2004 killing more than 250,000 people, MoveOn swung into action, asking its members to email Congress requesting assistance for the victims of the disaster. MoveOn members also donated $2.4 million to rescue relief. In 2005, when Hurricanes Katrina and Rita devastated the Gulf Coast, MoveOn Advocacy Director Ben Brandzel came up with the idea of asking its members to provide housing to New Orleans refugees. Within 24 hours, MoveOn had started HurricaneHousing.org. The idea caught on, and soon The Democratic National Committee, John Kerry, True Majority, and other organizations were on board was well. Collectively, the groups would ultimately offer 30,000 desperately needed beds to the refugees, some for as long as a year.[29]

The idea to use the power of MoveOn's Internet list to supply serious relief to the Katrina refugees was genius, but their next area of expansion was much more about courage than innovation. MoveOn had long discussed whether or not they should get involved in Democratic primaries; there were, after all, a lot of less-than-progressive Democrats who they thought their members might want to do without. They had even sponsored the 2003 MoveOn online primary, but ended up not endorsing any candidate when no one got a majority. But they were wary of primaries: they could be exhausting, disappointing, and could pit one MoveOn member against the other. And primaries really got under the skin of Democratic leaders, who liked their fellow incumbents to be able to hoard their resources for the main battle with Republicans. Besides, MoveOn leaders wanted to keep the focus where their members' passion was – in stopping Bush and the Republicans.

But some Democrats were actively interfering with their goal of stopping the Bush agenda. Most prominent was Connecticut Senator Joseph Lieberman. National progressives were furious that Lieberman, Gore's vice presidential nominee, had become such a Bush sycophant when it came to promoting the war in Iraq. Even though Lieberman continued to vote as a progressive on many domestic issues (with the notable exception of opposing a filibuster against Bush Supreme Court nominee Samuel Alito), he provided important Democratic cover for Bush's false claims about the Iraq war, and could be relied upon to go on Fox News to defend the Bush administration's foreign policy almost no matter how badly Bush was screwing up. Despite the disillusionment in progressive circles, it looked like it would be hard to mount a credible challenge against Lieberman – he was well financed, popular across party lines, and had all the power of incumbency behind him.

But then Tom Matzzie, MoveOn's Washington director, spoke at Yale University in November and found his anger at Lieberman shared by the students and New Haven citizens in attendance. So a few weeks later, when he was interviewed by a *Hartford Courant* reporter, he said that MoveOn would support a primary challenger against Lieberman if a majority of MoveOn members in

Connecticut demanded it. It was a gutsy move on Matzzie's part – he hadn't received authorization from the rest of the organization to announce the threat, but it hit a chord nonetheless – and was soon picked up by the national media. The stories about Matzzie's threats, however, dismissed the likelihood of any primary challenger succeeding against the well-financed, well-liked Lieberman. But to Ned Lamont, an anti-war cable millionaire, Matzzie's statement was music to his ears. He was already contemplating a primary challenge to Lieberman – having MoveOn's grassroots power on his side could be a significant boost to his campaign. Meanwhile, DC insiders led by Democratic Senatorial Campaign Committee Chair Chuck Schumer were doing all they could to prop up Lieberman – urging Lamont to drop out of the race, channeling millions of dollars to his campaign, and getting even Senate progressives like Barbara Boxer to make appearances in Connecticut on Lieberman's behalf. Of course, from an insider's perspective, this was a smart move, even for Democrats like Boxer who strongly disagreed with the way Lieberman had backed Bush: chances were Lieberman was going to win and they wanted to preserve good relations with him when he did. What's more, most incumbent Democrats, regardless of their ideological leanings, didn't particularly like the idea of primary challenges of any kind against incumbent senators.

But MoveOn – like the progressive blogosphere that was at the same time warming to Lamont's candidacy – didn't have the same constraints. It could do what it felt was right and damn the consequences – it wasn't particularly worried about how insider Democrats would react. But this was still a new step – and MoveOn wanted to test its members out. On February 14, they sent a survey to the membership asking them, "Should we take on right-wing Democrats? We think this makes sense but it's a big decision so we wanted to check with you and other MoveOn members. What do you think?" The question was biased, but the MoveOn membership's response was an unambiguous yes – 84 percent said they wanted to challenge Democrats. When MoveOn asked its Connecticut membership which candidate it should endorse, 85 percent of respondents said Lamont. And the respondents backed it up with cash, sending $250,000 into Lamont campaign coffers overnight. It was a clear demonstration of how MoveOn is fueled by the courage of crowds: freed from the insider calculations and fears that affected, by necessity, even progressive champions like Barbara Boxer, MoveOn members were able to take a stand that Washington Democrats, no matter how much they shared MoveOn members' frustrations with Lieberman, would never have found the courage to pursue.

As the August 12 primary date neared, Lamont's campaign became a national cause célèbre for progressives. While the newly powerful blogosphere got a lot of the attention, it was MoveOn that was providing the lion's share of the Lamont campaign's grassroots power. When a *Wall Street Journal* reporter visited Lamont headquarters in West Hartford, she reported that nine of 11 volunteers were MoveOn members. MoveOn was changing the face of Connecticut politics. A rally on the New Haven Green drew hundreds, shocking old Connecticut Democratic hands who'd never seen anything like it. "I literally knew only three or four people" there, said 20-year state politics veteran and state representative John C. Geragosian.[30] Those new people helped bump turnout in the Democratic primary to record levels and delivered Lamont a narrow 52-48 victory. Lamont's win had an electrifying effect on official Democratic Washington. Schumer, Reid and almost every other Democrat enthusiastically endorsed Lamont for his general election repeat matchup against Lieberman, who had decided to run as an independent. Hillary Clinton called Lamont and offered him "financial help and any other help he needs." It was a signal that Democrats in Washington were beginning to recognize that they ignored the politics of courage at their peril. The win demonstrated to other Democratic candidates that aggressively opposing the Bush agenda could pay big dividends in 2006.[xxxv] Not everyone was happy about this validation of the politics of courage. Not every Democrat was as excited about this new force in American politics. "They're the modern McGovernites," DLC founder Al From was heard yelling at a Beltway event around this time. "They're going to drive the party over the cliff."

Supporting the Lamont-Lieberman campaign wasn't the only way MoveOn made Democrats more aggressive during the 2006 election cycle. As early as 2005, Wes Boyd and the rest of the political team started to sense that the variety of Republican corruption scandals, growing frustration at the lack of suc-

---

[xxxv]Unfortunately, Ned Lamont didn't seem to entirely learn the lesson of his own victory. Rather than riding the anti-war platform he'd won with in the primary, he brought in Hillary Clinton adviser Howard Wolfson and started practicing the politics of fear. In an attempt to change the subject, Lieberman was accusing Lamont of being a one-issue candidate. Under Wolfson's guidance, Lamont took the bait – and started emphasizing other issues, not even bringing up the war unless he was asked about it. The switch robbed the Lamont campaign of its essence. The whole basis for his campaign was that Lieberman was too close to the very unpopular Bush. But on issues besides Iraq, Lieberman had often aggressively opposed Bush; on most other issues, Lamont's stances were barely distinguishable from Lieberman's. It allowed Lieberman to show that he wasn't just the Bush lackey Lamont had been painting him as. For independents, the election ceased to be a referendum on Bush and the Iraq War, and became instead a choice between two individuals. With all his experience, his record of delivering for the state, and his general progressive orientation, it was no contest for Lieberman, and he coasted to a comfortable victory that surprised the pundits who thought he was mortally wounded after his primary defeat.

cess in Iraq, and Bush's plummeting popularity were fundamentally altering the political climate – meaning that dozens of Republican seats that had previously been considered safe could suddenly up for grabs. But the Democratic leadership in Washington, particularly Democratic Congressional Campaign Committee chair Rahm Emanuel, seemed stuck with the idea that only those handful of seats that had been decided by less than 10 points in the previous election would be realistically in play – and were just looking at about 42 competitive seats, with the idea of ultimately investing major resources in 15 or 20. MoveOn set out to prove it to the Washington power brokers that the election could truly be transformative – and that they shouldn't be intimidated by Republicans boasting about their lack of vulnerability.

They needed to show that Republicans that the DCCC considered second or third tier targets could be beaten. And so they asked the membership to support an ad campaign that would tie what they thought were vulnerable representatives to Bush, Cheney, and Tom DeLay – and see what the impact would be. They came up with a series of "Caught Red Handed" advertisements aimed at some of the most established Republican members of Congress: 12-term incumbent Connecticut's Nancy Johnson, Indiana's Chris Chocola, Republican leadership member Deborah Pryce of Ohio, and Virginia's Thelma Drake. The ads showed grainy black and white pictures with their hands painted red – and implied that they had traded their votes in exchange for campaign donations from Halliburton or big drug companies. MoveOn put $1.2 million behind its first round of ads, enough to ensure that the average viewer saw them about 10 times. Then, they compared poll numbers in the districts from before and after the ads were run and compared those with control districts where they hadn't run any ads at all. The results showed that clear attacks on Republican incumbents on corruption could have a major impact: Nancy Johnson went down 11 points in MoveOn's polling after it ran the ads and Deborah Pryce went down 9 points, with smaller, but significant changes, for Chocola and Drake. They were so successful that MoveOn raised millions more to run subsequent rounds of "Caught Red-Handed" ads against the four targets – and were even noted for their effectiveness by Republican Leader John Boehner. He told the *Wall Street Journal* that the ads "certainly have had some impact."[31] Even more importantly, the ads achieved their mission – helping demonstrate to Democratic leaders that there were vastly more vulnerable Republican seats than insider Democrats had been forecasting – freeing up some money from the DCCC to make other races competitive. MoveOn's politics of courage was finally penetrating the Washington consensus

– and going big time.

And when Democrats won in November, it was even bigger – MoveOn volunteers had made over 7 million phone calls, organized 7,500 house parties, and 6,000 events in their congressional districts; in some districts, the calls volunteers made to voters far exceeded the margin of victory, suggesting that MoveOn may have provided the grassroots power that put candidates over the top in five or more districts (in Joe Courtney's race against incumbent Rob Simmons in Connecticut, MoveOn members made more than 100,000 calls in the district; Courtney won by 83 votes). [32] It was the politics of courage writ large.

In the wake of the election, MoveOn would start to think how it could grow even bigger. In a way, despite its phenomenal growth and increasing influence on Capitol Hill, the organization was still very narrowly focused: it had rarely departed from working on national politics through tried and true methods of online petitioning, fundraising, offline house parties, and some neighbor-to-neighbor grassroots politicking at key points. It rarely engaged in state and local politics and rarely developed any kind of depth on any one issue; it would flit from hot issue to hot issue, which was great for building its email list, but not so great for appealing to those members who wanted more sophistication and deeper impact. And it was limited: the overwhelming majority of its membership was white, well-educated liberals; so far, MoveOn hadn't figured out how to expand beyond that base demographic.

And even in the majority, sometimes MoveOn did things that made it difficult to move beyond its base. In September, 2007, the U.S. Commander in Iraq was scheduled to testify to Congress about the Iraq War. George Bush had been hiding behind Petraeus, claiming he was going to make up his mind about what to do in Iraq based on what Petraeus said during his visit to Washington. The media was buying into the gambit: reporters swooned for the "warrior-intellectual" with a chestful of medals and were reporting on Petraeus's upcoming testimony to Congress as if it would be the unvarnished truth. But Petraeus had another quality, in addition to being a media darling, that made him the perfect front man for Bush: the perfect mix of political ambition and loyalty. Based on the reports filtering out of Baghdad, no one really doubted what Petraeus was going to say: that victory was just around the corner if the American people just stuck with the war for another few months. But to get the media to look deeper than Petraeus's testimony about the real state of the war effort, MoveOn and its antiwar partners had to get the media to doubt Petraeus's commitment to the truth. It shouldn't have been too hard: Petraeus had provided plenty of evidence that he was willing to violate the military tradition of political neutrality and distort the situation in Iraq to service Bush's agenda. In 2004, just weeks before the election, Petraeus wrote an op-ed painting a rosy picture of the situation in Iraq, saying, for instance, that there were more than 100,000 trained and equipped Iraqi soldiers, giving the impression that those soldiers were actually ready for battle, when the truth was that only a tiny fraction were anything approaching a modern army.[33] And just before his testimony, he released a report showing reduced sectarian violence – something widely believed until media reported that Petraeus's formula excluded deaths by car bombs[34] and *The Washington Post* reported that assassinations only counted if the victim was shot in the back of the head, not the front.[35] Meanwhile, independent reports noted that Bush's troops surge was largely failing.[36] Indeed, in the days leading up to Petraeus's testimony, national media started reporting on the contradictions between Petraeus's expected optimism and the dire analyses of other government and journalistic sources; some even raised the issue of his political neutrality.

Sensing an opportunity to take it to the next level, MoveOn resorted to the time-honored tactic of running a hard-hitting *New York Times* ad to help change the direction of the debate – and its members responded with the cash to put it on the air. The ad they came up with asked "General Petraeus or General Betray Us?" and raised some of the evidence that cast doubt on Petraeus's neutrality. To be sure, the ad was cartoonish and maybe even a little over-the-top. But the response to it said more about the Democrats than about MoveOn. Not surprisingly, Republicans sensed an opportunity in the ad's personal attack on Petraeus. They mobilized the full force of their media echo chamber to try and put Democrats on the spot, demanding whether or not Democratic leaders supported, in Rudy Giuliani's words, an "abominable" "character assassination" on "a general in time of war." Republicans not only successfully distracted attention from Petraeus's testimony, but also intimidated many Democrats into shying away from asking Petraeus tough questions about the veracity of his claims (to her credit, Hillary Clinton was not one of those intimidated, telling Petraeus that trusting him required the "willing suspension of disbelief.") President Bush joined the fray, telling the press, "I thought the ad was disgusting. It was an attack not only on General Petraeus but on the U.S. military. I was disappointed that not more leaders in the Democrat Party spoke out strongly against that kind of ad…most Democrats are afraid of irritating a left-wing group like MoveOn.org – or more afraid of irritating them than they are of irritating the United States military."[37] It was exactly the kind of threat – being too close to progressives and against the military – that Politics of Fear Democrats are terrified of. And so it shouldn't be any surprise that the very next day more than half of Senate Democrats – including many who had received hundreds of thousands of dollars for their election and tens of thousands of hours of volunteer time from MoveOn members – voted to condemn the "liberal activist group" for its ad, which, the resolution claimed, impugned not only "impugned the honor and integrity" of Petraeus, but also "all members of the United States Armed Forces." Regardless of whether or not the ad was over the top, it was a little absurd to single out MoveOn for condemnation when the Senate had done nothing to condemn the 2000 Bush campaign's whisper campaign against John McCain (saying he had a "black baby" in reference to his adopted Bangladeshi daughter), Republican comparisons of Vietnam War triple-amputee senator Max Cleland to Osama bin Laden, or the Swift Boat attacks on war hero John Kerry. It was a symbolic fight to be sure, but one that showed that Democrats, even in the majority, even in control of the agenda, could be cowed into submission.

To start developing some of that depth and some extra reach, MoveOn spun off two new groups. Founder Joan Blades launched MomsRising.org, which works to organize mothers into an online political force that would help improve work, pay, and health care for mothers and their children. Former staffer James Rucker founded colorofchange.org to organize Black Americans around progressive issues – and make America's Black political leadership more aggressive in taking on the Bush administration and other members of the right-wing political establishment. Within a few months, both organizations had topped 50,000 members – and were already making waves in Washington.

Taking Courage Global

But most ambitious is MoveOn's plan to take its online progressive politics global. The organization has almost from its birth been popular overseas; about a third of its members live in other countries: although they never intended it, foreigners found stopping the Republicans' impeachment drive, heading off the Iraq War, and opposing Bush as appealing as American progressives. At home, however, MoveOn's large foreign membership made it vulnerable to Republican attacks that it was a front for "foreign interests," so MoveOn has consistently downplayed the international flavor of its email list – and been careful to only accept political contributions from Americans.

But the global enthusiasm demonstrated that there was an audience for MoveOn-style politics in other countries too. With support from the Service Employees International Union (which was working to organize workers globally), Greenpeace, Human Rights Watch, and others, MoveOn teamed up with the think tank Res Publica and launched Avaaz.org (the name means "Voice" or "Song" in Hindi and several other languages) in early 2007. It represents the Googleization of progressive politics: Avaaz has staff on four continents and sends out MoveOn-style emails in six languages on global issues like climate change, the Iraq War, and whatever else is hot in the global news. In other languages, this kind of politics is a novelty; Avaaz is finding that its response rates in non-English speaking countries are double that of English-speaking countries, where recipients are already inundated with political emails.[38] Although its politics are similar to MoveOn's, Avaaz is already pioneering methods that MoveOn hasn't even touched. Among them is what Executive Director Ricken Patel calls the "Idolization" of politics, referring to the American Idol singing competition that has sprouted national versions everywhere from Malaysia to Afghanistan. Everywhere there's an Idol show, thousands or millions of people spend significant amounts of money to vote for their favorite performers by text message. Avaaz is planning on sending text messages to its members for some instant fundraising: hit one on your cell phone and send $1 to Avaaz to fight global warming. This kind of organizing has already had some success overseas: in 2001, Filipino students used text messages to organize massive rallies that caused the downfall of then-president Joseph Estrada.

Whether it's a vigil in France, on a laptop in Starbucks, or a neighborhood activist meeting in suburban Philadelphia, MoveOn is proving that courageous progressive politics is increasingly powerful. They've shown that it can draw big money and volunteer enthusiasm that can outcompete big corporate donations and the cautious Politics of Fear of the Democratic Party's past. And it's not just raising resources only to fritter them away in a blaze of leftist bombast – increasingly, it's also winning big victories: the 2006 elections, and campaigns to stop Republicans from slashing funding for National Public Radio and PBS, or making sure that big telecom companies have to maintain equal access to the Internet (known as the Net Neutrality principle). Of course, the war in Iraq goes on and President Bush continues to refuse to do anything about global warming. But as the organization continues to grow, it's setting the stage for even bigger victories down the road.

Courage in Chadds Ford

Indeed, the best place to glimpse MoveOn's future – and the future of the progressive politics it practices – is not in Washington, DC or even at Wes Boyd and Joan Blades's house in Berkeley. It's in the hundreds of communities where progressives have gotten involved in politics through MoveOn and used the communities they've built and skills they've learned to change politics on the local level. One such community is Chadds Ford, Pennsylvania, a Philadelphia suburb in Delaware County. The town is dominated by the many pharmaceutical companies that have headquarters and research facilities in the area. And until recently, it has been about as Republican a town as is possible to find outside of Utah. Not only has it traditionally voted heavily Republican, its Republican machine actively excludes Democrats from civic life – going so far as to blackball Democrats even from neighborhood associations and clubs.

But in the last few years, disenchantment over Bush's extremism has seeped into even this prosperous, corporate-dominated suburb. Typical is Branch Heller, a prosperous and voluble retired pharmaceutical executive. "I was a lifelong Republican until I saw that the Republican Party and I were two different people," Heller said at recent Delaware County MoveOn council planning meeting, where participants' seething political fury belied their comfortable surroundings. "I joined the party of Lincoln and have ended up in the party of Tom DeLay and George Bush," he said Even though he says he's benefited financially from Bush's tax cuts, Heller and many others like him eventually found their way on the Internet to the one group they felt was channeling their passion and giving them an easy outlet to do something about it: MoveOn. Pretty soon, MoveOn's Chadds Ford meetings started drawing dozens of people – most of whom were surprised to find a single other ardent Democrat, let alone a roomful of people sick of not only Bush but also the local Republican machine.

Pretty soon, they started organizing. They played a big role in helping Democratic candidate Joe Sestak oust 20-year Republican congressman Curt Weldon, initially considered one of the safest Republican seats in the country. And for the first time in decades, the Democratic congressional candidate received more votes in Chadds Ford than the Republican. Even more impressive, the MoveOn group had an impact on the local level too: its previously apolitical members started getting involved in the moribund local Democratic Party – within months, they'd help elect a Democrat to the town's three member Supervisor board, ending a decades long Republican monopoly. It was MoveOn politics going deep. And it might just be a taste of the future – not just in Congress, or towns and cities across America, but around the world.

TOM DASCHLE
CIRCUMSTANTIAL COWARDICE

★★★★

It's hard not to feel sorry for former Democratic Senate leader Tom Daschle. Okay, maybe not too sorry — the guy *is* pulling down a million dollars a year at a DC lobbying firm. But still. Daschle was always so nice, so mild-mannered, and the Republicans seemed to derive some special glee from tearing him to shreds. It was difficult to watch him, pulled in so many directions as he was. On the one hand, he was always trying to appear like an independent in tune with his state's Republican politics and parochial demands. And on the other there was his responsibility as the Democratic Party leader – the antithesis of an independent – who was supposed to think of the country and speak for his party. He was perpetually twisting this way and that. But it never really worked out. More often than not, he just twisted himself into some absurd political pretzel just waiting to be devoured by a GOP attack dog. One day, he'd defy most of his caucus and vote to pass the Republicans' latest legislative abomination just because it contained some pork barrel spending destined for his home state of South Dakota. The next day he'd try to rally the Democrats, in his quiet way, to oppose some other Bush atrocity that happened not to be loaded up with lard destined for South Dakota. He looked craven, he looked cowardly, and in the end, he just looked ridiculous.

While Daschle never seemed to manage his predicament very well, it's hard to imagine many politicians doing much better. Daschle may not have been the most courageous politician ever, but he also wasn't the most cowardly. Yet he led the Democrats in the most shrinking way possible. He rarely challenged Republicans and almost never really pushed members of his own caucus to vote with him, whether he was fighting for progressive values or giving into Bush. He delivered defeat after defeat to the Democratic agenda, and ultimately went down in ignominious failure himself: the first sitting party leader beaten in an election since Barry Goldwater downed Ernest McFarland in 1954. What happened to make such an average politician – neither particularly skilled nor abysmally incompetent – such a disastrous failure?

In truth, Daschle's failures are less a condemnation of any personal weakness on his part and more a commentary on the Democrats who chose him as their leader – and who put him in the impossible circumstances that led to his defeat, their disgrace, and the country's shame. That is where this chapter begins: in the Democratic caucus room on December 2, 1994, as the senators met to choose their future leaders and contemplate the young South Dakotan presenting himself for the Senate's second most powerful position.

It was a sorry bunch of Democratic senators who filed into the caucus room that day. Not only had their own numbers dwindled from 57 to 47 in the 1994 Republican tsunami, but they now faced a Republican Party dominated by ruthless right-wingers determined to humiliate and isolate Democrats. Many of the Democrats in the room weren't just sad, they were scared. They would be up for re-election in two years – if the country really had experienced a revolution of the right, like the Republicans were saying, what would that mean for their own political survival?

They faced a fundamental question that day: how were they to respond to the expected barrage of Republican attacks? They needed an answer quick. In the wake of the elections, one of the Democrats' number, Alabama senator Richard Shelby had already abandoned the party. Another, Colorado's Ben Nighthorse Campbell, was rumored to be considering the same. And they couldn't rely on the Clinton White House for leadership or direction; the deeply unpopular Clinton was already signaling his "triangulation" strategy of distancing himself from congressional Democrats who he felt had "shackled" him during the first two years of his administration.

The senators had two options. The first was the Politics of Fear approach: accept the verdict of the 1994 elections, keep their heads down, minimize conflict with the Republicans, and hope that voters wouldn't see the Democrats as getting in the way of the right-wing change they had voted for. In the words of one unnamed Democratic senator quoted on ABC's *World News Tonight*, "After the shellacking we took in the election, all we need now to finish us off is to be known as the party of gridlock."[1] The second strategy would be to fight back, hard.

The less confrontational approach had a clear candidate in South Dakota Senator Tom Daschle. Daschle had started running for Democratic Leader in March of 1994, after then-Majority Leader George Mitchell announced his retirement. Daschle was variously described as "mild," "low-key," "unassuming and "bland," but he'd been able to turn these characteristics to his advantage in the ego-charged Senate. His self-effacing style allowed him to ingratiate himself with older, more powerful senators much faster than some of his more attention-seeking colleagues. He was the rare senator who was usually willing to allow other senators to take the national spotlight, and he had no problem listening wide-eyed as one of the Senate's senior windbags expounded on a pet topic. As Daschle's deputy, Harry Reid, would describe it later, Daschle was a master of "convincing each senator that he or she is his favorite."[2]

There was another reason Daschle was so willing to let his fellow senators have the national spotlight – he knew that spotlight might not shine so kindly on him. Because South Dakota was so Republican – with the exception of Lyndon Johnson's landslide

1964 victory, South Dakota hadn't voted for a Democratic candidate for president since FDR in 1936 – voters didn't tend to support politicians too closely identified with the national Democratic Party. Indeed, South Dakota voters had even rejected their native son, Democratic Senator George McGovern, when he ran for president in 1972 against Richard Nixon. Eschewing the national spotlight and the national party was a strategy shared, more or less, by all of Daschle's fellow Dakota Democrats: Byron Dorgan, Tim Johnson, and Kent Conrad. The four compiled generally liberal voting records, but confined their public statements largely to non-partisan Dakota issues like farm policy. It was a strategy that worked: they got elected over and over again in overwhelmingly Republican states even as they took on powerful behind-the-scenes Democratic Party roles in Washington. For Daschle, in some measure, avoiding confrontation wasn't a choice – it was a political necessity.

So why did Daschle want to be Democratic Leader in the first place? Outside of simple ambition, being the Democratic leader would deliver one major asset that was very important to Daschle's Dakota Democrat brand of politics: the supposed ability to funnel federal spending, back to his home state. That was an important power for a state as addicted to federal largesse as South Dakota (South Dakota receives about $1.49 in federal spending for every dollar it sends to Washington in taxes[xxxvi3]). Daschle also argued that bringing in someone from a Republican state would increase the national Democrats' popularity in Republican areas. "There is a vast part of the country out there that would go unrepresented if we didn't have some member of the leadership to serve there," he told CNN's Bernard Shaw. "I intend to be a very aggressive and articulate spokesperson for the West and Midwest, but I think we've got to represent the whole country in our leadership."[4]

Daschle made that statement because his opponent in the race for Democratic leader, Connecticut senator Chris Dodd, was everything Daschle wasn't: eastern, urbane, and above all, aggressive. Not only did Dodd drive a Ford Mustang (golf bag in trunk), he was known as an enthusiastic companion of Ted Kennedy on the East Coast party circuit. More substantively, he'd won a reputation for being someone who would joust with the Republicans with gusto. Dodd was looking to blow his opponent away by impressing his fellow senators with his ability to go toe-to-toe with new Republican Whip Trent Lott and his charismat-

---

[xxxvi]In the event, being Minority Leader didn't help Daschle much in boosting his state's share of the spending significantly. In 1994, South Dakota was receiving $1.31 in federal spending for every dollar it contributed in taxes, and that level didn't start rising until 1999. But when he became Majority Leader, he was able to elevate it to a high of $1.60 for 2002.

ic wing-nut colleagues. While Daschle was trying to curry favor and wrangle up commitments in private, Dodd went public. A top Dodd strategist laid out his team's misgivings about Daschle for the *Hartford Courant*: "Daschle has no presence. It was one thing to ask for support, but how could you know if he should be your leader until you've seen him on TV?"[5] Dodd set out to show that he could provide the national megaphone that Daschle wouldn't. While Democrats were still licking their wounds from the election, Dodd broke the Democratic silence with appearances on NBC Nightly News, PBS's Charlie Rose, and Don Imus. He opened a well-attended news conference the next day with a none-too-subtle shot at Daschle's reticence: "I'm Chris Dodd and I'm a Democrat. You haven't seen many of us recently," he said. Then, Dodd took the lead in defending President Clinton when Republican Jesse Helms asserted that Clinton didn't have the support of the military. He went on CBS's Face the Nation, ABC, CNN, and said that Helms was "aiding and abetting insubordination."[6] Dodd's forceful approach won accolades all around. *Newsweek* lambasted Daschle and wrote of Dodd in its "Conventional Wisdom Watch" that "Conn senator feistier than dull Daschle in minority leader race. This Chris can hiss."[7] This was the kind of politics that Republicans had ridden to victory in 1994 and Dodd was clearly signaling that it was the kind of confrontational politics he would bring to the job too.

There was another big difference between the two men. Dodd was from Connecticut, one of the country's more progressive states, where Democrats outnumbered Republicans by more than 200,000 voters. Because Connecticut's east coast culture wasn't all that dissimilar from Washington's, Dodd wouldn't have to worry about accusations that he'd "gone Washington" because of his leadership role. South Dakota, in contrast, was both reliably Republican and somewhat more parochial. If Daschle were to win, there would be an inevitable tension between his identification with the national Democratic Party and his desire to be seen as an independent voice in South Dakota. Daschle would be far more likely than Dodd to find himself in a position where South Dakota politics would suggest one approach or policy position, and national politics another.

Part of the reason Daschle faced a tension between his own liberal ideology and his constituents' feelings was that he had done very little to persuade Dakotans to embrace his own more progressive views. True, every summer, he'd go on his famous summer road trip, visiting all of South Dakota's 66 counties alone in his 1971 Pontiac Ventura, visiting Norwegian farmers, Native Americans, and credit card call center workers. He'd pull up to a café, a grain silo, or an office and listen. And then listen some more. He did little talking. He was simply, and sincerely, trying to understand his constituents so that he could better reflect their concerns in Congress – and make sure they knew that he hadn't taken on any fancy airs since going to Washington. He wasn't organizing and he wasn't persuading – he lacked both the courage and the inclination to really try and change the hearts and minds of South Dakota. But listening alone was enough to get him elected so long as he stuck to the tried and true Dakota Democrat strategy of keeping his head down in Washington and keeping his eye always firmly fixed on South Dakota.

And so when the senators went into the caucus room that clear December day, they faced a clear choice: Brash versus Bashful. East vs. West. Advocacy vs. Listening. Daschle had something of a head start because he had begun campaigning so early, which gave him more time to lock up senators' pledges. But public pledges weren't that important in a secret ballot race. When Robert Byrd ousted Ted Kennedy from the Democratic whip position in 1971, Kennedy thought he had 31 votes – more than enough to put him over the top. After coming up with just 24 votes, he told the press with a wry smile, "somebody lied."[8] No, in a secret ballot race with politicians as the voters, what mattered most was who senators thought would be the best leader for them: who would represent the party well, who would best help them get re-elected, who would be sympathetic to their own agenda, and who they just plain liked better. The decision would say as much about the Democratic Party as it said about the two candidates for Majority Leader.

With the future of the embattled party on the line and everyone aware of the closeness of the leadership race, the room was tense as the senators were handed ballots, filled in their choices, and stuffed the slips of paper into the box. Virginia senator Charles Robb read out the names as he pulled them out of the ballot box, and Rhode Island senator Claiborne Pell made the tally. It was a tie, 24-24. But there was one vote left to count, that of Colorado Senator Ben Nighthorse Campbell, which was in a separate envelope because Nighthorse Campbell wasn't present.

Daschle already knew what the result would be. The previous day, Daschle's counts of his fellow senators made him believe that he was going to win. But this man who ran four miles every morning even in the bitterly cold South Dakota winter wasn't about to leave anything to chance or rest on his laurels. "My attitude is that only the paranoid survive," he later told *USA Today*. "You've got to think of every possible thing that could go wrong and try to figure out how to address it."[9] He went around from senator to senator to check and recheck their commitments. As he was doing his last check-ins the day before the vote, he happened to come upon Colorado senator Ben Nighthorse Campbell mounting his Harley Davidson motorcycle in the Capitol parking lot. Campbell had pledged his support to Daschle long ago, but that didn't stop Daschle from double checking. To Daschle's surprise, Campbell, who was involved in a bitter feud with home state Democrats, said he wouldn't come to the caucus meeting, no matter what. But Daschle deployed his prairie patience, and persuaded Campbell to fill out a proxy ballot on the spot before he roared off into the sunset. Now, that proxy ballot would be the deciding vote.[10]

Robb opened the envelope and declared Daschle the winner. It was an election with lasting consequences: Daschle would go on to lead the Democrats for the next 10 years. In a painful twist for Dodd, the vote that put Daschle over the top would not have been there just a few months later, when Nighthorse Campbell defected to the Republicans in early 1995. Despite the closeness of the victory, the Democrats put up a united front. Although the campaign had been spirited, the two competitors had kept any direct criticism of each other private.

Daschle's victory represented a kind of senatorial version of Bill Clinton's Triangulation strategy. It was a signal that the Senate Democrats preferred attempts at conciliation with the Republicans to fighting them. But they would ultimately pay a high price for their choice of Daschle. For circumstances would one day – when it mattered – put those klieg lights squarely on Daschle, no matter how self-effacing he tried to be. When that happened, they would force him to make the choice he had spent his entire senatorial career trying to avoid: to be the leader that the national Democratic Party needed, or to be the senator that South Dakotans wanted. It was an impossible choice for someone like Daschle – his response to it ultimately made him look ridiculous and paralyzed by fear.

But that national attention – and the difficult bind it put Daschle in – came only six years later, when Bill Clinton left office. For the remainder of the Clinton years, Daschle was able to keep his head down, largely because no one was paying attention to him. Clinton not only sucked up most of the media oxygen available to Democrats, he purposefully shut congressional Democrats out of many of the most important negotiations with the Republican leadership. In his memoir *Herding Cats,* then-Republican Senate Leader Trent Lott says that the Senate Democrats under Daschle were "like a fifth wheel. We didn't need them."[11] The media picked up on Daschle's irrelevance and Daschle was able to go on being the Dakota Democrat he aspired to be – working behind the scenes and spending his congressional recesses driving around the state listening to the concerns of South Dakota voters, and working to channel as much pork as possible to his state.

Strength Behind the Scenes

But in 2000, two events occurred that would ultimately spell the end for Daschle's Dakota Democrat strategy. First, Bill Clinton left a Republican in the White House to replace him. With Clinton gone, there was suddenly a lot more media oxygen to go around for Democrats. Second, Daschle's Senate Democrats were able to take advantage of the unpopularity of several Republican incumbents and some prolific (though allegedly corrupt) fundraising by New Jersey Democrat Bob Torricelli to pick up four seats – leading to a 50-50 Senate tie with the Republicans. With the Republicans and Democrats at parity, Daschle was suddenly wielding real power for the first time. Despite Daschle's new clout, the media continued to largely ignore him for the first few weeks after the election. They remained obsessed with the Florida recount battle and its aftermath and had little space left over for the power struggle in the evenly divided Senate.

That was the way Daschle liked it. Hidden from public scrutiny, Daschle proved he could be a tough behind-the-scenes negotiator. He insisted that even though Vice President Dick Cheney was the tie-breaking vote in the Senate for the Republicans, Democrats would be treated like a co-majority: they'd get equal representation on committees, equal budgets, and the ability (usually reserved solely for the Majority Leader) to bring legislation directly to the Senate floor. Daschle received some indirect praise for his negotiating when hard-line Republicans blasted Lott for what they saw as overly generous concessions to Daschle. Conservative movement leader Paul Weyrich said of Lott in the press, "I don't think anybody has disappointed me more in public life" while Lott's fellow senator Phil Gramm told *USA Today* that he was wondering if Lott had "given away the store."[12]

"I hope you'll never lie to me"

The media might have been ignoring the newly powerful Daschle, but George W. Bush certainly wasn't. With their ability to filibuster legislation to death, the Senate Democrats were the one group that had the power to stop his agenda cold. Bush was determined to cajole and cow them into submission, relegating national Democrats to the same kind of enduring minority status to which he had condemned easily intimidated Texas Democrats. And so during Bush's first private meeting with Daschle, Bush felt him out to see how this he would respond to the charm, bullying, and attack combo he had perfected in Austin.

Bush started off the meeting by recalling his close relationship in Texas with Democratic Lieutenant Governor Bob Bullock. "We got to be very close. I'd like to see if we could do that, too," Bush told Daschle. It was less an appeal for friendship than it appeared on the surface. Bullock won Bush's "friendship" largely by doing Bush's bidding. That was the kind of relationship Bush was hoping for with Daschle. Then, Bush made a more brazen parry. "I hope you'll never lie to me," he suddenly blurted. "I hope you'll never lie to me either," Daschle responded. Bush's remark was, as Daschle would later remark, an "unusual" statement with which to launch a new relationship, and it made Daschle realize the extent of Bush's swagger.[13] Then, during a joint public appearance with the other congressional leaders after their private meeting, Bush opened his remarks with a "joke" that cast a bit of light into what he thought might be the best way to conduct his presidency. "I told all four that there are going to be some times where we don't agree with each other, but that's OK," Bush said. "If this were a dictatorship, it would be a heck of a lot easier, just so long as I'm the dictator." Daschle and the rest of the audience responded with nervous laughter – it seemed Bush's joke might represent something more.

Daschle responded to Bush's bullying assays exactly as Bush had hoped. On PBS that night, anchor Jim Lehrer asked Daschle if Bush had treated him as an adversary in their meeting. "There was no adversarial tone at all," Daschle lied. "It was a very conciliatory one, and I thought exactly the kind of positive approach that you'd expect for a first meeting between two people."[14] It was a sign to Bush that Daschle might be exactly the kind of Democrat he was hoping for – one who would respond to his attacks by covering up for him and saying how nice he was.

That early encounter with Daschle was indeed an indicator of what was to come. Although Bush had run on a "compassionate conservative" platform, he began touring the country promoting a hard-right agenda notably lacking in any hint of compassion. He unilaterally withdrew the United States from all international efforts to stop the emerging global climate crisis, pulled out of the Anti-Ballistic Missile treaty, and started pushing a massive $1.6 trillion tax cut primarily for the ultra-rich. And he nominated extreme right-wingers like John Ashcroft and Gale Norton to his cabinet, guaranteeing fights with the Democrats. Ashcroft in particular proved to be a lightning rod. He had opposed desegregation of public schools while governor of Missouri; blocked Clinton's nominee for Ambassador to Luxembourg, James Hormel, who is gay, because, Ashcroft said, "he had been a leader in promoting a lifestyle;" and had smeared Ronnie White, a black Clinton nominee for a federal judgeship, who he said had "shown a tremendous bent toward criminal activity" because he had voted 18 times to reduce death penalty sentences (and 41 times to uphold them).

It was exactly these stances, though, that made Ashcroft a favorite of right-wingers, who were determined to force him down the Democrats' throats. If they could pass through an extremist like Ashcroft, they'd show that Bush's agenda would be unstoppable. They thought they could soften up Daschle by going after him in his home state and ran a series of television advertisements urging him and Johnson to support Ashcroft, characterizing any decision to vote against him as surrender to Democratic "party extremists."

Despite the ads, Ashcroft's extremist record was all too much for Daschle. Daschle had voted only one other time to oppose a presidential cabinet nominee – Defense Secretary nominee John Tower in 1989. But on January 30, he took to the Senate floor and delivered a long speech, passionate by Daschle's standards, clearly denouncing Ashcroft. "Senator Ashcroft misled the Senate and deliberately distorted his record," Daschle said of the Ronnie White affair. "John Ashcroft has shown a pattern of insensitivity through his public career."[15] They were tough words, but Daschle had already limited their significance. Days earlier, in an attempt to avoid upsetting the air of post-Election collegiality, he had assured Bush that all the president's nominees, including Ashcroft, would be approved. In this case, it meant that even though 42 senators – enough to support a filibuster – were opposing Ashcroft, he would let the nomination go to a vote. He was trying to appear non-partisan and civil, but in this case the obligations of Daschle's version of civility meant letting one of the worst nominees for a cabinet position ever take office.

Suddenly Spotlighted

The Ashcroft ads were only a taste of what the right-wing had in store for the newly powerful Daschle. In April, *National Review Online* ran a story entitled "Tom Daschle's Love Affair With Arsenic." It led by asking, "What is it about poisoning the nation's children that Senate Majority Leader Tom Daschle enjoys?" after Daschle voted to allow the Bush administration more time to clean up arsenic pollution in the water supply.[16] The Republicans also did to Daschle what they had had so much success doing to Al Gore, and would later find success with John Kerry – attacking him on his strongest point.[xxxvii] For Daschle, they went after his reputation as a relatively non-partisan senator who generally tried to build consensus and avoid battles. That could be particularly deadly. If Daschle lost his reputation as a consensus-oriented leader, he wouldn't have much to fall back on: he didn't have deep support among progressive activists and he didn't have the chutzpah to force an agenda through with strong armed lobbying.

Taking their lead from the Republican National Committee, conservatives began repeating the claim that Daschle was a "ferocious partisan." From now on, he would be an "ultra-partisan" to *The New York Times* conservative columnist William Safire and a "hyper-partisan," to *The Wall Street Journal* editorial board. Daschle was rapidly becoming the Republicans' new Clinton: their all-purpose whipping-boy. Republicans' bitter attacks on Daschle surprised those pundits who had erroneously and repeatedly attributed Republicans' vituperation toward Clinton to some kind of Clinton-specific baby boomer jealous rage. Of course, the Republican assaults on Clinton really had little to do with him personally. They were more about tearing down Democrats so Republicans could get more power. It had worked with Clinton. If they could get Daschle to buckle anywhere near as much, they would achieve near-total control over the country.[xxxviii]

Even though he had lived through the Clinton years, Daschle was shocked that he was now the target. In his memoir of the 107th Congress, *Like No Other Time*, Daschle talks about returning home to South Dakota after going to Florida to support Gore during the post-election debacle. "I was shocked by what I encountered that day," he wrote. "Outside the hotel where I was to speak, there was a massive anti-Gore and anti-*Daschle* demonstration. This was the first time in my life this had ever happened to me. People pushing in from all sides. Angry faces shouting and waving signs and placards..."[17] Over the next four years, Daschle would be "amazed," "shocked," and "surprised" over and over again at the zero-sum hardball the Republicans were willing to play and the degree to

---

[xxxvii]With Gore, the Republicans had convinced voters that the Boy Scoutish vice president was actually dishonest by distorting his comments about his huge role in the creation of the Internet and by nitpicking their way through some tiny errors in Gore's debates. With Kerry, they would manufacture conspiracy theories to generate doubt about his Vietnam War heroism.
[xxxviii]Thanks to Chris Mooney's review of the attacks on Daschle in his article "The Secret War on Tom Daschle" in *The American Prospect Online*, July 2, 2001.

which they were willing to go after him personally.

The paradox of Daschle's new prominence was that the better the Democrats did at the national level, and the more publicity he and they got, the more he drew Republican attacks at home. Most politicians want to get more airtime. For Daschle, however, more airtime put him exactly where Republicans wanted him: identified as the leader of the liberal national Democratic Party, for which South Dakotans felt little affinity. It might have been different if Daschle was aggressively working in South Dakota to build a powerful Democratic Party more closely aligned with a national progressive agenda that could support his actions as a national leader. But that had never been his style. Nor was his home state a fertile ground for such action; and now he was reaping the bitter harvest.

This was Daschle's quandary when Bush, in a nationally televised address to Congress, rolled out his first major domestic policy initiative, a $1.6 trillion plus tax cut targeted mainly at the ultra-wealthy. In a speech immediately following Bush's, Daschle and Gephardt harshly criticized the tax cut. Daschle described how Bush had used overly optimistic projections as governor of Texas; when they didn't work out, the state plunged into debt. "If his budget predictions now are as faulty as they were then, his tax cut would bring huge deficits, increase the national debt and put our economy back in the ditch," Daschle said. While voters in a less Republican state might have been proud to see their senator helping represent one of the nation's two great political parties in front of a huge countrywide audience, South Dakota was different. Politically, the address helped remind South Dakota voters that Daschle's loyalty was now divided between them and national Democrats. Daschle's South Dakota opponents began to argue that Daschle was putting the national Democratic Party first. Typical was a letter published shortly after Daschle's address in the Sioux Falls newspaper, *The Argus Leader*. "Daschle is in Washington, DC to represent South Dakotans, not the Democratic Party," wrote one Sioux Falls resident in a letter largely cribbed from Republican talking points. "I understand he has certain responsibilities to the party. However, Sen. Daschle will become Mr. Daschle very quickly if he continues to disregard the will of the people he was elected to represent."[18]

Bush himself decided to bring this contrast right to South Dakota voters immediately after the speech, scheduling a trip to the state as part of his nationwide tax-cut barnstorm. When he arrived, Bush avoided his usual ultra-incendiary rhetoric, but used his sneer and famously flexible face to get his message across silently and clearly to the partisans filling the hangar at the Sioux Falls Air National Guard in frigid 21-degree weather. "I appreciate the dialogues we have had," Bush said of Daschle. "He treats me with respect. I will treat him with respect," but said it in a way that caused the crowd to erupt in jeers.[19] Bush went on to make his case for big tax cuts for the top earners (very few of whom lived in South Dakota) and wasn't shy about exhorting his adoring audience to pressure their senators. "You're just an email away from making a difference in somebody's attitude," Bush told the crowd. At first, Daschle did strike back relatively hard at Bush – pointing out that 63 percent of South Dakota families made under $30,000 a year and so would receive no tax cut.

But Bush kept up the drumbeat over the next month, and Republican-affiliated groups like the Club for Growth gave him heavy air coverage. They flooded the airwaves with ads that played a 1962 speech in which John F. Kennedy touted a tax cut, and then asked why Daschle and fellow South Dakota Democratic senator Tim Johnson weren't supporting a tax cut when even Democrat Kennedy had found it in his heart to push one. (The ads didn't mention that Kennedy was arguing for lowering the top tax rate from 91 percent to 70 percent, not from 39 percent to 33 percent as Bush was doing). The combination of the airwave assault and Bush's ongoing barnstorm put Daschle so on the defensive that he felt he had to reach into his own campaign treasury to counter the ads. The spot Daschle came up with was one of the mildest ads in American political history. Not only did it not compete with Republicans for artistry or gimmickry (Daschle, alone in a suit in front of an American flag, spoke straight to the camera), it also didn't contest the President's turf. He didn't attack Bush or his tax cut and didn't even try to change the agenda from tax cuts to Daschle's other priorities.

> I want to thank President Bush for coming to South Dakota to hear first-hand the concerns of our state. I'm sure he'll hear, as I've heard, your desire for us to set aside partisan differences and work together. President Bush and I both support a tax cut. We differ on the details, yet I'm confident that we can agree on a plan that benefits all Americans, not just the wealthy.
>
> A tax cut not based on a risky 10-year projection, but one that pays off our national debt, protects Social Security, strengthens Medicare to cover prescription drugs and leaves money for other important priorities like agriculture, and building the Lewis and Clark and Mni Wiconi and Mid-Dakota water projects so vital to our state's health and economy.

In a way, it was classic Dakota Democrat – an attempt to portray Daschle as someone with Republican values, but without the rough edges. But while the content may have been similar to messages that had worked before for Daschle and the Dakotas' other Democrats, the environment in which they were broadcast was suddenly far, far different. Daschle's conciliatory tone was a hard sell when just a few weeks before, for a national audience, Daschle had attacked Bush's tax plan in far harsher terms. Republicans followed up by making sure that the stark difference between what Daschle said in Washington and what he said in South Dakota was under more scrutiny than ever before.

With the stridency of Daschle's (and many other Democrats') opposition crumbling in the face of the administration's aggressive campaign, it was only a matter of time before Bush passed his tax cut. Democrats got a few concessions – the size of the tax cut was reduced from $1.6 trillion to $1.35 trillion, but the overwhelming majority of the benefits still went to the ultra-rich. Indeed people earning more than $100,000 a year accounted for 63.7 percent of the benefits of this and Bush's later tax cuts; people making over $1 million got 19 percent of the benefit.[20] Although Daschle voted against the measure, he didn't back it up with any of the confrontational rhetoric, grassroots appeals, or strong arm lobbying that might have been able to stop Bush's plan cold. Indeed, his opposition was so weak and the Bush juggernaut so strong that Bush picked up 12 Democrats in support of his plan, including even Daschle's fellow South Dakotan, Tim Johnson.

Partisan Success, Partisan Fury

It was a major defeat and showed early on that it would be difficult for the party to stop a full-court press from President Bush. But there was a downside to these successes – or rather, the blustering way in which they were achieved. Although Daschle was accommodating enough, or afraid enough, to put a friendly gloss on Bush's private bullying and public arrogance, it didn't work so well with some of the Senate's flintier members – notably Vermont's Jim Jeffords. Jeffords was part of a dying breed – the Northeastern liberal Republican. Though he had always been a Republican partisan, he would frequently vote with Democrats on issues like environmental protection and expanded children's health care. Every time Bush rammed through another element of his far-right agenda, Jeffords felt increasingly isolated, powerless, and angry. When the White House wouldn't support his relatively modest demands for education and health funding, and his fellow Senate Republicans began to freeze him out because he wasn't toeing the party line (even "forgetting" to invite him to performances of the Republican singing group he had started), it pushed him over the edge. During a meeting with Chris Dodd, he broached the idea of switching parties. A week later, he had declared himself and independent and handed control of the Senate to the Democrats. Daschle was now the Majority Leader. It was great news for Democrats eager for more power with which to stop Bush, but it was dangerous for Daschle, who began to attract even more national attention.[xxxix]

Hopeful and Inspired

All this partisan warfare seemed suddenly small-bore to Daschle when the September 11th hijackers flew their airplanes into the Twin Towers and the Pentagon. Members of Congress of both parties tried to top each other's declarations of unity. Daschle took these commitments at face value – especially after he became a direct target of terrorists himself when a still unidentified attacker sent an envelope filled with anthrax to his office, exposing several members of his staff to the potentially deadly spores. With lives so immediately at stake, Daschle didn't believe that anyone would try to use the moment for political advantage. Daschle would later remark in his diary about "how hopeful and inspired I was by the solidarity and teamwork displayed by Congress and the White House in the wake of such a tragedy, how refreshing it felt to see partisanship and politics put aside as our government and our people stood together to respond to the needs of our nation."[21]

Yet even as Daschle was indulging this reverie on the apparent new mood in Washington, Republican leaders were plotting to use the attacks as an excuse to advance their policy agenda, including items that had very little relation to

[xxxix]By his own admission, Daschle played only a small part in convincing Jeffords to switch. Republican snubs and Dodd's charm played a much bigger role. But Daschle's behind-the-scenes strength did play an important role in preventing Jeffords's switch from being rendered moot by a successful Republican raid on Democratic ranks. That was a real worry – Georgia Democrat Zell Miller had refashioned himself as a right-wing extremist after a moderate eight years as the Peach State's governor and was subject to Republican entreaties to switch parties himself. It wasn't just policy differences – his rhetoric was filled with sneering contempt when he discussed his own nominal party. "My Democrat friends need to be reminded and return to those days of yesteryear when they supported cutting tax rates and did not engage in this endless class warfare that they have today become a Johnny-one-note on," he told the conservative group Empower America, using the Republican pejorative for the Democratic Party. But Daschle had the stomach to swallow the abuse and avoid pushing Zell into the Republicans' hands. He even went so far as to tell Fox News, "Zell Miller's got a bright future in our caucus." Of course, had Daschle worked to punish Miller at the first sign of apostasy, there's a chance he would have cut off Miller's lurch to the right – but that was never Daschle's style and could indeed just have pushed the prideful Miller away much faster. Daschle's unassuming style was awarded in this case when, immediately after Jeffords switched parties, Miller issued a statement saying he would stick with the Democrats, keeping Daschle majority leader.

September 11th. In his memoir, Trent Lott (Daschle's GOP counterpart) would call this period "a legislative treasure trove that helped launch President Bush's war on terrorism and usher in a new political era."[22]

"Daschle Told Us to Fold"

The first piece of this trove was the anti-terrorism bill known as the USA Patriot Act, which expanded the government's ability to spy on American citizens, and made important changes to immigration laws. Everyone agreed that some of the changes were necessary, but Republicans saw the bill as an opportunity to pass far-reaching limits on civil liberties. Whenever Democrats spoke publicly to raise concern about the erosion of individual freedoms, or even just to demand fuller congressional consideration of the proposed changes, Republicans accused them of helping al Qaeda. "Talk will not prevent terrorism," Ashcroft said on CBS's Face the Nation. "We need to have action by the Congress."[23] Under this withering assault, Daschle was worried about appearing insufficiently security-conscious even though he also had serious concerns about the reach of many of the bill's provisions. Just one month earlier he had fought to keep some of the same restrictions on civil liberties out of Bush's war powers act, but this time he personally forced through the same changes with little scrutiny and less dissent. He even maneuvered on the Senate floor to table Wisconsin Senator Russ Feingold's amendments aimed at curtailing some of the most egregious assaults on civil liberties, such as permitting warrantless spying for up to 96 hours, instead of the unlimited period the Bush administration was pushing for. Daschle also prevented consideration of those amendments that the Bush administration had indicated it was willing to accept. "The clock is ticking," he argued, echoing Republican arguments he had rejected just a month earlier that the legislation was needed immediately to give the security apparatus the legal tools they needed to prevent future terror attacks.[24] In part, Daschle did this because he was concerned that opening the bill up to debate might imperil some of the small changes the White House and Republicans had agreed to, like a sunset provision that would cause the law to expire four years later. But that didn't satisfy those Democrats who thought they could have got a bill that enhanced security without including the most extreme attacks on civil liberties contained in the bill. "Daschle told us to fold," Feingold was later quoted saying about the episode. "It was a low point for me in terms of being a Democrat and somebody who believes in civil liberties."[25]

Fresh from this victory, Republicans sensed that it might be even easier than they had imagined to transform national unity into Democratic passivity. Democrats were being even more accommodating than usual in the face of pressure. A moment like this could mean only one thing: more tax cuts! Conservative mouthpieces like the *National Review* and *The Weekly Standard* and conservative media guru Frank Luntz urged Republicans to cast aside bipartisan goals and pursue instead a broader right-wing platform repackaged as part of a "security agenda." The White House quickly jumped aboard the campaign, despite the fact that many independent economic analysts were urging the government to rescind some of the recently passed tax cuts to help pay for the burgeoning costs of the war on terror. On October 4, Bush equated the fight against Al Qaeda with tax cuts. "We need to counter the shock wave of the evildoer by having individual rate cuts accelerated and by thinking about tax rebates," he said. He'd go on to link the war with oil drilling in Alaska's Arctic National Wildlife Refuge, privatizing Social Security, and cutting food stamps.[26] As usual, Daschle was taken aback by Bush's cynical opportunism. "It was hard for me to imagine what some journalists and pundits had begun to assert – that this administration would actually exploit this situation to advance the broader agenda that had been slipping from its grasp before September 11th," he wrote.[27] Daschle never really could get his head around the idea that the Republicans wouldn't play according to the same prairie polite rules he did.

Despite his professed surprise, Daschle initially showed some resistance to some of the more extreme elements of the new Bush "security agenda." Under Daschle's leadership, Democrats refused to rush to confirm far-right judicial nominees like Miguel Estrada, whose own boss in the Solicitor General's office described him as "so ideologically driven that he couldn't be trusted to state the law in a fair, neutral way."[28] Daschle and others also hesitated to expand Bush's tax cuts even further. But it was only that – hesitation. In late January, Daschle sent President Bush a letter outlining a possible compromise that would include some tax cuts, though not as much as Bush was demanding. Bush rejected it and Daschle was forced to shelve the bill. "I could call the Republicans obstructionists, but I wouldn't do that," he told the *Washington Post*. "It wouldn't be fair."[29]

A Funny Kind of Obstructionist

Republicans, however, saw any resistance at all – even the mild resistance Daschle was offering – as both heresy and opportunity. However tenuously,

Daschle was standing in the way of their agenda – now they had to make him crack like they'd done so many times before. It didn't seem like it would be too hard. Just choose a characteristic that Daschle didn't have, attack him for having it, and then sit back and watch him try to prove extra hard that really - no really, look guys! - he didn't have it. It had worked when they accused the relatively bipartisan Daschle of being a "hyper-partisan" – he'd tried to prove that really he and George Bush shared the same goals and stopped putting up any credible opposition to Bush's tax plan. Now, on Luntz's advice, they decided to tar him as an "obstructionist" – and wait for Daschle to step whatever minor obstruction he might have been doing. On December 9, 2001, Vice President Dick Cheney lobbed the first "obstructionist" charge on *Meet the Press*; Trent Lott followed by blaming Daschle for making the Senate into what he called a "black hole of inactivity." If Daschle was an obstructionist, he was a very odd kind of obstructionist – not only had he greased the Senate wheels since September 11th, he'd been giving in to Bush since their first meeting in January 2001.

At first, Daschle tried to laugh off the obstructionist accusations as "an amusing overreaction." But when the Republican attack machine got hold of a notion, no matter how ridiculous, it was not easy to laugh off. Republicans great and small accused Daschle of obstructionism every chance they got. Republican-affiliated organizations made sure South Dakotans got the message by running dozens of anti-Daschle radio and television ads labeling him as such – this in a year when he wasn't even up for re-election! The Family Research Council (an ultra-right Christian group) ran an ad that juxtaposed photos of Daschle and Saddam Hussein, asking: "What do Saddam Hussein and Senate Majority Leader Tom Daschle have in common?" The answer: "Neither man wants America to drill for oil in Alaska's Arctic National Wildlife Refuge." Daschle's spokesman offered an appropriately livid response to the Hussein comparison, calling it "an outrageous, extremist attack at a time when the nation is unified." "I don't know that I've ever had attacks of this intensity directed at me in a non-election year," he said in the *Aberdeen American News*. "I guess I'm beginning to find out how broad and wide the territory is [when you're Senate majority leader]."[30] But Daschle remained a bit baffled by all the vituperation targeted at him. By the spring of 2002, the Republican strategy started to work: Daschle had stopped trying to laugh them off or spin them away and started trying to disprove them by giving into Republican demands to let Bush's agenda through.

Getting Out of the Way

Daschle set to looking for areas where he could show that he wasn't the obstructionist Republicans said he was. He used all his behind the scenes power to get the Senate to pass an energy bill, one of Bush's priorities. Daschle's bill started out as a measure to encourage clean energy production and reduce America's reliance on foreign oil: it would have increased fuel efficiency standards for cars and trucks, reducing oil consumption and saving drivers money, and required utilities to start getting some of their energy from clean energy sources like wind and solar power. It was a very different measure than the polluter bonanza favored by Bush. But as soon as Daschle's bill hit the Senate floor, polluter lobbyists pulled strings with sympathizers in both parties to load up the bill with billions in subsidies for the coal, oil, nuclear, and agribusiness industries and remove the fuel efficiency standards. The result was a far different from what Daschle had originally introduced – instead of protecting the environment, increasing energy security, and helping consumers, it now did the opposite.

But the bill still contained massive ethanol subsidies, a huge boon for South Dakota farmers who grew the corn that was its main ingredient. Daschle was in a familiar bind: on the one hand, he was the leader of the whole U.S. Senate, charged with looking out for the country's interests as well as those of his party. From that perspective, the energy bill was bad news: it would exact a heavy environmental and financial cost and anger many members of his own party. On the other hand, part of the reason that Daschle brought up the energy bill in the first place was to avoid looking like an obstructionist. How would it look if he now turned around and voted against the underlying bill he himself had proposed, no matter how twisted it had become?

There was one more consideration of increasing urgency to Daschle. Although he wouldn't be on the ballot in 2002, his fellow South Dakota Democratic Senator Tim Johnson would. Johnson was facing a formidable opponent in John Thune, a telegenic, charismatic, and completely ruthless Republican operative who was the state's lone congressman. The media was portraying the Johnson-Thune race as a proxy fight between Daschle and Bush. The Johnson campaign based its message on the idea that Johnson would vote to keep Daschle Majority Leader, thus ensuring that Daschle kept the pork flowing. "Can we afford to lose Daschle's position," asked one typical Johnson ad.[31] It would significantly undermine Johnson's message if Daschle did anything – like voting against an energy bill loaded with ethanol subsidies – that diverted the landslide of lard flowing from Washington to South Dakota. And so Daschle spoke on the floor in favor of the perverted version of the energy bill he had originally offered. But the vote had its political costs: environmentalists felt betrayed and angry, and Senate Democrats like Dianne Feinstein were furious at the way Daschle had put his state's interests ahead of the nation's. "I am upset because he knows how much I cared about this issue," Feinstein said of Daschle. "It's hard to have this kind of thing done by somebody you thought was a friend."[32]

Daschle faced this same tension between doing what was in the perceived self-interest of Johnson's campaign and doing what he believed was right over Iraq. During the Bush administration's rush to war, Daschle made clear that the Bush administration should have to sincerely work to win international support for the war and ensure that America put at least as much planning into the aftermath of an invasion as it did into the invasion itself. "Now we're not going to just blindly say whatever it is you want, you've got," he told *The New York Times* on September 14, after Bush urged the United Nations to confront Iraq about Saddam's alleged weapons of mass destruction.[33] Despite his serious reservations, Daschle was wary of outwardly opposing Bush on such a high profile matter. So even when he expressed his doubts, he rhetorically couched them in a way that never really challenged Bush's framework.

On September 26, Bush escalated his rhetoric even further when he told a crowd in New Jersey that "The Senate is more interested in special interests in Washington, and not interested in the security of the American people." Prompted by furious Democrats, Daschle went to the floor and made what was probably the single most passionate speech of his career.

> Not interested in the security of the American people? You tell Senator Inouye he's not interested in the security of the American people! You tell those who fought in Vietnam and in World War II they're not interested in the security of the American people! That is outrageous! Outrageous! We ought not politicize this war. We ought not politicize the rhetoric about war and life and death.

Bush, despite Daschle's demands, didn't apologize. Instead, Trent Lott asked, "Who is the enemy here? The president of the United States or Saddam Hussein...It's time we get a grip."

Daschle's outrage was effective, but it didn't persuade Republicans to discontinue their barrage of attacks against him and Johnson. Republicans were running ads accusing Tim Johnson of standing "with one of the most dangerous antimilitary groups in America" because he had accepted campaign donations from the pro-peace, anti-nuclear proliferation group Council for a Liveable World. Thune trotted out military veteran supporters on September 17 to highlight how Johnson had opposed the Gulf War in 1991 and had even sued President Bush, Sr. to challenge his authority to wage war without explicit congressional authorization. "I would hope [Johnson] won't do it again," said Thune supporter and Korean War veteran Bob Jamison. "We cannot risk American safety by allowing Saddam Hussein to continue building his weapons of mass destruction."

Johnson had repeatedly expressed doubts on the campaign trail about the wisdom of unilaterally invading Iraq – and the resistance that troops could encounter once they got there.[34] That wasn't just politics for Johnson – his son had already served a tour in Afghanistan and was now serving in an army unit that had been identified by U.S. commander Tommy Franks as likely to lead the charge into Iraq. But, eventually, whether from fear or conviction, Johnson gave in. On September 26 he delivered an emotional speech saying unambiguously that he would support any resolution that gave Bush the authority to invade Iraq unilaterally – even if it meant sending his son back to war and harm's way.[35]

Johnson's move and Dick Gephardt's Rose Garden deal, which gave Bush unlimited authority to invade Iraq, put Daschle in a bind. To oppose war now would not only make it appear that the Democratic leadership was divided, but that he and Johnson couldn't even agree on a subject as important as the Iraq war. Even so, Daschle kept stating his deeply felt reservations. But he was boxed in. Like so many of his colleagues, he ended up voting to give Bush authority to make war on Iraq at a time and in the manner of his choosing. Daschle loaded up his floor statement announcing his support for Bush with dozens of admonitions and reservations, but they were just rhetoric. Indeed, in a news conference after his speech, Daschle acknowledged the ridiculousness of his position. A reporter asked him if he was confident that "the administration will not look at this resolution as some big green light," and he admitted that in all likelihood they would see it that way.[36]

Daschle – like many other Washington Democrats – had completely given into Bush despite his own doubts. The ambiguity and meaninglessness of his rhetoric helped neither him nor Johnson. Given the political pressures, Daschle's position is understandable. But it's also important to note that Daschle did little to shape those circumstances: with the single exception of his outburst on the Senate floor in response to Bush's accusation that the Senate didn't care about the security of the American people, Daschle had spoken mainly about the need to support Bush in his challenge to Saddam – despite what he acknowledged was the lack of evidence that Saddam possessed weapons of mass destruction. "There is no conclusive evidence to suggest that the situation warrants greater level of concern with regard to the weapons that we know to exist within Iraq," Daschle told PBS's Gwen Ifill on September 17, 2002. "We can argue about how conclusive it is. But that doesn't change what ought to be the action of the United States. The action of the United States is exactly as the administration has presented it."[37]

With the Iraq vote behind him, Daschle tried to turn his attention to helping Johnson win re-election. Johnson was running a textbook Dakota Democrat campaign: though he had compiled one of the more liberal voting records in the Senate (his Americans for Democratic Action score was a 90), he'd done so quietly; in the campaign he emphasized his ability to work with Republicans and his ability to deliver federal money to the state. Bush himself inadvertently gave a boost to Johnson's independent, Dakota-focused image when he visited South Dakota – and didn't mention the drought that was at the top of everyone in the state's minds, probably because he opposed the $5 billion drought relief plan being pushed by Daschle and Johnson. As a result, Bush's visit undermined Thune's claim that he had pull with the White House – if he did, he should have been able to deliver the kind of drought relief pork Daschle was pushing for. "That cost him 500 votes right there," former state GOP president Jason Glodt said later, only half-joking.[38]

In a state of just 761,063 people, 500 votes could make a big difference – and they did: Johnson edged out Thune by just 524 votes. Although the election was a squeaker, Johnson's victory was nevertheless quite an accomplishment. Even in this most Republican of states, while Republicans across the country were grabbing Democratic seats, Johnson was able to win. It was the ultimate validation of the Dakota Democrat strategy.

Dakota Democrat or Democrat's Democrat?

Daschle recognized that this Dakota Democrat strategy would be the path of least resistance to win re-election to his own seat in 2004. But it wasn't clear if it would be available to him anymore. His role as Democratic leader meant that, like it or not, he was a spokesman for the national Democratic Party. As the Iraq war unraveled and Bush's popularity declined, Democratic calls for a more confrontational leadership intensified. Daschle was pulled ever more in two competing directions: be the quiet, accommodating, Dakota Democrat that could win his Senate seat in 2004, or be the national Democratic leader who would stand up to Bush. It was an impossible situation for a politician like Daschle, and it would soon show itself to be an impossible situation for the Democrats as well.

After the 2002 election results came in and it was clear that Senate Republicans had picked up seats, Al Gore called for a "major regrouping," in what was widely interpreted as a challenge to Daschle. Probably the best thing that could have happened to Daschle – and the Democrats – at this point was if Senate Democrats had heeded Gore's call and replaced Daschle with someone more confrontational and suited to the growingly polarized political environment.

The Democrats could have given Daschle their top spot on a powerful or relevant committee like Appropriations or Agriculture so that he could still claim DC clout and still channel spending towards his home state, but be free from the obligation to publicly take on Bush and the Republicans. But the appeal that had won Daschle the Democratic leader's post in the first place remained as strong in 2002 as it had in 1994. The majority of the Senate Democrats remained in thrall to the politics of fear – even as they were becoming privately angrier and angrier at Bush's abuses and failures, they were wary of choosing a leader who would confront Bush too much and aggressively advance progressive values. After all, the nation had gone for hard right Republicans in yet another election and Bush remained popular. And so – although losing the majority had frequently been a time to change leadership – Senate Democrats reelected Daschle by acclamation. It was a disastrous victory.

The Biggest Loser

The looming disaster – and the competing pressures that created it – became apparent when Senate Republicans introduced their own even dirtier version of the 2002 energy bill (the House and Senate had never reconciled their competing versions of the bill, leaving it in legislative limbo). The price tag for the original energy bill had been about $38 billion; the Republican version ballooned to more than $50 billion (including such multi-million dollar subsidies as producing energy by incinerating turkey carcasses). It would have allowed a massive increase in global warming pollution, allowed oil and gas drillers to ignore the Clean Water Act, paved the way for offshore oil drilling and shifted responsibility for tens of billions of dollars of pollution cleanup from oil companies onto state and local taxpayers.[39] In *The Washington Post,* the U.S. Public Interest Research Group dubbed it a "10-course orgy" for big polluters.[40] Daschle himself acknowledged that the bill "does almost nothing to increase energy security," but Daschle wasn't thinking about national interests like security – he had corn on the brain. Among those polluter subsidies were billions for ethanol. According to Daschle, that money could finance every third row of corn in South Dakota. Daschle was making his support for ethanol a campaign issue – featuring gushing ethanol manufacturers in his campaign commercials. No matter how dangerous the energy bill was for America and the planet, for Daschle, corn was king, and he announced his backing for the bill.

It was a declaration that Daschle had finally ended any pretense of truly national leadership; he was now using his national power for purely local ends. He had ceased to be Senate Leader for America, and was acting like the Senate Leader for South Dakota. Daschle's move infuriated progressives. Environmentalists, civil rights groups (worried about the bill's high cost to consumers and pollution in minority communities), labor unions, and even churches were outraged that Daschle would prioritize such a small component of the bill – the ethanol subsidies – over the health of the country and the planet. "It's a tremendous failure of leadership on his part," said Friends of the Earth Legislative Director Sara Zdeb. "It is clear he supports the bill for narrow parochial interests he has put ahead of the public's interest and the environment."[41] The nascent progressive blogosphere went ape at Daschle's unwillingness to tell South Dakotans that while one part of the energy bill might be economically beneficial to the state, the rest of it was a disaster. "I want to cut him some slack, given that he faces a potentially tough re-election battle, but screw it," said one angry contributor to the DailyKos blog. "Screw Daschle. The nation's best interests have been abandoned to award corn growers a massive federal giveaway."[42] Other plains states Democrats were taking the same position, but their quiet stands didn't have national consequences in the way that Leader Daschle's did – and so they managed to avoid at least some of the progressives' ire.

Despite Daschle's support, the high environmental and fiscal cost of the energy bill was something that most Democrats and some Republicans just couldn't swallow. True to form, Daschle didn't do much to get other Democrats to back his position – arm twisting wasn't his style. And so the giant stinking bill began to rot and die. Bill supporters ultimately failed to break a filibuster of the bill. Because the bill failed, and farmers and ethanol manufacturers weren't seeing any additional money, Daschle didn't win major points with the very farmers he'd been attempting to seduce by backing the energy bill.

Republicans saw a golden opportunity to attack the Daschle campaign's main selling point: his effectiveness. "For the minority leader, the Democrat leader, Senator Daschle just to take a walk and not be able to get any more than a dozen Democrats who voted [in support of the energy bill], no thanks to him – it is just such an abdication and total neglect of responsibility," Republican senator George Allen told the *Rapid City Journal*.[43] "He claims to have the clout needed to get things done," State GOP chair Randy Frederick complained in the *Argus Leader*. "If Daschle could have even delivered one-third of his caucus, we would have won. From today forward, we always will know how much pull Senator [Daschle] has with his fellow Democrats."

Daschle's pull came under renewed scrutiny just a few weeks later when the Senate took up President Bush's $400 billion proposal to provide prescription drug coverage under Medicare and take the first steps toward privatizing health insurance for the elderly and disabled. Daschle opposed the plan as an expensive giveaway to the drug companies that would do little to drive down prescription drug costs. It was the kind of bread and butter prairie populist position he had always embraced and which played well in South Dakota, which had a graying population, low incomes, and a tradition of suspicion of far off corporate executives.

Over in the House, Nancy Pelosi was using all her considerable powers of persuasion to get Democrats to fall into line – threatening to hold committee assignments hostage according to how lawmakers voted. And she succeeded, keeping all but 16 out of 205 Democrats on board. Daschle's approach was more laid back. "Daschle's response inside the caucus meetings [during the Medicare debates] was to let it be a free-for-all, let each individual senator have their own say and vote their conscience, rather than structuring an argument for why we should vote the way we should as a party," an unnamed Senate Democratic staff member told *National Journal*. "It was left to...others to try to fill that leadership vacuum and to make the case for why [defeating the legislation is] not just in the party's interest, but in the interest of the program itself."[44] Unsurprisingly, it didn't work. The big drug company lobbyists were twisting and breaking Democratic senators' arms by tacitly (and sometimes not so tacitly) threatening to withhold campaign contributions. Republicans were gearing up to attack any senator who opposed Bush. Democratic senators needed some counter-threat if they were going to stay in line and vote against the bill. But Daschle wasn't the type who would give one, and 11 of 48 Senate Democrats broke party ranks to support Bush's bill, giving Republicans the votes they needed to overcome a filibuster.

Progressives were disappointed that Daschle hadn't fought hard enough, and Republicans criticized him for alleged apostasy from his claims to independence. "Today, Tom Daschle clearly showed his allegiance," South Dakota Republican Party Chairman Randy Frederick said in the *Argus Leader* following the Medicare vote. "Unfortunately, it was to Ted Kennedy and not South Dakota seniors."[45] For the second time in as many legislative battles, Tom Daschle found himself on the losing side of an important debate. He had gone from alleged obstructionist to ineffective legislative doormat to wannabe obstructionist, and failed at it all. Meanwhile, President Bush and conservative Republicans had won an important victory, pre-packaged for use in 2004 election speeches. Republican campaign funds benefited too, from huge contributions from the pharmaceutical industry. Under Daschle's schizophrenic leadership, his image was suffering and Democrats were losing.

"From the Arms of Michael Moore into the Arms of the President"

With Daschle under attack from all sides, it was clear that he would be very vulnerable in his 2004 re-election race. As a result, the man who everyone thought would make the best challenger – the defeated John Thune – jumped into the race. Thune was an even better candidate than he had been when he faced Johnson in 2002. He had 99 percent name recognition, and he was even more polished and confident than when he first ran. And with President Bush on the ballot, Republicans were sure to be motivated to come to the polls. But perhaps Thune's greatest advantage was that he had hired the notorious Dick Wadhams as his campaign manager. Wadhams was known for two things: cutthroat tactics and a string of impressive victories. He had just come off one of the most brutal Senate races in the country by reelecting Colorado Republican Wayne Allard against strong challenger attorney Tom Strickland.

Wadhams said it didn't take him long to figure out how to beat Daschle. "His party leadership position in many ways was the cause of his ultimate defeat, because the deeper he got into leading the Democrats in the Senate, the more out of touch he got with South Dakota voters," he said. "I knew that many South Dakotans obviously liked and respected Senator Daschle, but they were uncomfortable with how far left he was going. He was not the same guy they voted for 26 years ago." Wadhams wasn't being entirely accurate – Daschle had always had a relatively liberal voting record. His liberal scores at the end of his career were no higher than they were at the beginning, with a lifetime score of 83. But before 2000, he hadn't been *perceived* as a liberal because he'd kept his head down in Washington and generally confined his public remarks to South Dakota concerns and spoken in an independent fashion. After his rise to prominence, that was no longer an option.

TOM DASCHLE: CIRCUMSTANTIAL COWARDICE

Thune made the contrast between his "South Dakota values" and what he alleged were Daschle's "Washington DC values" the center of his campaign. "South Dakotans know Democrats support an agenda of higher taxes," said one typical Republican ad. "And as Democrat leader, it's Tom Daschle's responsibility to push that agenda. If he didn't, he wouldn't be the Democrat leader. Tom Daschle: loyal to a national Democrat agenda at South Dakota's expense."[46] Instead of defending the progressive votes he had taken, Daschle resorted mainly to trying to prove that he really wasn't the partisan obstructionist Republicans were making him out to be. After Republicans attacked Daschle for attending the premier of filmmaker Michael Moore's anti-Bush movie *Fahrenheit 9/11* and alleged that he had embraced Moore, he went to great lengths to make sure everyone knew that he had not in fact hugged Moore. Then, he left the Democratic National convention in Boston two days early, in what was widely perceived as an attempt to distance himself from the Democratic Party, of which he was a top leader. His campaign manager bragged about a study saying that Daschle had voted with President Bush 75 percent of the time – infuriating progressives for whom allegiance to the Bush record was not something to tout. Many of his ads emphasized his conservative positions like his opposition to "partial birth abortion" and his apparent belief that "marriage is a sacred union between one man and one woman," rather than highlighting the negative consequences for South Dakotans of Thune's extremist Republican agenda. And finally – and most famously – Daschle actually ran a full 60-second ad that began, "Tonight the president has called us again to greatness, and tonight we answer that call" and then actually featured an image of Bush hugging Daschle. The Republican National Committee called on Daschle to pull the ad. To say the least, the message was confusing; at worst, it appeared craven.

Before Daschle started his absurd effort to link himself to Bush, Republicans had largely confined their attacks to calling him liberal. Now they added that he was deceptive and weak. John Thune himself led the charge. "I don't know how you can project leadership and strength and, at the same time, run for tall cover any time anybody challenges your record," Thune said of Daschle following one televised debate.[47] "In Washington, DC, you know, he's attacking the president, you know, blocking the president's agenda, and in South Dakota, he's hugging the president. And, you know, the remarkable thing about it is how quickly he was willing to throw John Kerry overboard in order to help himself in South Dakota. I mean, I don't know very many party leaders that would do what he just did by running that ad."[48]

On Election Day, the almost $33 million spent on the election had its effect – more than 80 percent of South Dakota's registered voters went to the polls. Through Election Day, Tom Daschle showed the prairie persistence that had got him as far as he'd gone. He was making individual get-out-the-vote calls until 9 pm, when the polls closed. But his efforts weren't enough. Ultimately, the combination of Bush's popularity, the high quality of the Thune campaign, and the conflicts that had torn Daschle for the previous four years delivered Thune a narrow 51 to 49 victory. The exit polls showed the consequences of Daschle's conduct. Thune won 61 percent of the vote of those voters who said they decided their vote primarily on whether or not the candidate was a strong leader, 70 percent of those voting on honesty, and 62 percent of those voting for the candidate with clear stands on the issues (though Daschle picked up 90 percent of those who voted for change and 59 percent of those looking for a candidate who "cares about people like you").[49] Given the overriding importance of strong leadership in voter choice, Daschle's Potomac zigzag had been fatal.

And the losses weren't confined to Daschle's race. Dismal Democratic performance (and voters' preference for Bush) helped Senate Republicans pick up four seats. (In the House, by contrast, Republicans picked up just three seats – out of 435![xl]). Perhaps the only good news for Democrats was that they finally learned from the disastrous Daschle years and chose Harry Reid to be their leader for the 2005-2006 Congress. Though Reid had been Daschle's deputy, and shared his red state origins and his quiet manner, he waged politics in a far different manner. He always put his duties as national leader first, emphasizing his differences with President Bush over his similarities. And this former boxer was always willing to corral his fellow members to vote the Democratic agenda. It was the kind of leadership that Democrats had lacked for a decade and it produced results – helping set the stage for the surprise Democratic takeover of the Senate in 2006.

As for Daschle, he made a graceful valedictory speech, and then embarked on a new career in policy, landing a fellowship at the Center for American Progress think tank and a position working with former Republican Leader Bob Dole at the Alston & Bird law firm in Washington. There, he advised his new corporate clients how to pass or defeat legislation; he was even willing to help them repeal parts legislation he had supported in the Senate aimed at preventing repeated future Enron and of WorldCom frauds. He even contemplated running

---

[xl]Indeed, if the Texas legislature hadn't reapportioned its seats to favor Republicans, Democrats would have actually gained two seats.

TOM DASCHLE: CIRCUMSTANTIAL COWARDICE

for president in 2008. But the circumstances that had forced Daschle into the Politics of Fear, and made him one of its highest profile practitioners, had ceased to exist. Democrats were no longer looking as much for conciliation with Republicans – they were finally ready to take them on. And so – finally – there wasn't much room left for Daschle or his politics.

NANCY PELOSI AND THE DEMOCRATS OF 2006

★★★★

Just as Tom Daschle's replacement by Harry Reid signaled a new, at least marginally tougher breed of leadership for Senate Democrats, the rise of Nancy Pelosi to become the leader of House Democrats was a sign that Democrats would no longer be satisfied by the compromising, capitulating leadership of the past. Gone was Dick Gephardt, the man who had leaped at the chance to sign a Rose Garden deal with George W. Bush endorsing the Iraq War without even the support of a majority of his caucus (and who repaid him for his disloyalty to them with frequent disloyalty to the party leadership). As Gephardt left public service for a lucrative career as a lobbyist for polluters like Peabody Coal (as well as investment giant Goldman Sachs and the nation of Turkey), Democrats elected in his stead Nancy Pelosi, a woman with a style less suited to capitulation than combat.

Even as minority leader, Pelosi had charmed, persuaded, and threatened her famously ideologically diverse caucus into falling in line behind her unapologetically progressive agenda. If a member told her that he couldn't be with her on a vote, she'd say "We can't be with you either" – and would withhold campaign donations, perks, and power from even some of the most powerful house "bulls" – the committee chairmen formerly unchallenged within their fiefdoms.[1] When Brooklyn Democrat Edolphus Towns voted with Republicans for President Bush's Central American Free Trade Agreement and then failed to show up for a budget vote Republicans won by a margin of two, she threatened to remove him from his prized seat on the Energy and Commerce committee. Her tactics got results: after meeting with Pelosi, Towns stuck to the party line on subsequent votes.[2]

This kind of toughness – largely foreign to other recent Democratic leaders – helped Pelosi make Democrats more unified than they have been in 50 years. Under Pelosi's leadership Democrats voted the increasingly progressive party line 87 percent of the time, the highest levels of party unity Democrats recorded since *Congressional Quarterly* started compiling them in the 1950's.[3] Getting Democrats to stick together in the minority forced Republicans to cast some very uncomfortable votes. Pelosi held Democratic defections on the Central American Free Trade deal to just 15 members – far fewer that Republicans had been anticipating (and far fewer than they had been able to get on previous trade votes). As a result, to pass the agreement, several Republicans from contested districts had to break their pledges to vote against the agreement, making them seem like unprincipled slaves to the increasingly unpopular Republican leadership at a time when most were trying to portray themselves as independent of that leadership.

In one case, Pelosi's ability to keep Democrats in line even caused a criminal investigation into Republican behavior: when unexpected Democratic loyalty forced Republicans to keep a House vote on President Bush's Medicare legislation open for three hours, Tom DeLay allegedly illegally offered Representative Nick Smith his endorsement in Smith's son's race for Congress in exchange for switching his vote. Perhaps Pelosi's greatest achievement came immediately after the 2004 elections when Republicans were riding high and Bush was trying to spend his "political capital" on privatizing Social Security. Pelosi kept getting pressure from the media, the Republicans, and many members of her own caucus to offer a Democratic Social Security plan. Worried that doing so would play into Republican claims that the system needed to be immediately reformed, Pelosi refused. By standing strong, she successfully prevented every Democrat except one from offering an alternative Social Security reform – leaving the Bush plan to wither under increased scrutiny.

Courage Rising

In large part due to Pelosi's leadership, the party was markedly more courageous than it had been even two years prior. Increasingly, both candidates and Democratic leaders are saying what they believe without apology – and they're convincing people to support them and their agenda as a result. That courage (as well as Republican unpopularity) helped Democrats win in 2006. The importance of courage in the 2006 elections could be seen in the divergent fates of two southern Democratic candidates widely dubbed by the media centrist or conservative. In a December 15, 2006 article, the cognitive scientist George Lakoff, famous for his groundbreaking works *Don't Think of an Elephant* and *Moral Politics,* analyzed how Democrats could win in the south. He compared the loss of Tennessee Senate candidate Harold Ford, Jr. to the surprise win of North Carolina congressman Heath Shuler, who ousted long-time arch-conservative Charles Taylor. Lakoff notes that while both Ford and Shuler were anti-choice, anti-gay marriage, and anti-gun control, they presented themselves in very different ways. Lakoff cites an NPR interview in which reporter Melissa Block asked Shuler if his conservative positions on social issues would "fit in" with the Democratic Party. "It isn't about, necessarily, the social issues," Shuler replied. "It's about protecting American families and American jobs, making sure that we increase the minimum wage and that we do things that encompass the entire nation and that will bring our nation together...[making] sure that we protect our country, and our God's great creation, be good stewards of the land, and start providing health care that everyone can afford."[4] Shuler's response deemphasized those issues on which he was more conservative and instead emphasized the progressive agenda that helped get him elected. And he stuck to that once he started casting votes – sticking with his party on 83.6 percent of party loyalty votes, tending to vote with the party on economic and environmental issues, but leaving them on social and some national security issues.[5]

Ford, in contrast, tried to win by convincing voters that he was the more conservative option, basing his platform on conservative issues and a conservative framework. "He ran enthusiastically using conservative code words," Lakoff writes. "*Personal responsibility, strong moral values, character education, pro-family, a constitutional amendment defining marriage as a union between a man and a woman, eliminate abortion,* and so on. He was trying to convince good 'ol boy Tennesseans that he was one of them...he didn't come across as authentic, and authenticity is the name of the game."[6] Ford played the "Who's more conservative?" game – not surprisingly, the real conservative Republican won. Meanwhile other red staters (like Montana's Jon Tester) were able to take advantage of the anti-Republican climate by running on a progressive agenda and emphasize their differences with Bush and the Republicans. So while Tester beat a heavily-financed incumbent in a state more Republican than Tennessee, Ford couldn't do it even though his race was an open seat.

Despite Ford's disastrous strategy and defeat, James Carville actually spearheaded a campaign to make him DNC chair and replace Howard Dean (who had been largely responsible for the 50 state strategy of distributing resources around the country that helped relative dark horses like Shuler and Tester to win), where he could bring his losing politics to the nation. Fortunately, the Democrats actually in charge of electing the DNC chief decided they didn't want a loser to replace a winner, and kept Dean on. But the Democratic Leadership Council had no such compunctions about hiring a loser. And so on January 25, 2007, the DLC named the Ford to be its head. It was a perfect match between an organization that had brought a failing strategy to the Democratic Party and a man who had ridden their failing strategy to actual defeat – and apparently hadn't learned his lesson.

Majority Courage

Since leading her caucus to the majority, Pelosi has been even more courageous about articulating a progressive agenda and keeping Democrats in line fighting for it. Before assuming the chairmanship of the House committee with jurisdiction over climate policy, John Dingell, a long-time Democratic auto industry lackey, told *Grist Magazine*'s Amanda Griscom Little that he wasn't sure if global warming existed. Traditionally, that would have cast an immediate pall on the likelihood of any action. Until Pelosi, Democratic chairmen held almost entirely unalloyed power within their respective fiefdoms. But Pelosi was unwilling to let anyone hijack the Democratic agenda – even Dingell, who had first taken office in 1955 and was feared around Capitol Hill for his ruthlessness, his intimate knowledge of the levers of power, and the alacrity with which he could slip a political knife between the ribs of his enemies. And so she slapped him down in a way that sent shockwaves through the Capitol and let everyone know that things had change. Pelosi decreed the creation of a new Special Committee on global warming under the direction of environmental champion Ed Markey.

There were limits, however, to how far Pelosi could or would go. Her father had been Mayor of Baltimore, and, as such, the head of an old line urban political machine. Pelosi grew up respecting political dues paid, age, and length of service – sometimes regardless of the quality of the service, or even the honesty of the person doing it. Pelosi had worked her own way up the House ladder through loyalty and a willingness to make non-ideological allies and was loyal to those who had put in their time. She was loath to oust a senior member like Dingell no matter how much he aroused her pique. And so at the same time that she established the competing special committee, she also continued to allow Dingell (and his pro-coal deputy Congressman Rick Boucher) jurisdiction over great swathes of energy and climate legislation. Similarly, Pelosi backed her close ally John Murtha for the Majority Leader post in gratitude for his past support of her and his opposition to the Iraq War - even though Murtha had widely engaged in ethically questionable practices like brazenly funneling contracting dollars to companies in his district, and had been videotaped discussing a possible bribe with an undercover FBI agent during the 1980's AbScam sting.

Nevertheless, standing up early and hard to someone as powerful as Dingell sent a strong signal to the rest of her famously fractious caucus: abandon the progressive agenda at your peril. And for a few months, episodes like the Dingell slap-down worked to win Pelosi powerful backing for her progressive agenda: When Congressional Quarterly tallied party loyalty at the end of August, 2007, they discovered that the average House Democrat voted with Pelosi 91 percent of the time – a formidable achievement.[7] The Politics of Courage had arrived in

Congress and progressive Democrats were reaping its dividends.

World's Worst Negotiators

But it couldn't last. During the spring and summer of 2007 Pelosi and other top Democrats started slipping back into the cycle of capitulation and connivance that had so often ensnared them in the past. It was almost as if they couldn't help themselves, that no matter how much success it brought them, they could be brave for only so long. They had been having success sticking it to Bush over his failures in Iraq, his unwillingness to implement the September 11th commission's recommendations, and his refusal to do anything real about gas prices, pollution, and energy security. But Bush and the Republicans knew their opponents well, and knew how to operate effectively in the minority. Just as Republicans had done in the first two years of the Clinton administration, they decided to block as much of the Democratic agenda as possible, and try to label the Democrats as ineffective. They hoped Democrats would respond by trying to prove how effective they were by agreeing to pass legislation – any legislation, even Republican legislation – so long as they could tell Republicans that they were too getting something – anything! – done. And so Republicans used the power of the filibuster and the threat of President Bush's veto pen to shut down the poll-tested Democratic agenda. Of course, that meant obstructing the very popular agenda Democrats had run on in 2006, but Republicans knew something that Democrats still haven't learned: that most voters care little and know less about even the most high-profile policy issues – as a result, it often doesn't matter what position you take on an issue if fighting it serves a broader political purpose – in this case attempting to label the Democrats ineffective.

So when Republicans blocked up clean energy legislation, a minimum wage hike, the recommendations of the September 11th Commission, a measure giving workers greater freedom to form unions, and above all an end to the Iraq War, they didn't see their popularity plunge further: instead, at the same time that their own intransigence was preventing the Democrats from being effective, they had the incredible, and incredibly successful, chutzpah to blame the Democrats for getting little done. "The dozens of promises made by Democrats last fall were all pushed aside once they actually had the power to act on them," said Republican House Leader John Boehner, in a typical attack. "Whether it was a pledge to increase access to affordable health care for uninsured Americans, or a commitment to help lower gas prices and reduce our dependence on foreign oil, the majority has demonstrated a total inability to govern."[8] Perhaps even more incredible was the Democratic response. Rather than launching a sustained campaign to paint the Republicans as corrupt obstructionists blocking the clear mandate of the American people, Democrats got scared that Americans were starting to believe Republican rhetoric that Democrats were unable to fulfill their new governance duties, that they began grasping desperately for any legislation to pass, even if that legislation came not from their list of priorities but from the list of the president whom the American people had so clearly repudiated during the 2006 elections.

And so, on May 10, Pelosi, Reid and other leading Democrats gleefully announced that they had reached a trade deal with President Bush to expand free trade rules to Panama and Peru, one of President Bush's top priorities. Advocates of the trade pacts argued that even though the agreements' environmental and labor protections were weak and the agreement could result in significant job losses and deforestation, the fact that there were any protections at all was a step in the right direction and that it could produce modest economic growth. Even if one accepts that dubious argument, it's hard to argue that the trade pact was good overall politics for the entirety of the Democratic agenda. Democrats could have said, "Pass the minimum wage, clean up government, and make at least some concession on Iraq – then we can talk about trade." But instead, they said, "Hey – you're blocking our entire agenda? No problem. Let's put that aside and cut a deal on your top priority and give President Bush and big corporations a deal on trade." That wasn't a big enough rebuke to progressives to get them to abandon the Democrats entirely, but it did signal the start of a new phase in what had been the increasingly close and copacetic relationship between the Democratic leadership and the progressive base: it meant that the progressive Democrats providing the bulk of the energy and a great deal of the money to Democrats started to focus their energy less on bolstering the party in its battle with Republicans and diverting their time and money to try and make sure Democrats didn't betray them. "We're going to go on a jihad and make sure every Joe Labor guy knows that the Democrats sold them out on this," a senior trade deal opponent told me immediately after the deal was announced.

Things quickly deteriorated when, days later, top Senate Democrats announced they'd okayed a White House "Grand Bargain" on immigration – along with the trade deal, President Bush's single top domestic priority. Again, it would have been bad enough if it was what the deal-cutting Democrats said it was: a compromise that would have enhanced border security and made it slightly easier to regularize currently illegal immigrants. With what supporters admitted were only very marginal upsides like these, it was hardly sending the right signal to the Republicans to allow them to push an immigration deal when they'd stymied Democrats on Democratic priorities. But that wasn't all the immigration deal contained – it quickly emerged that the White House and its corporate backers had gotten almost everything they wanted in the "Grand Bargain" while progressive priorities were left out. Most egregiously, the bill created a "guest worker" program that was little more than indentured servitude: workers would come to this country for two years and then be required to return to their home country without having the opportunity to take on higher paying work or join a union that could fight for increased wages and political rights. Not only would that be bad for the "guests," it could be disastrous for American workers at large, who would be forced to compete with a low-wage legal work force with few political rights, who would have little recourse against low wages and poor working conditions. That could force a race to the bottom for immigrants and non-immigrants alike. In addition, the bill was a human and environmental disaster: it would have mandated the construction of 370 miles of double-layered concrete wall on the U.S.-Mexico border. Although the wall would have done little to enhance border security (as a spokesman for Senator Harry Reid put it, a 10-foot wall won't do much to stop someone with an eleven foot ladder), it would have been an insurmountable obstacle for the endangered wildlife of the American Southwest like jaguars, ocelots, and the Sonoran pronghorn antelope, whose populations have been driven so low in the United States that they need some access to breeding populations in Mexico to survive as a species.

Democrats immediately recognized the problems with the bill. "I have serious concerns about some aspects of this proposal, including the structure of its temporary-worker program and undue limitations on family immigration," Harry Reid told reporters immediately after the contents of the bill were revealed. But like many other Democrats who initially criticized the bill, Reid got seduced by an idea being pushed by the DLC-affiliated think tank Third Way: that voters were demanding the White House version of immigration reform embodied in the Senate bill. "The bottom line is that our findings show that progressives should support comprehensive reform legislation, not only because it is right substantively, but also because – when messaged correctly – it is consistent with the wishes of their constituents," wrote Third Way Vice President Jim Kessler in a memo to senators.[9] Talking short-term politics rather than substance was the language spoken by Reid and other Democratic leaders, and it had an almost instant impact. Soon, Reid was touting the legislation as if it was the most perfect compromise conceivable. "The people who are talking about the negativity of this legislation I do not think understand how good it is," he said on the Senate floor.[10]

The polling data was actually highly ambiguous and shouldn't have given much succor to either side of the debate. For instance, two thirds of respondents said they favored creating a guest worker program in the bill, but only 15 percent favored relying primarily on constructing walls and fences. More broadly, 48 percent favored some controls on immigration, but the remaining population was equally split between support for open borders and support for a total ban on immigration.[11] But the long-term impacts would have a serious impact. The consequences of a bill written by and for Big Ag and other exploiters of cheap labor were serious for Americans. By inviting lots of immigrants to America, denying them political rights, and sending them back to their home countries before developing the social capital that could allow them to get ahead and demand equality, the bill would have put immigrants in direct competition with other low-wage Americans, driving down wages and working conditions and putting lots of people, and especially lots of Democrats, out of work. Fortunately for Democrats (and immigrants and jaguars), xenophobic Republicans saved the Democrats from themselves and voted down the bill with the help of a handful of courageous progressives like Barbara Boxer and Bernie Sanders willing to buck the idea that voters were so eager for immigration reform that they wouldn't care what the contents of that reform were. "I know how hard my colleagues have worked – on both sides of the aisle – to put this immigration bill together," Boxer said. "But I believe that this bill, as it currently stands, is unworkable and unfair...I believe we can achieve an immigration bill that will be fair and just to all, and the best chance for that is to vote against cloture and continue working as long as it takes to get it right."[xli]

The Iraq Collapse

Working to end the war in Iraq had been a central piece of the Democrats' platform in 2006. Under Pelosi and Reid, they did make some initial moves in that direction and twice tied Iraq funding bills to fairly mild requirements that troops start redeploying. But even as they were debating the legislation, Bush taunted Democrats with veto threats – and kept up a steady drumbeat claiming that it was the Democrats who were cutting off funding for troops – even though

---

[xli]Unfortunately, Senate Democrats used $3 billion in funding for the border wall as an inducement to get Republican support for a Homeland Security appropriations bill.

the Democrats were passing the bills that funded the troops and Bush who was vetoing that funding. "It is irresponsible for the Democratic leadership in Congress to delay for months on end while our troops in combat are waiting for the funds they need to succeed," Bush said.[12] But Bush knew Democrats would blink. Leading Democrats were publicly saying they would. Most notoriously, Armed Services Committee Chairman Carl Levin repeatedly told reporters that Democrats would write Bush a blank check for the war if he vetoed their attempts to force troop withdrawals. Democrats quickly went from tough talk to surrender. "What the president invited us to do was to come to his office so that we could accept without any discussion the bill that he wants," Pelosi said on April 10 in response to an invitation from President Bush to Reid and Pelosi to join him at the White House and discuss the terms of Democratic surrender. "That's not worthy of the concerns of the American people, and I join Sen. Reid in rejecting an invitation of that kind."[13] But secure in the knowledge that Democratic defiance had a limited shelf life, Bush almost mocked the Democrats' empty posturing. "Democratic leaders in Congress are bent on using a bill that funds our troops to make a political statement about the war," he said the same day. "They need to do it quickly and get it to my desk so I can veto it, and then Congress can get down to the business of funding our troops without strings and without further delay."[14]

Bush managed to make it seem like it was the Democrats who were cutting off funding for the troops when it was actually he who was vetoing troop funding bills. And pretty soon he had Democrats parroting this thinking, taking the responsibility on themselves. "What you don't want to do is to play chicken with the president, and create a situation in which, potentially, you don't have body armor, you don't have reinforced humvees, you don't have night-vision goggles," Obama told Wolf Blitzer on CNN's Late Edition at the beginning of the showdown.[15] With Democrats taking this burden onto themselves, it was only a matter of time before they rendered Bush their abject surrender. And so they did on May 22, when they announced that they would strip out the timeline for withdrawal as well as other measures that Bush objected to (though they did succeed in requiring Bush to issue reports on specific benchmarks for progress in Iraq). Democrats tried to paint their capitulation as strategic savvy. "The problem is that we have to provide money for the troops, and if we don't, the Democrats will be blamed," Congressman James Moran told Congressional Quarterly. "Bush has the bully pulpit, so he will define who is responsible."[16] Democrats also said they were nervous that although they had won previous votes for a timeline to end the war, Republican support was shaky and they might lose the backing of Republican senators Chuck Hagel and Gordon Smith, meaning the timeline would no longer be able to muster a majority of Senate votes – making it seem like support for ending the war was losing ground. However, in accepting that logic, they were also passing up the opportunity to force Smith and other GOP senators facing re-election in antiwar states to either endorse Bush's war management or betray their party leadership.

The results were considerable division within the caucus and fury among grassroots progressives. Even Nancy Pelosi, who helped shepherd the deal through, said "I would never vote for such a thing," and released members of her caucus to make up their own minds on the deal. It also caused a great deal of dismay and disillusionment among progressives. "There has been a lot of tough talk from members of Congress about wanting to end this war, but it looks like the desire for political comfort won out over real action," said Senator Russ Feingold, the leader of the faction urging Democrats to keep escalating the confrontation with Bush until he agreed to withdraw American troops from Iraq. "Congress should have stood strong, acknowledged the will of the American people, and insisted on a bill requiring a real change of course in Iraq." Feingold's sentiments were echoed throughout the progressive blogosphere, which almost immediately lit up with tirades against what was seen as the Democrats' (not altogether unexpected) capitulation. "Voters think Democrats are weak – and I'm in this camp – because if Democrats don't fight for what they believe in, then what will they fight for," wrote Markos Moulitsas Zúniga. "How can we trust them to do what's right when they'll jump at shadows?" Perhaps most memorably, MoveOn.org asked their members to send Harry Reid teabags in the mail to protest his acceptance of a deal that he had dismissed as "weak tea" only a few weeks earlier. In part because of progressive disenchantment over the Democrats' failures, the congressional Democrats' ratings fell into the low 30's, about the same level as Bush (though still about 10 points higher than congressional Republicans').

Animal Politics

Throughout the summer, Democrats' willingness to stand up to Bush and the Republicans seemed to oscillate like a sine curve: they passed an expansion in children's health care (forcing Bush to defend his opposition to the measure by saying that sick children can "always just go to an emergency room"), the recommendations of the September 11th commission, and an energy bill that redirected $16 billion in subsidies from the oil and gas industry to clean energy sources like wind and solar power. But they also responded to a full pressure White House campaign by allowing the passage of a bill to legalize the Bush administration's warrantless wiretapping of American citizens. As usual, the Democrats' willingness to challenge Bush and the Republicans fit a pattern: they'd do it where, as with energy and children's health care, polls told them they had overwhelming majority support; but when polls showed an electorate against them or evenly split, as was the case on the wiretapping authority, Democrats tended to cave. It showed that despite some major advances, the Politics of Fear was still alive and well in the Democratic Congress in 2007.

I think progressives deserve a small bit of blame for the Democratic capitulations – largely for ignoring Pelosi and the Democrats' small successes when they happened. Even though Democrats passed strong energy legislation, the recommendations of the September 11th commission, increases in health care funding, and major ethics reform legislation, many progressives responded like a nagging spouse: Instead of celebrating Democratic victories, most progressives took them for granted and ignored them. Then they trashed Democrats for their shortcomings, often reinforcing Republican claims that the new Democratic majority isn't actually getting anything done.

Meanwhile, with no one touting the Democrats' achievements, congressional approval numbers plummeted to below those of President Bush. Top Republican presidential candidates were running just a few points behind their Democratic counterparts in hypothetical matchups. In adopting a pure-criticism attitude, progressives were ignoring basic political psychology that's as true for chimps as for senators. Animal trainers know that it's impossible to motivate our furry and feathery friends to do what we want with criticism alone. As author Amy Sutherland put it in a now famous op-ed in *The New York Times* last summer, "The central lesson I learned from exotic animal trainers is that I should reward behavior I like and ignore behavior I don't. After all, you don't get a sea lion to balance a ball on the end of its nose by nagging." Sutherland's insight was to apply the lessons she'd learned from her days in animal trainer school to one particular exotic animal, her husband Scott. And she found that it worked – she'd keep silent when he left socks on the floor, but gushed when he put even one article of clothing in the hamper even if others remained strewn around their bedroom. Pretty soon, in Sutherland's telling, Scott became tidier, calmer, and less ornery, a model for American husbandhood.

Well, what's true for the primate we know as spouse can be just as true for the primate we know as politician. After all, strip them of the attendant consultants, wonks, and $1000 dollar suits, and politicians are just chest-thumping apes with remarkably big hair. And whether you're teaching an orangutan to skateboard or a Democrat to show some courage, the basic technique is largely the same. You need to reward good behavior and punish the bad (for animals, ignoring them is punishment enough; for politicians, something significantly more painful is often required). Of course, that's easier said than done. It's natural for us to take the good for granted and go ballistic at the bad, whether we're dealing with a biting monkey, an untidy spouse, or a capitulating pol. But animal trainers will tell that you have to keep the rewards coming or expect old, unwanted behaviors to reemerge. I know if I go too long without giving my dog Calliope some cheese as a reward for retrieving a stick from the Potomac, she'll start dropping the sticks 10 feet before the riverbank, forcing me to wade in and get it (I can tell from the look on her face that she thinks this is hilarious). In the same way, if progressives respond only when Democrats betray our principles or commit acts of titanic stupidity, we might be able to drag some Democrats kicking and screaming to occasionally vote our way in Congress or insert a policy plank in a presidential platform, but we won't be creating the progressive champions we need. So the next time a Democrat does something right, even something small, throw him the political equivalent of a doggy treat: public praise or a big contribution. Pretty soon, the primates we know as Democrats will be jumping through hoops for the progressive agenda.

COURAGE RISING
★★★★

The Wonks Rise Again

T hey're ba-ack! In the introduction to this book, I discussed the rise of the Politics of Fear and its defense by strategists Elaine Kamarck and William Galston. Well, they're back, almost 20 years later, peddling the same trash political science to service their corporate clients. In 2005, Galston and Kamarck updated the paper that launched the Politics of Fear takeover of the Democratic Party, calling their new work "The Politics of Polarization." They argued that all those frustrated Democrats were wrong: it wasn't the caution, capitulation, and weakness of the Democratic Party that had paved the way for President Bush's election, the disasters of his administration and the 12-year domination of Congress by the Republicans: it was instead a failure to move sufficiently to the policy center. At the core of their case was the idea that more people identify as conservatives than liberals – meaning that Democrats have to capture the center to win: "With three conservatives for every two liberals, the sheer arithmetic truth is that in a polarized electorate effectively mobilized by both major parties, Democratic candidates must capture upwards of 60 percent of the moderate vote – a target only Bill Clinton has reached in recent times – to win a national election."[1] Their prescription for doing that: regardless of what they believe, Democrats should advocate centrist policies so that they don't – heaven forbid! – come off as liberals.

I've already discussed how shifting policy positions for political reasons can be politically lethal: it's not likely to help with average voters for whom a candidate's policies only factor a tiny amount into a voter's decision. It's likely to hurt when it comes to voters deciding who is (or isn't) a strong leader, and who does or doesn't have integrity, factors that do play mightily in voters' decisions. But let's imagine a Democratic candidate so good at masking his beliefs, or so devoid of beliefs in the first place, that he can successfully shift all the way from being a liberal to being a conservative without anyone doubting his sincerity. It won't help that much: ideology only accounts for about 11 percent of voter choice. Keep in mind as well that while shifting from liberal to conservative might make the 30 percent of voters who call themselves conservatives 11 percent more likely to support a candidate, it's going to make the 20 percent of voters who identify as liberals 11 percent less likely to support a candidate. In the end, a magician-politician would stand to gain only between 1 and 2 percent extra votes. For any non-magical candidate whose strong leadership and morality ratings would be hurt by such shiftiness, that 1 to 2 points is just not enough to make abandoning one's principles worth it.

That's what the Politics of Fear advocates have been reduced to: arguing that Democrats should sell their soul to pick up a maximum of one to two points at the ballot box. But the political landscape is shifting to such an extent that whatever advantage some conservative policies once had has been reversed in the face of growing disillusionment with Republican failures. Americans are increasingly supportive of the progressive agenda. According to a March, 2007 Pew Research Center report, 69 percent of people believe that government should care for those who can't care for themselves, the highest number recorded since 1987; additionally, majorities or supermajorities continue to support environmental protection, continued or expanded gun control, and a women's right to choose (Republicans still retain advantages on taxes and immigration).[2]

What's more, expanding the Democratic vote among self-defined liberal Americans is one of the greatest potential growth areas for Democrats. A 2005 Pew study found that only 33 percent of Democrats and Democratic leaning voters in the Pew study had an "excellent" or "good" view of the Party. While all segments of the party share this dissatisfaction, it's most acute among the biggest group in the Democratic-leaning tent – the liberals – a whopping three quarters of whom had a "fair" or "poor" opinion of the Democratic Party. Contrast that to the 51 percent of Republicans who had a positive opinion of their party, with the most support coming from the most hard-core conservatives. The problem is so bad that after almost two decades of Politics of Fear dominating the Democratic Party, many liberals don't even consider themselves Democrats – 41 percent consider themselves independents, and in 2004 13 percent of liberals reported they didn't even bother to vote (though those who did vote voted overwhelmingly for Kerry). Having 87 percent voter turnout might sound good, but not when compared to the two most hard core Republican groups: 94 and 96 percent of business-oriented and socially conservative Republicans turned out.[3][xlii]

Even as voters have become more progressive in their orientation, strong leadership hasn't lost its appeal. Voters continue to look for candidates who will stand up and fight for their principles – even if they happen to disagree with those principles. It's this phenomenon that explains why George Bush could win even though majorities disagreed with his policy positions on most issues in 2000 and 2004. For instance, 22 percent of Americans who believe that same-

---

[xlii]There's also significant room for improvement among lower-income Democrats, only 34 percent of whom give the party an "excellent" or "good" rating (13 percent of whom also stayed home in 2004). (The Pew Research Center for People and the Press. "The 2005 Political Typology: Beyond Red vs. Blue". May 10, 2005. P. 31)

sex couples should be allowed to marry voted for Bush, despite his opposition to gay marriage.4 Independent voters in particular responded to Bush's repeated assertion about himself: "Whether you agree with me or not, you know where I stand, what I believe, and where I am going to lead."[5] Indeed, it was that sentence that Bush communications director Nicolle Devenish pinpointed as "the most important words we uttered in the campaign" during a post-election debrief conducted by the Annenberg School of Communication.[6][xliii]

It was this quality that allowed Paul Wellstone to win too, even though his policy positions were often to the left of the Minnesota electorate. When he voted against both Republicans and President Clinton by opposing the 1996 welfare reform bill, supermajorities of people in his own state disagreed with his position on what was then one of the most important issues in the national debate. In 2002, he voted against the Iraq War resolution even though it too was favored by the majority of voters in his state and his own party leaders were predicting doom to any candidate who stood up to the president on the war. In both instances, his support surged after his unpopular votes – Minnesota voters wanted the kind of candidate who would stand up for what he believed in even when it was politically unpopular and even when they themselves disagreed with him. In contrast, Bill Clinton and Tom Daschle spent much of their careers trying to find the political center – regardless of their own beliefs. For Clinton, that led to some of the lowest "strong leader" ratings in recent political history; more importantly, it left his progressive friends feeling betrayed and his implacable Republican enemies emboldened – paving the way for the Republican takeover of Congress, his impeachment, and just enough progressive disenchantment with his administration to cause progressives to defect to Ralph Nader and put Bush within striking distance of victory in 2000.

If You're Going to Pander, Pander to People Who Care

There is one group of voters who do act based in a significant way on candidates' positions on the issues – the progressive base. These activists and the unions, environmental organizations, civil rights groups, and bloggers who form

---

[xliii]Bush's confident leadership helped him pick up an enormous amount of independent support for a candidate with whom majorities disagreed on almost every important issue. The same 2005 Pew study showed that because of Bush's enormous personal appeal with independent voters, he was able to transform key groups of "upbeat" and "disaffected" independents from a plurality favoring Bill Clinton in the 1990's to voting for Bush by 5-1 and 4-1 margins respectively. Even though only about 35 percent of these groups consider themselves Republicans, 71 percent of them said they had an overall positive personal opinion of Bush.

the progressive coalition can deliver the volunteers and financial resources progressive candidates need to win. Many of these activists follow issues closely or belong to organizations that follow issues and pay attention to what those organizations say about candidates. We all know these people: they're the ones who knock on doors, make phone calls, and throw neighborhood fundraisers around election time – and who often are always talking about a politician's latest betrayal of *the cause*. They're also the ones who are more likely to set litmus tests on candidates' positions on the issues before deciding whether or not they will expend their effort for him. Primarily, these activists and organizations are looking for politicians who will champion their causes (though they definitely factor in how likely a candidate is to win; there's little to be gained from endorsing a guaranteed loser, no matter how much he or she supports your agenda). MoveOn.org tapped these voters' hunger for proudly progressive leadership at a time when few Washington Democrats were providing it – and channeled it to become one of the richest and most powerful organizations in Democratic politics today. Similarly, Paul Wellstone was able to use progressive enthusiasm for his courageous stances to become the best-financed candidate in the country in 2002 and to build a formidable grassroots political movement. In contrast, Clinton and Daschle, who put the Politics of Fear at the center of their political strategy, could never count on significant grassroots enthusiasm to fall back and to support them when they challenged Republicans.

Courage Alone…

Before continuing, I want to make clear that courage alone cannot create a stronger progressive movement.Similarly, I don't want to pretend that fear alone is solely responsible for the past failures of the Democratic Party. The problems of the Democratic Party have many sources. Specifically, Republicans have built a more powerful and skillful media machine and have until recently been more willing to invest resources in the long-term health of their party. Many Democrats have a fatalistic view about these imbalances – they've embraced a culture of defeat. In sum, these critics argue, Democrats are basically doomed to failure if they have to fight well-financed people who can mouth the phrase "Praise the Lord and Pass the Ammunition" free of irony. But the facts show that while the Democrats certainly need to improve their political infrastructure, they're even with Republicans in most measures of political organization and ahead in many. Even the much-ballyhooed Republican financial advantage is small and shrinking.[xliv] In 2004, for instance, Republicans spent just 5 percent more than Democrats: $1.798 billion to $1.711 billion (in 2006, Republicans again outspent Democrats by just 5 percent, $1.4 billion to $1.3 billion.[7] By 2007, there were indications that the Republican financial advantage had been eradicated: the Democratic candidates for president outraised Republicans by $27 million in the first quarter. Even in 2004, Democrats were ahead when it came to raw grassroots turnout: in 2004, the Kerry campaign contacted a higher proportion of the electorate, and got more of the people they contacted to vote their way (these numbers, however don't reflect all the people the Bush campaign contacted through their pastors, real estate brokers, and bosses – contacts that gave the Bush campaign the advantage that put it over the top).[8]

Once a Democrat, Always a Democrat

One key to boosting Democratic performance is recruiting more people to identify as Democrats. As our analysis of voter data shows, and as political scientists have known for half a century, by far the strongest influence on a voter's decision is the voter's party identification. Democrats vote for Democrats and Republicans vote for Republicans. Independents split their vote right down the middle.[9] Even without these fancy analytical techniques, it's easy to see how strong this connection is. More than 80 percent of self-identified Republicans have voted for the Republican candidate in every election since 1972. Although Democrats tend to vote with less loyalty to their party, they've never given more than 26 percent of their vote to Republicans, with the sole exception of the disas-

---

[xliv]There's major potential for financial growth in the progressive movement infrastructure – the think tanks, training institutes, and media outlets that make up the permanent progressive establishment. Liberal foundations spend way more than their right-wing counterparts – the Ford Foundation, Rockefeller Foundation, Charles Stewart Mott Foundation, David and Lucille Packard Foundation, and other top liberal foundations have given away more than $11 billion in the last 10 years alone; unfortunately, almost none of this money is given to help build political organizations that can relatively affordably influence the trillions of dollars the government spends; instead, they try to replace government through direct charitable giving (or at best, policy advocacy). In contrast, far more efficient conservative foundations like the Richard Mellon Scaife, Coors, Bradley and Olin Foundations have established and maintained the Heritage Foundation, the Cato Institute, right-wing attack magazines like *The American Spectator, National Review,* and *Weekly Standard* for about $500 million (while leaving a little bit over to fund the DLC and its offshoots). If progressive foundations could start giving even a fraction of their direct-service money to progressive political institutions, the right-wing financial advantage would be erased overnight – and progressive donors would make way more efficient use of their money by leveraging it to influence government policy and spending. For more on this topic, see environmental organizer Ken Ward's essay "Murder by Numbers" about how this phenomenon affects the environmental movement: http://www.grist.org/comments/soapbox/2005/03/17/ward/. The good news is that The Democracy Alliance and other groups of wealthy donors are trying to change this balance by building up the progressive infrastructure.

trous 1972 McGovern campaign.[10] That's why recruiting people to the Democratic Party is so important and building that affiliation should be at the center
of any party strategy: once a Democrat, always a Democrat (for the same reason,
it's just as important to prevent people from becoming Republicans). People do
not easily discard their partisan affiliations. In 1965, researchers interviewed 728
parents of high school students about their partisan leanings, and then went back
and interviewed them about their voting behavior in 1982. In the 1980 election,
Ronald Reagan received support from 89.5 percent of the people who had originally classified themselves as Republicans in 1965 and from just 33.8 percent
of those who had classified themselves as Democrats. Though some had voted
against their partisan affiliation in the 1980 election, only 5.7 percent of the respondents had changed their partisan identification during the 17-year gap.

Partisans are also multipliers. The same study showed that even 30 years
after the Republican parents were first interviewed, their *children* were 1.6 times
more likely to be Republicans than the rest of the population.[11] The importance
of partisan affiliation has enormous implications for political strategy. It shows
that the most reliable way to improve Democratic performance is to get more
Democrats to the polls and to create more Democrats. There are a lot of factors
that go into making somebody a Democrat or Republican, notably their parents'
political identification. But having Democrats consistently seen as courageous,
strong leaders is an incredibly important element not just to convincing voters to
support a single Democratic candidate in a single election, but to turn them into
loyal Democrats over time.[xlv]

The Politics of Selective Courage

There's a school of thought – I'll call it the "Politics of Selective Courage" –
that argues that courage is a good idea only on economic issues and environmental protection because Democratic positions on these issues are popular. Politics
of Selective Courage advocates argue that Democratic politicians should alter
their positions on some social issues, or at least not spend too much energy fighting on them, because of what they say is their unpopularity. Political consultants
James Carville and Paul Begala make this case in their otherwise compelling
2006 book *Take It Back*. Carville and Begala make a convincing and colorful case
for Democrats to stand up, fight hard, and take no prisoners for health care, for

---

[xlv]For a comprehensive, academic examination of the importance of partisan affiliation see Donald
Green, Bradley Palmquist, and Eric Schickler's comprehensive and readable 2002 book *Partisan Hearts
and Minds* (Yale University Press, 2002).

tax fairness, for the environment, but when it comes to issues like abortion and guns, they sound like the finger in the wind weasels they decry.

They criticize all the 2004 Democratic presidential candidates for opposing restrictions on a woman's right to choose an abortion, because a majority of the American people support increased restrictions. They also argue that Democrats shouldn't fight for more gun control, arguing that gun owners will see this as evidence that Democrats don't share their values. But this political analysis buys into the Politics of Fear. As I've demonstrated above, voters in general, and independents in particular, will tolerate differences on policy issues – what they won't tolerate is spinelessness. If you seem like you're just mouthing socially conservative positions to get elected, it's likely the very people to whom you're pandering will just choose a Republican who can argue against women's rights and against controls on gun ownership with conviction.

At the same time, taking socially conservative positions turns off Democrats' potentially most loyal supporters – the liberals who provide the votes, money, volunteer hours, endorsements, and enthusiasm that make campaigns run.[12] Here's another little acknowledged element of history of the last 30 years: for every southerner who abandoned the Democratic Party over its commitment to civil rights for blacks and women and its support of moderate gun control, there's a pro-choice, pro-gun control, pro-environment suburban woman who's joined it. Many of these voters have migrated to the Democratic Party because of their liberal stances on social positions – for better or worse, they're a lot more sympathetic to corporations and less sympathetic to a populist economic policy. They're not Democrats for pocketbook reasons – they're Democrats because liberal social policies keep their families safe from crime and pollution and protect their civil rights.

Support for liberal social policies like gun control isn't just confined to well-educated, upper middle class liberals – but actually includes much of the white, working class as well.

In a 2006 paper, Princeton political scientist Larry Bartels presents overwhelming empirical evidence showing that both working class and non-college educated white voters actually tend to share Democratic values on social issues and Republican values on economic issues – suggesting that for this segment of the electorate, at least, emphasizing progressive social values is helping Democrats. On gun control, for instance, 4 percent of voters said it should be easier to buy a gun, while 48 percent said it should be more difficult (with the rest supporting the status quo).[13][xlvi]

So if it's not social issues, why have working class white voters abandoned the Democratic Party? Bartels concludes that it's because these voters are voting on economic issues to a far greater degree than voters at higher socio-economic levels and ironically these working class voters actually tend to support the Republican economic agenda. You can see this in recent poll numbers that still show major Republican advantages when it comes to taxes: voters support repeal of the estate tax by a four to one margin, even though it only affects people who leave behind more than $3 million. It makes sense, of course, that low income voters vote on economic issues more than upper-income voters – they've got more bread and butter concerns and don't necessarily have the luxury to worry about other matters. But why do they support Republican tax cuts for the ultra-rich and other Republican anti-middle class policies? Probably because Democrats have done such a poor job of making a case for progressive economic policy, or even distinguishing their positions from the Republicans' positions on economic matters. These data show that the way for Democrats to pick up working class support isn't by abandoning their fight for liberal social policies (which actually gain them some support), but by persuading lower-income voters that progressive economic policies will help them – and fighting hard for those policies.

You Can't Spread the Gospel If You're Afraid of Speaking It

Here is the basic problem of anyone who practices the Politics of Fear: You can't spread the gospel if you don't speak it. Until Democrats everywhere are willing to stand up and articulate progressive values, all the advice in the world about how to do it effectively won't be worth a Harold Ford campaign button. Democrats have got to be willing to speak their values even when they're down in the polls. As I've laid out, it's hard to win independent votes without projecting courage and it's hard to do the key work of bringing more liberals into the party without fighting hard for their values. But it's also impossible to create new progressives unless progressives and Democratic leaders go about articulating those progressive values – and fighting for them.

Indeed, the political history of the last decade is a history of Republicans taking unpopular positions and using their media machine and clear messaging to convince the American people to support them, or at least to make other issues

---

[xlvi]In an earlier version of the paper, Bartels analyzed the behavior of white voters with family incomes in the bottom third.

a higher priority. It's how they were able to build, over the space of two months, supermajority support for the war in Iraq. It's how they passed the Central American Free Trade Agreement over the opposition of more than 60 percent of the American people. It's how they were able to move the number of Americans favoring the construction of a wall between the United States and Mexico from less than 15 percent to a majority as high as 80 percent at the key moment right before they voted on the fence (support has declined since then). Democrats and progressives have also shown an occasional ability to rally public opinion to their side. They were able to win over the country on civil rights, support for environmental protection, women's rights, and even protection from employment discrimination for gays. More recently, Democrats were able to maintain public opposition to President Bush's Social Security privatization scheme that would have given control of part of Social Security to Wall Street. They did it by consistently and unwaveringly criticizing the proposal and maintaining unity within their ranks.

That's the kind of effort required to beat back a bad proposal with powerful backing. But what about creating real progressive change in public opinion? 50 years of public opinion polling shows one thing: almost all big changes in public opinion on issues come slowly and in a similar way: when a determined group with a compelling message that doesn't much care what the polls say, says the same thing over and over and over again. And then says it again. This is true even on issues on which there have been the biggest national changes in sentiment. At no point did public opinion on civil rights undergo a sudden, dramatic shift – despite titanic national showdowns like *Brown v. Board of Education*, the Montgomery Bus Boycott, the March on Washington, the passage of the Civil Rights Act of 1964, and the assassination of Dr. Martin Luther King, Jr. Instead, it changed slowly over time as civil rights advocates on all levels explained their positions in the media and in personal interactions – helped along, to be sure, by the more dramatic points in the civil rights struggle that gained national publicity. Between 1942 and 1985, for instance, the percentage of people favoring allowing black and white students to attend the same schools rose from 31 percent to 93 percent, with an almost constant, uniform rate of change of 1.4 percent a year.[14] [xlvii] To be sure, persuasion wasn't the only force at play – the rising popu-

---

[xlvii]There are exceptions: support for the Iraq war has fallen off relatively dramatically: more than 30 points in three years, largely because the original rationale for the war – Hussein's possession of weapons of mass destruction – has been undermined. This falloff in support was similar to the a dramatic 20-plus point falloff in support for the Vietnam War that occurred in 1968 largely in response to the casualties suffered during the VietCong's Tet Offensive – which undermined American government arguments that the war was going well. In both cases, the decline wasn't related so much to increas-

larity of racial integration had to do with lots of old racists dying off. But as civil rights advocates became the dominant voice, young people coming of political age in the 1950's, 1960's, and 1970's grew up in an environment in which legalized racism was increasingly frowned upon.

Slow, constant change: Opinion about School Integration and Brown v. Board of Education[15]

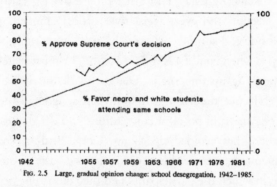

FIG. 2.5 Large, gradual opinion change: school desegregation, 1942–1985.

Reprinted by Permission from The University of Chicago Press from The Rational Public *by Benjamin I. Page and Robert Y. Shapiro. Copyright* © *1992, University of Chicago Press.*

At the beginning of the civil rights struggle, fighting for integration was not exactly a politically easy thing to do – it risked turning off the white supremacists who dominated in the South. Indeed, FDR, Eisenhower, and even Kennedy were all very cautious in their efforts to support integration, wary of angering southerners. But southerner Lyndon Johnson didn't have that fear – and used his political muscle and his considerable political skill to pass the Civil Rights Act of 1964 and the Voting Rights Act of 1965. He knew it could mean some temporary erosion of the Democratic power base in the South (though whether this is attributable to civil rights alone or not is highly debatable) – but it was a price he was willing to pay for social progress and for allowing Democrats further inroads into socially liberal areas in the North and West that had been represented by Republicans, as well as creating huge new groups of loyal Democratic southern blacks. It is Lyndon Johnson's courage in the 1960's that we have to thank for the fact that no one in America can be legally discriminated against at work, in school, or in public places on account of their race. And it's that kind of courage

---

ing casualties or political developments, but rather to the undermining of the government's and the president's integrity and credibility.

that will be required if Democrats are to effect the great changes needed today so that people 20 years from now will be grateful for how the courage of today's Democrats will have helped solve, for instance, the looming global climate catastrophe.

The Wimp Love Myth

Sometimes, exercising courage isn't pretty. LBJ had to break a lot of political arms to pass the civil rights act and other progressive legislation. It seems that during every election and every legislative battle Democrats missed the most basic lesson of political summer school: "It's hard for your opponent to say bad things about you when your fist is in his mouth."[16] Unfortunately, it's usually the Democrats coughing up fingernails. Democrats definitely had their collective foot in their collective mouth in 2004 when they ignored the entire accumulated history of American political conventions and decided to run a "positive" convention where they avoided criticizing George Bush. According to Carville and Begala, Democrats made this decision on the basis of one focus group in Dayton, Ohio in which the participants said they didn't like negative campaigning (the Kerry campaign operatives apparently didn't know that no one *likes* negative campaigning, but it sure is a great way to persuade people not to vote for the other guy). Apparently, Democrats think that their voters love wimps.

Not surprisingly, Democrats got at most a 2 percent bump from the convention – about one fifth the minimum bump parties usually get. The Republicans responded to the Democrats' smiley hug-fest with their usual political Napalm. They trotted out Georgia Senator Zell Miller, a Democrat in name only, to unleash his seething anger at Kerry with what is possibly the most rage-filled speech in recent American history. No southern courtliness here: just pure, unadulterated hatred – "For more than 20 years, on every one of the great issues of freedom and security, John Kerry has been more wrong, more weak, and more wobbly than any other national figure…This is the man who wants to be the Commander in Chief of our U.S. Armed Forces?! U.S. forces armed with what? Spitballs?!"[17] Though disgusting, Miller's rabid attacks worked – and gave the Republicans a 10 point boost in the polls.

This shouldn't have been a shock to Democrats. At their 1992 convention, speaker after speaker (including then-loyal Democrat Zell Miller) lustily attacked George Bush, Sr. for the total failure of his economic policy and the heartlessness of his right-wing social and environmental policies. Their attacks not only made a difference with the public, but so impressed independent candidate Ross Perot that he dropped out of the race (albeit temporarily), citing the "revitalization of the Democratic Party" and giving Clinton a record-setting 30 point boost in the polls. Unfortunately, even Clinton didn't seem to totally learn the lessons of his own convention and, as president, was often afraid to attack his opponents, even though they were much harsher than George Bush, Sr. ever was. When the Politics of Fear took over the Party, it hamstrung even those who had ridden courage to victory.

Fearing Fear

Indeed, by 2007, progressives and Democrats seemed to have once again forgotten the lessons of the 2004 convention and many had returned to inventing rationalizations for avoiding confrontational politics, which often involve evoking fear – fear of Bush, fear of climate crisis, fear of losing health care, or fear of war. These thinkers have embraced a new incarnation of an idea that seems to keep bubbling up in Democratic and progressive circles: that fear is either immobilizing or repellent and that everyone from environmentalists to health care advocates to Democratic candidates should always keep their messages up-beat and hopeful. It's an appealing conceit for the confrontation-adverse: if fear doesn't work, we can just go on doing the less emotionally taxing and controversial work of delivering happy little sermons. For that reason, just three years after running a cheerful and largely fear-free 2004 convention that was blown away by the Republicans' rhetorical mushroom clouds, lots of liberals are latching onto some recent psychological studies that suggest that anxiety has an expiration date.

These commentators note that President Bush's use of fear is generating diminishing returns: each time President Bush tries to evoke fear, it works less as more people clue into his deceptions. "Barring another assault on American soil, the moment of September 11th – and the reminder of mortality that it brought – may well have passed," wrote John Judis in a recent article in *The New Republic*. "And with it, too, the ascendancy of politicians who exploited the fear of death that lies within us all." Judis was interpreting a series of well known studies by psychologists Tom Pysczynski, Sheldon Solomon, and Jeff Greenberg that found clear evidence that evoking people's fear of death made them more defensive of their own world view, more hostile to foreigners, more willing to lash out violently at people of different political or religious beliefs, and more drawn to charismatic leaders. In one of their more memorable experiments, for instance, they found that reminding test subjects of their mortality by asking them to describe what would happen to their bodies after death, made them far more willing to surreptitiously feed people of opposing political views great quantities of painfully spicy hot sauce.

But these studies also found that it's possible to limit or reverse these effects. Urging people to make "careful" decisions rather than rash ones, priming people to think about the value of tolerance, or, critically, alerting them to the possibility of manipulation limits the ability of death to generate a defensive response. The anti-fear mongers have embraced this conclusion, arguing that Republicans' use of fear in the last 14 years has exhausted its ability to generate the intended response and that it may even be producing a backlash. But while it's true that the impact of politically motivated Homeland Security alerts and strategically timed al Qaeda-in-Buffalo arrests may be ebbing, that doesn't mean that dread is dead.

Indeed, one consequence of President Bush's monomaniacal focus on terrorism and Iraq has been to distract people from other lethal threats: disease, crime, state-sponsored nuclear attack, and the destruction of the natural world we rely on for life. Clever politicians who remind people of those threats will continue to leverage the immense political power of the fear of death. Leading Republicans know this and are desperately seeking something new that can trigger the fear of death in a way that turns people to the GOP. Some have turned to the prospect of a nuclear armed Iran to trigger people's defense mechanism. But more savvy Republicans recognize that the WMD threat, even if it's real this time, may not resonate with a war weary and cynical public. That helps explain the recent Republican obsession with painting immigrants as murderers, rapists, and lepers. If you can no longer get Americans to believe that a distant Middle Eastern country presents an existential threat, you might be able to get the same reaction by freaking them out about the gardener.

Many Democrats, on the other hand, have been reluctant to appeal to fear – either because they think doing so is somehow unethical, because they think fear doesn't work for Democrats, or, most commonly, because they lack the gumption to engage Americans' emotions, and not just their minds. Democrats who indulge these reservations, however, are forgetting the vital role fear has played in American politics from the beginnings of the nation – and how use of that emotion has been indispensable to both achieving progressive change and to electing Democrats. Indeed, the Founding Fathers were rarely shy about summoning the fear of death to achieve their political aims. Although we tend to remember the American Revolution as one fought primarily over economic and legal grievances, its authors knew that nothing short of the fear of death would inspire vast numbers of their countrymen to support a rupture with Great Britain and risk life and liberty in war. In the Declaration of Independence's famous catalog of grievances against King George III, Jefferson saves his most powerful indictment for last: that the King had "endeavoured to bring on the inhabitants of our frontiers, the merciless Indian Savages whose known rule of warfare is an undistinguished destruction of all ages, sexes and conditions," a claim that tapped into the most primal of fears for the white colonists clinging precariously to a fragile existence in the midst of a vast wilderness. It was Lou Dobbs for the Enlightenment.

In our own times, John F. Kennedy evoked the terror of nuclear holocaust to beat Nixon; George Bush, Sr. used his Willie Horton ad to evoke the fear of random crime (and black people in general), and in 1992 and 1996 Bill Clinton skillfully played on worries that Republicans would cut Medicare and Social Security to trigger the fear of dying from lack of resources to pay for health care. These politicians knew instinctively that politics is at least as much about scaring voters about the other guy as presenting a positive agenda. And it's an insight that has lately been validated by political science and psychological research.

In his 2006 book *Campaigning for Hearts and Minds*, political scientist Ted Brader found that fear in advertising worked far better than positive emotions like hope or enthusiasm. His research showed that fear is especially potent in prompting people to re-evaluate their existing beliefs. That's because when people are afraid, they stop relying on their preconceptions. A near crash causes us to rethink how fast to go; a study about the dangers of pesticides makes us reevaluate what we eat; a neighbor's mugging makes us avoid a certain area. In politics, fear produces the same kind of re-evaluation. Brader found that watching a single political ad that appealed to fear buried within a 30 minute newscast produced an eleven point jump in support of the candidate who ran the ad compared to a control group. It also had the more generally positive civic effect of prompting people to seek out additional, independent sources of information about the candidates – undermining more traditional views that negativity in politics suppresses interest and dumbs down the debate.   As academic reviewers of Brader's work universally remarked, what is so extraordinary about his results is that he was able to measure them despite showing his test subjects only one ad buried deep within a broadcast and doing it in a realistic setting: test subjects sat on a sofa eating snacks and watched a television newscast and weren't told the purpose of the study until after they'd completed it. With viewers seeing the typical political ad at least several times before voting, it's possible to imagine far greater effects.

In contrast to the powerful effects he measured from fear-inducing ads, Brader found that positive emotional ads aren't persuasive at all. Instead, they reinforce existing beliefs. People who already support a candidate become more enthusiastic after seeing an enthusiasm-inducing ad – that enthusiasm means they're more likely to actually get out and vote for the candidate as well as volunteer in the campaign. That makes them useful for candidates who are ahead in the polls or who are campaigning in areas where they already have majority support. The most famous hopeful ad in history, Ronald Reagan's 1984 "Morning in America," worked so well because Reagan was already so far ahead in the polls when it ran; its purpose and its effect was not so much to persuade Mondale voters or undecideds as to reinforce people's existing support for Reagan and make sure they actually got out to the polls for him.

But these hope and enthusiasm ads have a major downside as well – they're very polarizing. Surprisingly, when people see a positive ad for someone they already oppose, it actually makes them oppose that candidate even more. For that reason, the Morning in America ad wouldn't have worked when Reagan started his 1980 campaign behind in the polls against Carter – it would have reinforced people's anxieties about Reagan: that he was too extreme, that he lacked the level of responsibility to face down the Soviets. For that reason, all of Reagan's major 1980 television ads except one evoked fear and anxiety – and he rode that emotional response to the presidency. Brader's work suggests that it may actually be dangerous for a candidate to use positive messaging when he's either behind in the polls or speaking or advertising in areas where his support is less than overwhelming. Using fear and negativity may actually be the safe bet. Candidates should be wringing their hands not over negative ads, but rather ones that feature gooey spots of children running through sun-dappled fields.

Fear isn't just a good persuader: it's also good at conquering apathy, which is arguably the progressive movement's greatest enemy. To quote Samuel Johnson, "when a man knows he is to be hanged in a fortnight, it concentrates his mind wonderfully." Of course, it's easy to spur action with an immediate threat like a looming noose. But getting people to fear death from diffuse, long-term problems is just as essential to inspiring action. A study by Mark Lubell, Sammy Zahran, and Arnold Vedlitz in the September issue of the journal *Political Behavior* found that people's perception of how great a risk global warming is was the second biggest determinant of whether they would support pro-environment policies and take political action in support of those policies (the biggest determinant was their general environmental concern). Their risk perception, or to put it in emotional terms, their fear, trumped all other factors measured in the study like their level of knowledge about the issue, how much they thought they could influence the problem (their hope), or their level of education. It's important to note that the study found that outside of politics, fear isn't always the best motivator; the most important factor in motivating people to change personal environmental behavior – doing things like screwing in fluorescent lightbulbs or choosing a more fuel efficient car – was how likely people think those activities are to make a difference.

Fear is also a potent political weapon to deploy when dealing directly with politicians. Congress didn't pass civil rights legislation only because of the peaceful rallies, sit-ins, and lobbying; many Members of Congress were also afraid that if they didn't, angry blacks would lash out in a wave of black-on-white violence (in this case, however, fear had its limits: after the passage of the Civil Rights Act and Voting Rights Act in 1964 and 1965, protests and violence tended to produce more of a backlash in Congress than progress, according to a study by sociologist Wayne Santoro). A more extreme example of the power of fear was the anti-Vietnam War movement. A 2002 study by the respected sociologists Doug McAdam and Yang Su found that violent protest was the only kind that boosted Congressional opposition to the war.

Even when it comes to a complex problem like global warming, fear seems to trump reason – not just for the public, but for decision makers as well. In a study published in September in the journal *Social Forces*, University of Washington professor Jon Agnone studied the factors that affected passage of environmental laws from 1960 to 1998 and found that public protest was far more influential than either public opinion or insider advocacy.

As powerful as fear is, however, it's nowhere near as powerful as the combination of fear and hope. While Lyndon Johnson evoked the fear of death more powerfully and consistently than his opponent Barry Goldwater, he combined that message with one of security, warmth, and hope. We remember his "Daisy" ad for its blinding mushroom cloud, but forget the message Lyndon Johnson recorded over it: "We must love one another or die."

But evoking fear first is essential to tuning people into a message of hope. The politicians we remember as fonts of hope, Lincoln and FDR in particular, were ones who had no need to paint scary images with their language – fear already gripped the land. Even FDR used fear when he was trying to build popular and congressional support for aid to America's democratic allies before the attack on Pearl Harbor brought America officially into the war. FDR, Jefferson, and other successful politicians knew what some of today's cautious Democrats don't: there are things out there that are legitimately scary. People look to leaders to identify those threats and rally the nation to tackle them – and not cede the use of this most powerful of emotions to those who would exploit it for evil.

An unwillingness to play hardball isn't just damaging to politicians' electoral prospects; it's also crippling in the legislative fights that determine the shape of our society – and not just because it means Republicans are able to pass bad legislation or stop good legislation. Almost every major piece of legislation creates a new political constituency – or destroys an old one. Tax breaks for oil companies give those companies more money to give to Republicans – and more reason to give it. Passing laws that make it harder for victims of pollution and other corporate wrongdoing to sue corporations and hold them responsible defund trial lawyers – one of the Democratic Party's most reliable funders. Making it harder for unions to organize new members means fewer workers get to take advantage of unions' efforts on behalf of Democratic politicians. When Democrats fail to deliver by refusing to play hardball, they make it harder for their progressive base to get excited about voting for them or getting involved in their campaigns – it seems like it doesn't make a difference who wins. Playing hardball means using all the tools available – cutting deals, using the filibuster in the Senate, and holding people accountable. Republicans, of course, have taken hardball too far – crossing legal boundaries and fighting hard not for the public good, but to line their own pockets. But Democrats are nowhere near that point. With so much power lined up against them, they need to twist some arms to win. If they don't, voters will ask themselves: "If Democrats can't stand up to Rush Limbaugh and the Republicans, how will they ever stand up to Osama bin Laden?"

The Burning Tires of Fear

To most Americans during the early years of the Clinton administration, Hillary Clinton was the White House liberal. She was the public face of the drive for universal health care and was upsetting the tradition of a First Lady as subservient symbol and society queen. Even when she withdrew from a public political role in 1996, it didn't convince many people that she didn't remain an extremely influential voice in the White House – and not all Americans were sure they liked that influence. When Dick Morris started polling for Clinton in 1994, he found that of the voters who held negative opinions of Clinton, half thought he had few core beliefs himself – and looked to ultraliberal Hillary to provide them. "In effect, they believed that she was Example A of how weak he was, and that their marriage was a zero-sum game, where the 100 points of power would be divided

60-40, 70-30, 50-50," Morris told *New York Times* reporter James Bennett. "But they didn't understand the idea that in a strong marriage between two strong people, their strength augments one another rather than robs one another. They just saw it as who wears the pants in the family."[18]

Ironically, despite Clinton's media reputation as a raging ideological partisan, her record is anything but. Even when she was First Lady she was often a voice for caution and corporate-friendly policies (not surprising for someone who long sat on the board of Wal-Mart). It was she who convinced Clinton to bring in Republican political consultant Dick Morris as his main adviser, and she who, with Morris, encouraged Clinton to focus on small-bore issues like school uniforms, and she who advised and supported Clinton's decision to support the Republican welfare reform package. Her highly complex health care reform plan is exhibit A – rather than opting for the simple, low-cost, and effective single payer model of health care, Hillary concocted a system that would keep HMOs and the insurance industry profiting off of Americans' illnesses. To be sure, Hillary is usually a reliable liberal vote for progressive priorities – it's rare she bucks the party on the environment, expanding health care, or letting right-wing judges through. But even as she votes on a largely progressive platform, she's also adopted a conservative framework on some issues, teaming up with far right Republicans like Sam Brownback and Bill Frist to, for instance, sponsor a bill to ban flag burning. And while she usually ends up voting progressive, she is rarely willing to put herself at the vanguard of the Democratic Party's fights. During the fight to save Social Security, for instance, Hillary declined to take a leading role.

As a result, she's earned the contempt of many progressives who were hoping that she would aggressively confront the Bush administration's abuses. She'll have to overcome that contempt if she's going to triumph in the primaries. While progressives are angry because they don't see her as sharing their priorities or their tough approach to the Bush administration, the general public still considers Hillary a liberal. In 2005, at the height of Clinton's conservative positioning, a CNN/*USA Today* poll found that 54 percent of respondents viewed her as a liberal and just 30 percent as a moderate. That puts Hillary in a difficult paradox. She's viewed as a centrist by progressives and a liberal by the general public: in either case, she's out of step.[19] While perception of ideological differences alone won't sink her, what she will find challenging to overcome is the inconsistency: the general electorate thinks she's a liberal no matter how much she positions herself as a conservative – meaning that whenever she takes a conservative stance or adopts conservative rhetoric, no matter how sincerely, she'll come off seeming dishonest. And unless she abandons the Politics of Fear, she's unlikely to win many friends among the many progressives who have written her off.

You could see the deadly consequences of Clinton's Politics of Fear at work on November 15, 2006, when workers at the Ticonderoga, New York plant of International Paper started feeding old shredded tires into their massive incinerator – sending an acrid cloud loaded with deadly chemicals and heavy metals like mercury and cadmium into the air. It was the culmination of a three year battle between timber executives and Vermonters downwind from the plant worried about the health and environmental impacts of the toxic brew (the International Paper facility lies just a few miles across Lake Champlain from Burlington, Vermont), a battle in which Clinton weighed in decisively for the timber company. Tires are just about the most poisonous fuel known to man. They're particularly dangerous for children whose developing brains and immune systems are hypersensitive to pollutants like mercury and benzene. Exposure to burning tires can cut years off a child's life, according to the American Lung Association. But IP wanted to cut costs for running its mill (which already produced more pollution than the entire state of Vermont – including Vermonters' vehicles) and came up with the idea of saving money by cutting up old tires and burning them for energy.

Of course, it was immediately controversial – more than 5 million people would be downwind of the burning tires. Even Vermont's Republican governor was working to stop the tire burn. But IP had an ace up its sleeve in Hillary Clinton. Although Clinton had been chairman of the Children's Defense Fund and had made a huge issue out of the Bush administration falsely claiming that the Ground Zero site was safe enough for workers, she wanted to do anything she could to boost her margin of victory in upstate New York. The facts that she was pretty much guaranteed a landslide, outspending her opponent $41 million to $5 million in the most expensive Senate race in the country, and that burning tires would seriously jeopardize children's health, were secondary to the few hundred votes she might pick up from factory workers and others willing to do anything to keep IP's profits high. And so she lobbied to allow the tire burning. Given the choice between a few hundred additional votes and children's health, Clinton chose the votes (whether or not this actually helped her politically is an open question – lots of New Yorkers were downwind from the pollution as well). In the event, the burning tires turned out to be so polluting that the emissions exceeded even IP's extremely lax permit. IP was forced to suspend its test just three days after it had started the burning. They didn't go out of business, but

Hillary Clinton had racked up another example of the Politics of Fear – putting political expedience ahead of what was supposed to be her most cherished value – children's welfare.

The Baby Bond Boomerang

Once her presidential campaign started, Clinton couldn't get away from the politics of fear. She was consistently the last of the major candidates to offer detailed policy plans on almost any topic, cautiously waiting until everyone else had proposed plans and then offering her own. And she rarely strayed from mushy orthodoxy, an attitude reinforced by her strong standing in national polls, lulling her into a sense of security that she could avoid taking any confrontational stances. Even on one of the few occasions when she did show creativity and even a little courage by floating a progressive policy idea, she allowed right-wing Republicans to bully her into backing off it. On September 27, Clinton told the Congressional Black Caucus that "I like the idea of giving every baby born in America a $5,000 account that will grow over time, so that when that young person turns 18 if they have finished high school they will be able to access it to go to college or maybe they will be able to make that down payment on their first home." It won her praise from her audience and progressives. "I think it's a wonderful idea," said Representative Stephanie Tubbs Jones in response. "Every child born in the United States today owes $27,000 on the national debt, why not let them come get $5,000 to grow until their 18?" It would have meant a significant leveling of the playing field for young Americans. But Clinton's campaign staff was nervous that the idea might open her up to Republican attack and quickly sent out spokesperson Blake Zeff to tell the press that Baby Bonds were "not a firm policy proposal but an idea under consideration." Their instinct was right: the right-wing jumped all over the idea – freaked out about a program that, like the GI Bill before it, might give Americans reason to be grateful to the government for giving them a head start in life. Rush Limbaugh, the right-wing blogosphere, and Rudy Giuliani all blasted the idea for being "socialist" or for taking money out of people's pockets. The attacks worked, and Clinton soon backed off the idea. "It's just an idea I threw out," Clinton said on October 4, while proposing a retirement savings plan instead. "I'm looking for a conversation." The right-wing cooed how they had bullied her into retreat. "Remember the Hillary baby bonds," Giuliani chortled to a meeting of South Carolina Republicans. "We pointed out in strong terms how irresponsible this was…She gave them up in three or four days."[20] John Edwards jumped on the reversal as more evidence that Clinton was completely poll driven. "Apparently new polling data seems to have pressured the Clinton campaign to throw out the baby bond with the bathwater," he said.

Fear and Audacity

On January 19, 2007, *Saturday Night Live* opened its show with a sketch featuring a poll-obsessed Hillary Clinton explaining that she would institute a "specific trigger mechanism" to withdraw troops from Iraq: "For every one-point increase in Senator Obama's poll numbers, 7500 U.S. troops will have to be withdrawn. Of course, if his poll numbers should collapse or if he drops out of the race, the troops can stay in Iraq." It was a harsh indictment of Clinton's image – that she comes up with her plans based on what the polls at any one moment dictate she should do. The Clinton character then comments about Barack Obama, "He seems to take positions based on studying an issue and then following his convictions. Which is perfectly all right. But suppose he were to go to Iraq and conclude that the war was necessary, after all. He might decide to support it. Can we really trust someone like that?" The sketch perfectly captured a common liberal sentiment in 2007: that the election boiled down to a contest between Hillary's ultra-calculated, convictionless machine and Barack Obama's politics of principle.

Unfortunately, even a cursory glance at Barack Obama's record shows a politician who rivals Hillary as a practitioner of the Politics of Fear. That may be surprising given Obama's early and vociferous opposition to the Iraq War at a time when most Democrats had serious doubts but shied from expressing them. But his position on the war was more of an exception than an example of a regular tendency to be courageous when it came to backing progressive priorities. It should be noted, also, that at the time Obama was representing a heavily black, very progressive, anti-war constituency. It's difficult to know what Obama would have done if he had been in anything less than an ultra-safe state senate seat. But what is clear is that since entering the Senate, Barack Obama has made the politics of fear his gospel – avoiding confrontation with Republicans, President Bush, and corporate lobbies at key points – and even occasionally working to undermine populist, progressive organizing efforts.

I first got a sense that the inspiring Barack Obama we all saw at the 2004 Democratic convention might not be as courageous as he said he was when he spoke at an event put on by the environmental organization I was working for in early 2005, soon after he had taken office. While we were all very excited to have Obama there, our excitement was tempered by the fact that he'd been refusing to say for weeks whether or not he would vote for President Bush's "Clear Skies" bill, a giveaway to big coal companies and other polluters that would have involved a massive increase in pollution (and thousands of additional pollution-related deaths) compared to just leaving the Clean Air Act intact. His vote was the deciding one on an equally split Senate Environment and Public Works committee, so his stand was crucial. Obama had run on an environmental platform in 2004 and so we were all surprised when one of Obama's first acts as the newest Democrats on the committee was to declare himself uncommitted on Bush's bill because of his concerns about the coal industry in southern Illinois (all the other Democrats opposed Bush's pollution plan). The polluter lobbyists were surprised too – and launched a big, last-minute campaign in Illinois (with the collaboration of the anti-environment Teamsters union) to win Obama's vote. Meanwhile, we had to divert thousands of dollars and hundreds of hours of our organizers' time into persuading Obama just to oppose Bush's bill – money and time we would have preferred to spend persuading Republicans to vote against the bill.

Despite all the effort we'd expended and our frustration that Obama wouldn't go along with his fellow Democrats on the committee (including Hillary Clinton) in clearly opposing Bush, we were still excited when Obama used the occasion of our party to officially announce that he would in fact vote against Bush on this issue. But I sensed that this wasn't the first battle we'd have to fight with polluters or Republicans for Obama's vote: he explained his equivocation by telling us that in politics, "As you all know, sometimes you have to trim your sails" – meaning cut back on your goals for the sake of expediency. It's true that politics is the art of the possible, and that compromise is sometimes the only way to move forward, but effective actors always keep their goals of the kind of society they want to construct in mind, and don't let tactical compromises interfere with their dreams. At best, it was the wrong message for his audience. At worst, it was evidence that he would let bogus Politics of Fear considerations prevent him from pursuing solutions to the country and the world's problems.

My concerns about Obama were quickly borne out as he sought accommodation with Bush and the Republicans repeatedly during his first two years in office. Although he has accumulated a generally progressive record, at key moments he has shied from confrontation with Bush and the Republicans – and helped deliver defeats to progressives. In response to Republican attempts to tie Democrats to trial lawyers, he voted for President Bush's "tort reform" bill, which limited the ability of private citizens to hold major corporations accountable when they caused harm through pollution, unsafe working conditions, or allowing poison into your pet food. Not only will the bill make corporations less likely to instaill safeguards to prevent these kinds of damages, it's also political poison for Democrats: trial lawyers are the single most reliable and consistent big donors to the Democrats. By preventing citizens from having their day in court against big corporations, it also limits trial lawyers' income – meaning that there will be less money available for Democrats in the future. This is the main reason Republicans expend so mucheffort trying to limit citizens' abilities to hold big corporations accountable: they do want to shield those corporations from responsibility for their actions, but their primary concern is defunding the Democratic Party. Despite these drawbacks, it would have been possible that Obama just believed the Republican arguments: that allowing citizens their day in court burdens the justice system and is overly onerous for business – and was putting his concern before the financial interest of the Democratic Party. But his actions afterwards belied any notion that going along with Bush was an act of principle of any kind.

Following the vote, Obama met with a group of public interest lawyers, among them Public Citizen president Joan Claybrook. "We were worried about what his vote indicated about him for the future," Claybrook told *The Nation's* David Sirota. "And he told us, 'Sometimes you have to trim your sails.' And I asked myself, Trim your sails for what? You just got elected by a wide margin – what are you trimming your sails for?"[21] Obama would go on to "trim his sails" on a host of other issues, going along with Bush and the Republicans and often throwing mud not just in the eyes of progressive activists, but also the poor, the middle class, and the environment. He voted to allow credit card companies to charge usurious interest rates above 30 percent (he defended his vote by saying that the amendment was poorly written and went on to vote against the underlying bill that limited consumers' right to file bankruptcy and escape crushing debt). He is the Senate's leading Democratic supporter of "coal to liquid," a technology that can make gasoline out of coal. Only problem: it produces double the global warming pollution that regular old dirty oil does. As if that wasn't bad enough, Obama actually voted for George Bush's energy bill despite more than $27 billion in subsidies for the oil, nuclear, and coal industries, its weakening of clean air and water laws, and the fact that it gave electric companies the power to charge consumers higher rates while doing almost nothing to tackle global warming or increase consumer protections.

Why is Obama be so willing to "trim his sails" so often – despite the consequences to working and middle class Americans and the environment? It's not just that he apparently believes accommodation – even of right-wing extremists – can be both right and politically useful. It's something deeper. In his autobiography *The Audacity of Hope*, Obama admits he has a hard time feeling a truly pressing sense of urgency about the great issues of the day.

> My wife will tell you that by nature I'm not somebody who gets real worked up by things. When Democrats rush up to me at events and insist that we live in the worst of political times, that a creeping fascism is closing its grip around our throats, I may mention the internment of Japanese Americans under FDR, the Alien and Sedition Acts under John Adams, or a hundred years of lynching under several dozen administrations as having possibly been worse, and suggest we all take a deep breath. No, what's troubling is the gap between the largeness of our problems and the smallness of our politics – the ease with which we are distracted by the petty and the trivial, our chronic avoidance of tough decisions, our seeming inability to build a working consensus to tackle any big problem.

It's true that the wars, holocausts, and famine we read about in history (as well as the abuses Obama mentions) are horrible to contemplate. But today's national and planetary threats are at least as severe: nuclear annihilation, the global climate crisis, genocide, the destruction of the earth's tropical forests, and the decimation of the seas that are the cradle of life's beginnings. It's not that Obama would say that these aren't problems, even serious problems worthy of attention. It's that when push comes to shove, he doesn't get "worked up" about them – he doesn't feel that the fate of the country, the world, or even one life are hanging on his actions. Without that sense of urgency, it's a lot easier to rationalize giving into lobbyist pressure or prioritizing campaign donations over doing what's right.

In part, his lack of urgency stems from a certain arrogance about the process of politics. His standard campaign speech is more a plea for civility than a statement about how he will deal with the challenges of the country and the world. It's as if he believes the nature of the debates between pundits on MSNBC, Fox News, or CNN or in the halls of Congress are more important than the outcome of those debates. But the progressives who will determine Obama's fate in the 2008 primaries, however, have a different attitude: politeness is fine, but if the choice is between politeness and a living planet, or politeness and health care, or politeness and an end to genocide, it may be time for the rhetorical sucker punch that will get the job done.

Obama's blasé attitude and his willingness to let political fear trump planetary survival because of his temperament suggests he doesn't yet have a real sense of the tremendous responsibilities of the position to which he aspires. President Clinton had a similar attitude – because lacked a visceral feeling of how much was riding on his decisions, he was that much more willing to compromise, capitulate, or let things fester. And so it wasn't until late in his presidency that he grasped how wrong he had been when he failed to act in response to a cataclysm in his midst: the Rwandan genocide. He didn't have the sense of crisis about it that would have been required to stop it. As long as we live in what General Omar Bradley called a world of "nuclear giants and ethical infants," those who presume to defend us on that thin line between planetary life and global death will need both urgency and courage to pull the world back from the precipice.

No matter what Obama does between now and primary season, his caution and record of collaboration with the Bush administration are likely to haunt him when Iowa voters cast their first ballots on January 3, 2008. Obama is especially vulnerable because he has staked his claim on the nomination largely on his pledge to practice a "new kind of politics." The evidence that his record is actually one of accommodation of big corporate interests and the Washington establishment will signal that his "new kind of politics" is just so much empty rhetoric – in fact, his style of politics is the old kind of influence peddling, caution, and smallness that most Democrats reject. Something similar happened to Howard Dean during his run for the presidency. He had ridden a tide of enthusiasm for his opposition to the war and anti-Bush spirit to a leading position in the polls. But Dean had a centrist and occasionally acommodationist record as Vermont governor of which many of his liberal supporters were unaware. A 527 political committee set up by John Kerry and Dick Gephardt supporters knew about this record and polled caucus and primary voters to find out how it would affect their choices. It discovered that when primary voters found out about Dean's support for Nafta, Newt Gingrich's Medicare cuts, and his opposition to most increased gun control measures, support dropped 12 percent, moving him from a five point advantage against all his opponents combined to a 14 point disadvantage. The 527 (as well as the Kerry and Gephardt campaigns) did their best to get that information out to the progressive primary voters through hard-hitting television ads in Iowa like "Facts": "These two men have been given top grades by the National Rifle Association. One is George Bush. The other might surprise you. It's Howard Dean. That's right. In Vermont, Dean was endorsed eight times by the National Rifle Association, and Dean got an "A" rating from the NRA because he joined them in opposing common-sense gun safety laws. So if you thought Howard Dean had a progressive record, check the facts, and please think again."[22] Partly as a result of these attacks on his record, Dean's progressive support collapsed as caucus day approached, contributing to his unexpected third place finish and Kerry's victory.[xlviii]

So can Obama ever escape the grip of the Politics of Fear? It would be a good thing if he does: he is preternaturally eloquent and charming. If he could ever rid himself of his deeply flawed political strategy and political ennui, he could be an enormously successful politician and a formidable force for building the progressive movement. The good news is that others have beaten this path before, and left the Politics of Fear in the dust where it belongs. Unfortunately for Obama, one of those people is his rival, John Edwards. When Edwards ran for president in 2003 and 2004, he did it with a largely specifics-free platform that, like Obama, emphasized a message of sunny optimism to counter political cynicism. He won the same kind of media swoons that Obama is now garnering. But on caucus day, he came up short in the on-the-ground organization crucial to winning elections of any kind, but primary campaigns in particular. It was the kind of passion that John Kerry had inspired with his tough and specific attacks on Bush during the lead up to the Iowa caucuses. But Edwards learned from this experience and from being subjected to the full force of the Republican attack machine as Kerry's vice presidential nominee.

By the time he launched his 2008 campaign, it was a new John Edwards. Gone was the senator who avoided specifics, and who voted for the Iraq war even though he sat on the intelligence committee and knew first-hand that President

---

[xlviii]There were other factors that doomed the Dean campaign: John Kerry ran one of the greatest campaigns in history in the final six weeks before the Iowa caucuses, and received a huge boost when a Republican ex-Marine whose life he saved in Vietnam came out of the woodwork to campaign for Kerry. Dean ran some extraordinarily poor television advertising, and there's some evidence that Dean's vaunted field operation flopped because so much of it relied on out-of-staters without the local connections that the Kerry network had. Indeed, Iowa caucus entrance polls show that the strategy worked: Kerry outperformed Dean by nine points among self described liberals (though Dean edged Kerry out among the 17 percent of voters who said they were "very liberal".) Kerry won a whopping 71 percent of voters who said that having the right experience was the most important quality they were looking for in a candidate; interestingly, only 26 percent of voters said a candidate would could beat Bush was the most important quality they were looking for. (CNN Iowa Caucus Entrance Poll, January 19, 2004. http://www.cnn.com/ELECTION/2004/primaries/pages/epolls/IA/)

Bush's claims about Iraq's weapons of mass destruction were, at best, exaggerated. Gone too was the senator who would avoid confrontation by surrendering to special interests on key votes: although he had never given into the Bush agenda to the degree Obama has, Edwards had voted to make it harder for families to get out of bankruptcy, let oil companies violate the Clean Water Act with impunity, and subsidize coal companies even when they were tearing the tops off of mountains and sending the toxic waste into Appalachia's hollows. Now Edwards's gloves were off. He wasn't afraid to criticize Bush and also not afraid to draw sharp contrasts with his primary opponents. Most importantly, he had left small-bore ideas behind – proposing a sweeping plan to provide universal health care coverage, unveiling the first detailed plan to tackle global warming of any candidate – and winning major plaudits from labor unions, environmentalists, and journalists hungry for something deeper than the other candidates' bromides. "I, like all of you, have evolved," he said about his new attitude. "It is not enough to do small things. Baby steps and incremental change are not enough. We need transformational change." His new style brought far greater grassroots support. And he fully leveraged that support by pioneering a new model of campaigning in which local community groups organized through the Edwards campaign did service projects related to the campaign's themes. For example, they retrofitted houses with energy efficient appliances to highlight Edwards's plan to tackle global warming and signed up eligible children for the CHIP health care program. Not only did it appeal to service-oriented Americans, it also allowed Edwards to make a direct positive impact on communities, creating a good impression for voters. And though as of this writing he hasn't raised quite as much money as Hillary or Obama, he's likely to field a more formidable get out the vote operation than either of them.

From Debacle to Goracle

Al Gore has similarly made the journey from caution to courage. In 2000, his presidential campaign was hamstrung by almost every component of the politics of fear: Gore focused on narrow issues, he declined to emphasize the differences between himself and George Bush (his ad on education even began with the line, "George Bush and I actually agree on accountability in education"), and he shied from playing hardball to counter the Bush campaign's dirty tricks. Perhaps the saddest and most consequential example of this Politics of Fear was Gore's failure to fully compete for victory during the 2000 recount battle. While Republicans were sending a "Brooks Brothers mob" of Republican Capitol Hill staffers to successfully harass and intimidate vote counters, the Democrats refused repeated requests from civil rights, labor, and environmental groups to send their own members to the streets to demand protection of their most basic civil right – having their votes counted. They feared that newspaper editorial boards would criticize Gore for being too political. His campaign officials ordered their supporters to take off their campaign buttons. Even though newspapers were similarly admonishing Republicans to keep the process apolitical, the Bush team just laughed at the pundits' halcyon view of high stakes politics. While Republicans were campaigning to include absentee ballots that had been cast after Election Day in Republican counties and to exclude legally cast ballots in Democratic counties, vice presidential candidate Joe Lieberman went on Fox News to say that illegally cast overseas ballots should be given "the benefit of the doubt." Add one act of intimidation to another, and pretty soon Republicans had the presidency.[23]

It's entirely possible that the cards were so stacked against Gore, that nothing he could have done would have won him that fight – Republicans controlled the Florida legislature, governorship, the Secretary of State's office, both houses of Congress, and the Supreme Court. Though he might not have won the presidency, he could have seriously damaged Bush's credibility and support among the American people by continuing to question the legitimacy of Bush's election – and given a major boost to the Democrats' and his own hopes to win the presidency again in 2004. Instead, Gore, winner of the popular vote by a margin of more than 500,000 votes, gave not only his blessing, but his pledge of support to George W. Bush – a man who had for the last 37 days been using every legal and illegal tool at his disposal to tar Gore's own legitimacy – and who was about to unleash an assault on Gore's legacy of environmental protection, scientific innovation, and an America boldly engaged with the world. Gore's concession speech is painful to read:

> Now the U.S. Supreme Court has spoken. Let there be no doubt, while I strongly disagree with the court's decision, I accept it…And tonight, for the sake of our unity of the people and the strength of our democracy, I offer my concession. I also accept my responsibility, which I will discharge unconditionally, to honor the new president elect and do everything possible to help him bring Americans together in fulfillment of the great vision that our Declaration of Independence defines and that our Constitution

affirms and defends.[24]

With this concession, the Democrats proved that they had forgotten the lesson of Gore's fellow Tennessean, Andrew Jackson, who lost a similarly closely contested election to another presidential son, John Quincy Adams, in 1824. Jackson had won the popular vote, but lost the election to Adams when it was thrown to the House of Representatives because no one had won an electoral college majority. Jackson didn't urge his supporters to rally behind the new president in an act of patriotic high-mindedness. Quite the opposite: he and his followers immediately set about a campaign to destroy Adams's legitimacy. Jackson told the Tennessee legislature, "The people have been cheated. The corruptions and intrigues of Washington have defeated the will of the people." He kept it up. Previewing modern-day Republican message discipline, the Jacksonians repeated the words "corrupt bargain" over and over again for three years until everyone knew it – and started to believe it. While Jackson was organizing the first modern presidential campaign, Adams initially refused to campaign, saying, "If my country wants my services, she must ask for them."[25] Meanwhile, the Jackson campaign pummeled Adams with false allegations that Adams had procured a "young American girl" for the Czar of Russia's pleasure, and even that the stoic Adams had installed a casino and brothel in the White House.

Jackson didn't allow the fact that Adams was a man of rectitude or that the popular vote was meaningless at a time when most states didn't use it to bother him – he intended to win, and win he did. At a Harvard seminar following the conclusion of the 2000 election, Karl Rove himself remarked that because Gore hadn't followed Jackson's tradition of contesting the legitimacy of a closely-fought presidential election, he doubted that questions about Bush's legitimacy would continue to dog him: "John Quincy Adams was faced with an ardent opponent in the form of Andrew Jackson who spent four years beating him up over the so-called corrupt bargain, the view that there had been a deal…There may be on [Gore adviser Bob Shrum's] part, but not on Al Gore's part, a desire to spend the next four years being the new Andrew Jackson, touring the country and yelling about the corrupt bargain."[26]

Conferring on Bush legitimacy he hadn't earned was Gore's mistake. But to Gore's credit, once he realized it, he put the politics of fear behind him and staked out a position as one of the most passionate, aggressive, and courageous leading Democrats. He was the most high profile Democrat to challenge the Iraq War before it started, and did it with a clarity and fire that escaped the more measured criticisms of Beltways liberals. He eschewed the complex, corporate Clinton model of health care reform by endorsing the more sweeping and affordable single payer system, even though Democratic insiders had long ago written it off as overly ambitious. And most famously, he campaigned with extraordinary success and extraordinary gusto and perseverance for action to reverse the global climate crisis. "Why wasn't he like this before?" became a common phrase in progressive circles as Gore won the passionate accolades that had eluded him as long as he was a cautious Politician of Fear. He was now the Goracle – the Oscar-award winning, Nobel prize winner who was now changing the world more, perhaps, than any living politician.

Global Courage

In the great struggles that will define our country and our world's future, progressives everywhere will need courage – we face powerful opposition from corporations, and from the cultural conservatives willing to accept economic injustice and environmental destruction as the price for fealty to an agenda of hatred. This book is not just for Americans. I worry that liberal fear is a virus that knows no political boundaries. It's transported around the world, in part, by American political consultants-for-hire who provide campaign strategies to candidates around the world and take the best and worst of American politics with them, along with, all too often, the Politics of Fear. I hope that the lessons in this book will inspire progressives the world over to examine and challenge their leadership to be braver and more faithful to core principles – allowing courage to sweep not just progressive America, but the world. The good news is that courage is sprouting across the American political landscape: in Minnesota, where a movement of progressives inspired and trained by Paul Wellstone is inspiring and training the next generation of progressive leaders; in Chadds Ford, Pennsylvania, where ordinary Americans have used the lessons they learned from MoveOn.org to challenge their town's Republican machine; and now even in Congress where congressional Democrats are acting more boldly every day to deliver the worker, civil rights, and environmental progress the country is so hungry for. To be sure, there are large spheres, most notably American presidential politics, where fear still exercises its paralyzing grip. But as the histories of John Edwards and Al Gore show, national Democrats can learn and are learning. And if they don't, there are millions of courageous progressives across the country who will make sure they do.

★★★★

SUMMARY: WHAT'S THE IMPACT OF DIFFERENT FACTORS ON THE ELECTION?

Factor Category:	Share of Total Effect:
Party Identification/Ideology	38 %
Social Characteristics (Race, Gender, Etc.)	25 %
Candidate Traits (Leadership, Moral, Smart)	16 %
Economic Conditions	15 %
Issue Opinions	6 %
	Explained variation only.

DETAIL: HOW DO VOTERS DECIDE?

Different Factors Affecting a Voter's Decision:	Share of Voter's Decision:
Voter Party Identification (Democrat/Independent/Republican)	33%
Does Voter Think Candidate is a Strong Leader?	18%
Voter Liberal/Conservative Scale	11%
How Moral is Candidate?	8%
How Have Economic Conditions Been?	7%*
Voter Race (White vs. Minority)	6%
Voter Favors More or Less Government Spending	6%
Is Candidate Smart/Knowledgeable?	6%
Voter Education Level	5%
Is Voter a Member of a Union?	4%
Voter Marital Status	4%
Voter Opinion: Future Economic Conditions	4%*
Voter Position: Abortion	4%
Voter Personal Financial Situation	3%*
Voter Position: Defense	3%
Voter Position: Blacks	2%
Voter Position on Role of Government in Ensuring Employment	2%*
Voter Level of Church Attendance	2%*
Voter Position on Role of Women	1%
Voter Position on Universal Health Insurance	1%*
Voter Income Level	1%*
Voter Religion	1%*
Gender	0%*
Voter Homeowner Status	0%*
Voter Lives in Red or Blue State?	0%*
Unexplained Variation?	28%

Although these results are displayed in rank order, we regressed them according to a modified Shanks-Miller model (see J. Merrill Shanks and Warren E. Miller's 1990 article "Policy Direction and Performance Evaluation: Complementary Explanations of the Reagan Elections" in *The British Journal of Political Science* and Miller's 1999 methodological summary, "Temporal Order and Causal Inference" in *Political Analysis*.) In particular, we utilized the Shanks-Miller "funnel of causality", sequentially adding variables in order according to our assessment of which way causality proceeds between variables: deciding, for instance, that while race and gender can affect one's ideological disposition, ideological disposition cannot affect one's gender. More to the point, we accept the view outlined by Green, Palmquist and Schickler in their Dec. 1998 article "Macropartisanship: A Replication and Critique" in the *American Political Science Review* that party identification has more of an impact on, for instance, vote choice and issue opinion than one's vote choice or issue positions have on party identification. Our funnel of causality follows.

Social Characteristics
Ideological Predispositions
Party identification
Policy-related preferences
Evaluations of Economic Conditions
Perceived Candidate Traits
Vote Choice

Linear Probability Analysis of National Election Survey Data, 1984-2004; Margin of Error +/- 4%. All entries except those labeled with an asterisk are statistically significant with at least 95 percent confidence. Data presented are standardized coeffiecients.

Unlike Shanks and Miller, we exclude most direct measures of respondent incumbent approval, and instead included a variable (not shown in this table) to control for annual election results that, in effect, controls for a voter's aggregate opinion of an incumbent candidate or party as reflected in their vote choice. Regardless, in constructing the model used here, we tested several variations in the order of regression and found no change that would alter the conclusions presented here.

ENDNOTES
★ ★ ★ ★

Introduction

[1] www.mediatransparency.org

[2] Dreyfuss, Robert. "How the DLC Does It." *The American Prospect*. Vol. 12, No. 7. April 23, 2001.

[3] Baer, Kenneth S. *Reinventing Democrats*. University Press of Kansas, 2000.

[4] *Gallup Poll*, November 7-10, 20905

[5] 2004 *CNN Exit Poll*.

[6] Guber, Deborah Lynn. The Grassroots of a Green Revolution: Polling America on the Environment. Cambridge: *The MIT* Press, 2003.

[7] Green, Donald, Bradley Palmquist, and Eric Shickler. *Partisan Hearts and Minds*. New Haven: Yale University Press, 2002. p. 27-28.

[8] See especially McCurley, Carl and Jeffrey J. Mondak. "Inspected by #1184063113: The Influence of Incumbents' Competence and Integrity in U.S. House Elections." *American Journal of Political Science*. Vol. 39, No. 4. Nov. 1995, p. 864-885.

[9] Menand, Louis. "The Unpolitical Animal" *The New Yorker*. August 30, 2004.

[10] Gelpi, Christopher, Jason Reifler and Peter Feaver. "Iraq the Votre: Retrospective and Prospective Foreign Policy Judgments on Candidate Choice and Casualty Tolerance." *Political Behavior*. June 2007, p. 162-163.

[11] Kenski, Kate and Jamieson, Kathleen Hall. "Issue Knowledge and Perceptions of Agreement in the 2004 Presidential General Election." *Presidential Studies Quarterly*. Vol. 36, No. 2. June, 2006. P. 243-259.

[12] Page, Benjamin I. and Shapiro, Robert Y. *The Rational Public*. Chicago: the University of Chicago Press, 1992.

[13] Alvarez, Michael R. and Franklin, Charles H. "Uncertainty and Political Perceptions." *The Journal of Politics*. Vol. 56, No. 3. August, 1994.

[14] Williams, Leonard and Wollman, Neil. "Remember the Way it Was?" *Roll Call*. April 1, 1996 and Williams and Wollman, "Why Democrats Won Control of Congress: the Real Story." Buzzflash. January 17, 2007. http://www.buzzflash.com/articles/contributors/727

[15] Galston, William and Kamarck, Elaine Ciulla. "The Politics of Evasion: Democrats and the Presidency." *Progressive Policy Institute*, September, 1989, p. 2. http://www.ppionline.org/documents/Politics_of_Evasion.pdf

[16] "The Politics of Evasion", p. 2.

Paul Wellstone

[1] Clift, Eleanor and McCormick, John and Barrett, Todd. *Newsweek.* "Crashing the Capitol Club" January 14, 1991. p. 26.

[2] Ceol, Dawn Weyrich. "Wall of resentment greets Wellstone." *The Washington Times.* January 4, 1991, p. A1.

[3] Clift, Eleanor and McCormick, John and Barrett, Todd. *Newsweek.* "Crashing the Capitol Club" January 14, 1991. p. 26.

[4] "Wellstone and the Pitfalls of Incumbency," *The National Journal.* April 13, 1991. Vol. 23, No. 15, p. 860.

[5] Lillehaug, David. PersonalInterview with Author. Minneapolis. November 30, 2005.

[6] *St. Paul Pioneer Press.* "Wellstone Regrets Using Memorial to Viet Vets for Press Conference." April, 4 1991. p. 1 D.

[7] Elvin, John. "Inside the Beltway." *The Washington Times.* June 19, 1991, p. A6.

[8] Cadwell, Clark. "Witnessing an Atomic Bomb Explosion" September 19, 2003. From Atomic Veterans History Project at http://www.aracnet.com/~pdxavets/caldwec.htm

[9] Kizer, Kenneth W. (Undersecreatry of Health, Department of Veterans' Affairs). Testimony before Senate Committee on Veterans' Affairs. April 21, 1998 *and* Gensler, Martin. Testimony at United States of America Advisory Committee on Human Radiation Experiments. March 16, 1995.

[10] Wellstone, Paul. "National Atomic Veterans Day" *Congressional Record.* April 6, 1995, P. S5520,

[11] Parrish, Albert "Smokey." Personal Interview. January, 2006.

[12] Wellstone, Paul. News Release: "Wellstone Bill to Aid Atomic Vets Passes Key Hurdle in Senate." July 27, 2000.

[13] From *Conscience of a Liberal*, p. 164.

[14] *Conscience of a Liberal*, p. 166.

[15] Aetna. January, 1992. From *Polling the Nations.*

[16] Wellstone, Paul. "Workers' Freedom of Association: Obstacles to Forming a Union" Health, Education, Labor, and Pensions Subcommittee Hearing Statement. June 20, 2002.

[17] Henry, Marty. Personal Interview. December 2, 2005.

[18] Henry, Marty. Personal Interview. December 2, 2005.

[19] Right to Organize Act of 2001 (S. 1102). Introduced June 26, 2001 by Senator Paul Wellstone.

[20] *Minneapolis Star-Tribune.* April 2, 1995.

[21] Wellstone, Paul. "Senate Concurrent Resolution 66 – Relative to Welfare Reform." *Congressonal Record.* June 27, 2996. p. S7191.

[22] Smith, Dane. "Facts take some punch out of 'Senator Welfare' label" *Minneapolis Star-Tribune.* May 25, 1996. p. 2B.

[23] Grow, Doug. "It's a new game, but he's the same." *Minneapolis Star-Tribune.* February 11, 1996. p. 2B.

[24] Toner, Robin. "Political Briefing: The States and The Issues." *The New York Times.* July 25, 1996.

[25] Smith, Dane. "Wellstone on centrist turf more often," *Minneapolis Star Tribune.* August 4, 1996. p. 1B

[26] Maki, James R. Personal Interview.

[27] Wellstone, Paul. *Conscience of a Liberal.* New York: Random House, 2001. p. 99-100.

[28] Center for Responsive Politics. 1990 fundraising report available at http://www.opensecrets.org/1994os/osdata/wellspau.pdf; 1996 report available at http://www.opensecrets.org/1996os/geog/S0MN00013.htm and http://www.opensecrets.org/1994os/osdata/wellspau.pdf.

[29] Keller, Ed and Berry, Jon. *The Influentials.* New York: The Free Press, 2003.

[30] Smith, Dane and Lopez Baden, Patricia. "Boschwitz raises question of Wellstone burning flag," November 2, 1996. p. 1A.

[31] "Minnesota's Race for the U.S. Senate: How Minnesotans Voted and Why – Star Tribune/VNS exit poll results" *Minneapolis Star Tribune.* November 6, 1996. p. 17A.

[32] Lofy, Bill. *Paul Wellstone: The Life of a Passionate Progressive.* Ann Arbor: University of Michigan Press, 1995.

[33] Stern, Eric. "Wellstone's speech stirs labor activists." *Waterloo-Cedar Falls Courier.* August 13, 1998.

[34] Hotakainen, Rob and Craig Gustafson. "Critics, allies react to Wellstone's decision to seek third term," *Minneapolis Star-Tribune.* January 18, 2001. p. 12A.

[35] October Harris, Gallup, CNN, CBS, AP Ipsos, ABC News/Washington Post, Zogby, Fox News/Opinion Dynamics found that Bush's national approval rating during October, 2002 was between 60 and 67 percent.

[36] Shesgreen, Deirdre and Dine, Philip. "United We Stood, Until Good Will Gave Way" *St. Louis Post-Dispatch.* September 5, 2002. p. A1.

[37] Lopez, Patricia. "Coleman, Wellstone camps argue defense issues" *Minneapolis Star Tribune.* September 20, 2002, p. 5B

[38] Republican Party of Minnesota/Mercury Group. "Defense Cuts" transcript from *National Journal,* October 16, 2002.

[39] Von Sternberg, Bob. *Minnesota Star-Tribune.* "Qualified support for Bush; Most favor ousting Saddam as long as Congress approves." September 1, 2002 p. 1A and Fox Broadcasting/Opinion Dynamics Minnesota Poll. November 4-5, 2002.

[40] Lieberman, Joe. "Media Availability Transcript." September 19, 2002. Shown on Early Today,

CNBC. September 19, 2002.

[41] Edwards, John. Statement on Iraq. Congressional Record, September 12, 2002. p. S8553.

[42] Wellstone, Paul. Senate Speeches – April 28, 1993 (Congressional Record p. S4991) December 13, 1995, p. Congressional Record p. S18522; Jouzaitis, Carol. "Clinton focuses on limits to U.S. role in Bosnia," May 2, 1993 P. 1.; McGinnis, Colin. Personal Interview, December 16, 2005.

[43] McGinnis, Colin. Telephone Interview, December 16, 2005

[44] Confidential email, September 16, 2002.

[45] McGinnis, Colin. Telephone Interview, December 16, 2005.

[46] McGinnis, Colin. Telephone Interview. December 16, 2005.

[47] Fiore, Faye and Stephanie Simon. "Wellstone's Beliefs May Imperil His Political Career" *The Los Angeles Times.* October 4, 2002, p. 1.

[48] Wolowitz, Elana. Email to Bill Lofy. February 9, 2007.

[49] Byrd, Robert. "A Robust and Tenacious Spirit" November 13, 2003. *Memorial Addresses and Other Tributes…Paul Wellstone, Late a Senator from Minnesota.* Washington: U.S. Government Printing Office, 2003.

Bill Clinton

[1] Krauss, Clifford. "THE NEW PRESIDENCY: Attorney General-Designate; A Top G.O.P. Senator Backs Nominee in a Storm" *The New York Times.* January 15, 1993.

[2] Schneider, William. "Majority of Americans Polled Line Up Against Zoe Baird," *CNN.* January 21, 1993.

[3] Woodward, Bob. *Shadow: Five Presidents and the Legacy of Watergate.* New York: Touchstone, 2000. p. 229.

[4] Berke, Richard. "Judge Withdraws from Clinton List for Justice Post," *The New York Times.* February 6, 1993. p. 1.

[5] Lewis, Neil A. "The Guinier Battle; Clinton Tries to Cut Losses After Abandoning a Choice." *The New York Times.* June 5, 1993.

[6] Berke, Richard L. "Clinton Backs off From Policy Shift on Federal Lands." *The New York Times.* March 31, 1993.

[7] Drew, Elizabeth. *On The Edge; The Clinton Presidency.* New York: Touchstone Books, 1995. p.110.

[8] Clinton, Bill and Gore, Al. *Putting People First: How We Can All Change America.* New York: Times Books, 1992. p. 64.

[9] Kelly, Michael. "The 1992 Campaign: Undeclared Candidate; Perot Shifts on Homosexuals in Military" *The New York Times.* July 10, 1992. p. A18.

[10] Clinton, Bill and Mitchell, Andrea. "The MacNeil/Lehrer Newshour" Transcript. November 16, 1992.

[11] Powell, Colin L. Letter to Representative Patricia Schroeder. May 8, 1992. Reprinted in *Congressional Record*

[12] *Los Angeles Times* poll of military personnel, February 13, 1993. From *Polling the Nations*.

[13] Apple, R.W. "The Economy's Casualty". *The New York Times*. November 4, 1992.

[14] *Putting People First*. p. 5.

[15] Federal Reserve Study, 2006.

[16] Woodward, Bob. *The Agenda*. New York: Simon and Schuster, 1994. p. 121.

[17] Egan, Jack. "Ruthlessly raising rates? Not so far". *U.S. News and World Report*, May 23, 1994

[18] *The Agenda*. P. 109.

[19] Woodward, Bob. *The Agenda*. New York: Simon & Schuster, 1994. p. 165.

[20] Drew, Elizabeth. *On the Edge* New York: Touchstone, 1994. p. 112-116.

[21] Dewar, Helen and Thomas Cooper. "ords
and Thomas Cooper. Stimulus Defeat Alarms Clinton Loyalists on Hill" *The Washington Post*. April 23, 1993.

[22] *On the Edge*, p. 286.

[23] Clinton, Bill. "Address to the nation on the economic program." August 3, 1993.

[24] Lewis, Kathy. "White House stages all-out media blitz" *Dallas Morning News*. August 5, 1993. p. 23A.

[25] Warren, Robert Penn. *All the King's Men*. Restored Edition, Edited by Noel Polk. Harcourt, 2001. p. 324-325

[26] *The Agenda*. P.310.

[27] Clinton, Bill. "President Clinton's Remarks on the Senate Budget Vote." DC Federal News Service Transcript. August 6, 1993.

[28] Gladwell, Malcolm. "The Risk Pool" *The New Yorker*. August 28, 2006.

[29] "History of the National Partnership for Reinventing Government; Accomplishments, 1993 – 2000.

[30] Quoted in MacArthur, John R. *The Selling of Free Trade: NAFTA, Washington, and the Subversion of American Democracy*. New York: Hill and Wang, 2000. p. 158.

[31] Johnson, Haynes and David S. Broder. *The System. Boston:* Back Bay Books, 1997. p. 123.

[32] *On the Edge*. p. 287-289.

[33] Gore, Al. "President Clinton Receives the National Performance Review from Vice President Al Gore" DC Federal News Service. September 7, 1993.

[34] *My Life*. Volume II: The Presidential Years. p. 120.

[35] MacArthur, John R. *The Selling of "Free Trade"* New York: Hill and Wang, 2000. p. 263.

[36] Public Citizen's Global Trade Watch. "The Record on Deals for Trade Votes: Don't Get Fooled

Again" December, 2001. http://www.citizen.org/documents/fast_track_deals.PDF

[37] *The Selling of Free Trade*, p. 150.

[38] Teixera, Ruy. "Who Deserted the Democrats in 1994?" *The American Prospect.* September 21, 1995.

[39] Public Citizen. "NAFTA-Trasitional Adjustment Assistance (1994-2002)" http://www.citizen.org/trade/forms/taa_search.cfm?dataset=1

[40] Clinton, Bill. "Remarks by President Clinton, President Bush, President Carter, President Ford, and Vice President Gore in Signing of NAFTA Side Agreements" September 14, 1993.

[41] Schott, Robert E. "The high price of 'free' trade" Economic Policy Institute Briefing Paper. November 17, 2003.

[42] Gallagher, Kevin P. "Mexico, NAFTA, and Beyond." Interhemispheric Resource Center. September 17, 2004. p. 2.

[43] Vaughan, Scott. "How green is NAFTA? Measuring the impacts of agricultural trade" *Environment.* March, 2004.

[44] Schott, Robert E. "The high price of 'free' trade" Economic Policy Institute Briefing Paper. November 17, 2003.

[45] Hufbauer, Gary Clyde and Ben Goodrich. "Lessons from NAFTA" *Free Trade Agreements.* Institute for International Economics.

[46] World Trade Organization. Environmental Disputes in GATT/WTO. http://www.wto.org/English/tratop_e/envir_e/edis00_e.htm

[47] CBS/New York Times poll (December 7, 1993); NBC News Poll (December 14, 1993), Institute for Health Policy and Health Services Research, January, 1994.

[48] Steinmo, Sven and J. Watts, "It's the Institutions, Stupid!: Why the United States Can't Pass Comprehensive National Health Insurance," *Journal of Health Politics Policy and Law.* (1995) Vol. 20, No. 2, p. 329-372.

[49] *The System*, p. 197.

[50] *The System.* p. 205.

[51] Kristol, Bill. "Memorandum to Republican Leaders. Defeating President Clinton's Health Care Proposal." Washington, DC: Project for the Republican Future. Washington, DC. December 2, 1993. Quoted in Skopcol, Theda. *Boomerang: Health Care Reform and the Turn Against Government.* New York: W.W. Norton, 1997 *and* American Health Line. "Strategies: How GOP Can "Erase" the Clinton Health Plan" December 2, 1993 *and* The Hotline. "GOP Group Wants Total Defeat of Clinton Plan" December 2, 1993.

[52] Jehl, Douglas. "Coverage of 95% Might Not be Enough, Clinton Concedes" *The New York Times.* July 20, 1994.

[53] Business divided its donations exactly 50-50 to Democrats and Republicans in 1992 and 1994. Source: Analysis of data provided by Center for Responsive Politics, July, 2006.

[54] Census Bureau. Historical Income Tables. Table H-6. Regions—All Races by Median and Mean Income: 1975 to 2004. http://www.census.gov/hhes/www/income/histinc/h06ar.html

[55] Teixera, Ruy. "Who Deserted the Democrats in 1994?" *The American Prospect.* September 21, 1995.

[56] Williams, Leonard and Neil Wollman. Article in *Roll Call*, April 1, 1996.

[57] *The System*, p. 557.

[58] Smothers, Ronald E. "A Disillusioned State Gives Up on Democrats" *The New York Times.* November 15, 1994

[59] *My Life* p. 214-215.

[60] Carville, James and Begala, Paul. *Take It Back.* New York: Simon & Schuster, 2006. p. 243.

[61] *Showdown.* P. 39.

[62] *Showdown,* p. 105.

[63] Purdum, Todd. "Clinton Says G.O.P. Rule Cutting Would Cost Lives" *The New York Times.* February 22, 1995.

[64] *Showdown,* p. 105.

[65] Besharov, Douglas J. "Two Cheers for Welfare Reform" American Enterprise Institute, August 22, 2006.

[66] Pratt, Sharon and Sherman, Arloc. "TANF AT 10 Program Results are More Mixed Than Often Understood" Center for Budget and Policy Priorities. August 17, 2006.

[67] See March 17, 1996 ABC News/Washington Post poll; April 19, 1996 Gallup Poll, May 14, 1996 NBC News/Wall Street Journal Poll; Aug 4., 1996 *Washington Post/ABC News Poll;* August 10, 1996 *Newsweek* poll; June 25, 1996 *NBC News/Wall Street Journal* poll; September 5, 1996 ABC News/ Washington Post poll.

[68] *Showdown,* p. 217.

[69] Clinton, Bill. "Remarks of President Bill Clinton to Students and Educators at Automated Graphic Systems," White Plains, Maryland. *Federal News Service.* May 17, 1995.

[70] Pope, Carl. "Ways and Means" *Sierra Magazine.* November/December 1995.

[71] The Wilderness Society. "Bush's Forest Plan: Salvage Rider Resurrected." August 30, 2002. http://www.wilderness.org/Library/Documents/upload/Bush-s-Forest-Plan-Salvage-Rider-Resurrected.pdf and Egan, Timothy. "As Logging Returns, Recrimination on Why" *The New York Times.* December 5, 1995 and Farmer, Jared. "The salvage rider – down, but not quite out." *High Country News.* July 22, 1996.

72 *Showdown,* p. 233.

[73] CNN 1996 Exit Poll. http://www.cnn.com/ALLPOLITICS/1996/elections/natl.exit.poll/index1.html

[74] Clinton, Bill. "Address to the Nation by President Clinton Re: Administration Budget Proposal" Federal News Service. June 13, 1995.

[75] Purdum, Todd. "Battle Over the Budget: The Overview; President Offers Plan to Balance Federal Budget." *The New York Times*. June 14, 1995.

[76] Lambro, Donald. "Republican strategy: Divide and conquer; Budget rift opens door for more cuts" *The Washington Times*. June 16, 1995. p. A1

[77] Clinton, Bill. "Remarks at a Presidential Gala Dinner in Houston" Federal News Service. October 17, 1995.

[78] Purdum, Todd. "Clinton Angers Friend and Foe in Tax Remark" *The New York Times*. October 19, 1995.

[79] Clinton, Bill. Statement Regarding Republican Legislative Actions on Medicare and the Budget. Federal News Service. October 19, 1995.

[80] Thomas, Evan et. al. "Decision '96" *Newsweek*. November 18, 1996.

[81] Clymer, Adam. "Americans Reject Big Medicare Cuts, A New Poll Finds" *The New York Times*. October 26, 1995.

[82] *All Too Human*, p. 402.

[83] Clinton, Bill. "Text of Clinton government shutdown address" CNN Transcript. November 14, 1995.

[84] Knight-Ridder News Service. "Gingrich says snub influenced shutdown" Tampa Tribune. November 16, 1995.

[85] ABC World News Tonight Transcript. November 16, 1995.

[86] *All Too Human*. p. 407-408.

[87] *All Too Human*, p. 407-408

[88] Clinton, Bill. State of the Union Address. January 23, 1996.

[89] University of Michigan Index of Consumer Sentiment. (http://www.sca.isr.umich.edu)

[90] Bureau of Labor Statistics. Table A-1. "Employment status of the civilian noninstitutional population 16 years and over, 1969 to date."

[91] U.S. Census Bureau. "Table H-6. Regions--All Races by Median and Mean Income: 1975 to 2004"

[92] Clinton, Bill. Address to the Democratic National Convention, Chicago. August 29, 1996. Transcript from U.S. Information Agency.

[93] Morris, Dick. *Behind the Oval Office*. New York: Random House, 1997. p. 319.

[94] Analysis by Center for Responsive Politics, July 2006.

[95] *Shadow*, p. 252-253.

[96] *Shadow*, p. 338.

[97] President Clinton's Deposition. August 18, 1998. (For complete text see http://www.washingtonpost.com/wp-srv/politics/special/clinton/stories/text081898.htm)

[98] *A Vast Conspiracy*, p. 243 -244

[99] Clinton, Bill. Remarks on Grand Jury Testimony and Investigation by Independent Counsel

Kenneth W. Starr. Printed in *Washington* Post, August 18, 1998. For complete text see http://www.washingtonpost.com/wp-srv/politics/special/clinton/stories/text081898.htm

[100] *ABC News Special Report.* Transcript. August 17, 1998.

[101] *NBC News Special Report.* August 17, 1998, 10:00 pm ET.

[102] *Nightline.* August 17, 1998.

[103] *Los Angeles Times* poll, August 21, 1998; *ABC News* poll August 20, 1998; Harris Poll, August 20, 1998; *NBC News Poll*, August 20, 1998; Time/CNN poll, August 19, 1998; CBS/*New York Times* poll August 18, 1998. Pew Research Center poll, August 27, 1998. *ABC News/Washington Post* poll August 23, 1998.

[104] Connolly, Ceci. "Gephardt Says Clinton Could Be Impeached: House Leader Won't Rule Out Process" *Washington Post.* August 26, 1998.

[105] Wolf, Gary. "Weapons of Mass Mobilization" *Wired.* September, 2004.

[106] *Shadow,* p. 479-480.

[107] *Shadow,* p. 497.

[108] "Last Round of Ads Hit Clinton" *The Hotline.* October 28, 1998.

[109] Transcript from *CNN Capital Gang.* October 31, 1998.

[110] Orin, Deborah and Brian Blomquist. "Newtie's Cutie Couldn't Keep a Secret" *The New York Post.* August 14, 1999.

[111] The Institute of Politics, Harvard University. *Campaign for President: The Managers Look at 2000.* Hollis, New Hampshire: Hollis Publishing Company, 2002. p. 23-25 and 190-198

[112] The Labor Research Association. "U.S. Union Membership 1948-2004" (http://www.laborresearch.org/charts.php?id=29)

[113] Harris Poll. "Party Affiliation and Political Philosophy Show Little Change, According to National Harris Poll, March 9, 2005.

MoveOn.org: The Courage of Crowds

[1] Marech, Rona. "Grass Roots From Berkeley Sprout Online" *San Francisco Chronicle.* December 29, 2000.

[2] "Anti-impeachment website gets 400,000 to sign petition" *Allentown Morning Call.* December 17, 1998.

[3] Erickson, Creed. Personal Interview. February 26, 2007.

[4] Boyd, Wes. Pesonal Interview. February 1, 2007.

[5] Boyd, Wes. Personal Interview. February 1, 2007.

[6] The Pew Research Center for People & the Press. "Columbine Shooting Biggest News Draw of 1999." December 28, 1999. (http://people-press.org/reports/print.php3?ReportID=48)

[7] Flack, Dick. "mobilize now to protect civil rights and liberties" December 26, 2000. (http://

web.archive.org/web/20010205052100/www.actionforum.com/national/goals.html)

[8] Pugh, Tony. "Some college students, liberal groups, religious leaders urging U.S. not to retaliate." *Knight Ridder.* September 21, 2001.

[9] Pariser, Eli. "Notes to Address Power Session" Environmental Grantmakers 2003 Fall Retreat.

[10] Ibid.

[11] http://web.archive.org/web/20010922040606/www.actionforum.com/forum/index.html?forum_id=220

[12] Schmitt, Eric. "Iraq is Defiant as G.O.P. Leader Opposes Attack" *The New York Times.* August 9, 2002.

[13] Matzzie, Tom. Personal Interview.

[14] Musgrove, David. Personal Interview.

[15] Bush, George W. "New SEC Chairman Sworn-In" White House Transcript. February 18, 2003.

[16] Pingree, Chellie. Personal Interview. February 26, 2007.

[17] Von Drehle, David. "From Screen Savers to Progressive Savior? Newsbytes" *The Washington Post.* June 5, 2003.

[18] Von Drehle, David. "From Screen Savers to Progressive Savior? Newsbytes" *The Washington Post.* June 5, 2003.

[19] MoveOn.org PAC. "No Candidate Wins Majority in MoveOn.Org PAC First-Ever Democratic Online Primary" June 27, 2003.

[20] *Washingtonpost.com* "The Hitler Analogy" January 5, 2004.

[21] Darman, Jonathan. "Censored at the Super Bowl" *Newsweek.* January 30, 2004. (http://www.msnbc.msn.com/id/4114703/)

[22] O'Reilly, Bill. "CBS Bans MoveOn.org Commercial" *The O'Reilly Factor* January 16, 2004.

[23] Bolton, Alexander. "527 surge takes Kerry past Bush" *The Hill.* April 20, 2004.

[24] Rutenberg, Jim. "Activist Group Plans New Ads Attacking Bush in Swing States" *The New York Times.* February 12, 2004.

[25] Alterman, Eric. "The Soros Slander Campaign Continues" *The Nation.* June 17, 2004. (http://www.thenation.com/doc/20040705/alterman)

[26] Cassidy, John. "The Ringleader: How Grover Norquist keeps the conservative movement together" *The New Yorker.* August 1, 2005.

[27] Pariser, Eli. "Because of you, there is hope." Email to MoveOn members. November 3, 2004.

[28] Frederick, Dinae. Interview. March 16, 2007.

[29] Pariser, Eli. "Hurricane Housing.org: How It All Started" in Dawn, Laura. *It Takes a Nation.* San Rafael, CA: Earth Aware Editions, 2006.

[30] Cummings, Jeanne. "Left Turn? In a Key Primary, MoveOn's Revolt Divides Democrats" *Wall Street Journal.* August 1, 2006.

[31] Cummings, Jeanne. "Left Turn? In a Key Primary, MoveOn's Revolt Divides Democrats" *Wall Street Journal.* August 1, 2006.

[32] MoveOn.org Political Action. "Taking Back the House."

[33] Petraeus, David H. "Battling for Iraq." *The Washington Post.* September 26, 2004.

[34] Krugman, Paul. "Time to Take a Stand." *The New York Times.* September 7, 2007.

[35] De Young, Karen. "Experts Doubt Drop in Violence in Iraq." *The Washington Post.* September 6, 2007.

[36] Walker, David. "Securing, Stabilizing, and Rebuilding Iraq." Testimony Before the Committee on Foreign Affairs, House of Representatives. September 5, 2007.

[37] Bush, George. "Press Conference by the President." September 20, 2007.

[38] Patel, Ricken. Personal Interview. February 9, 2007.

Tom Daschle

[1] Cochran, John. "New Senators Prepare for Changes." *ABC World News Tonight.* November 30, 1994.

[2] Waller, Douglas. "Capitol Grudge Match" *Time* June 10, 2002.

[3] The Tax Foundation. "Federal Spending Received Per Dollar of Taxes Paid by State, 1981-2004" March 16, 2006. http://www.taxfoundation.org/research/show/347.html

[4] Shaw, Bernard. "Tom Daschle Says He's Qualified to Be Minority Leader" *Inside Politics.* CNN. November 25, 1994.

[5] Lightman, David. "Dodd's Near Miss Comes After Slow, Steady Climb." *Hartford Courant.* P. A 1.

[6] Kast, Sheila. *World News Tonight Sunday.* November 20, 1994.

[7] Cited in *The Hotline*, November 28, 1994.

[8] Germond, Jack and Witcover, Jules. "Too soon to count votes to replace Sen. Mitchell" *Baltimore Sun*, March 25, 1994.

[9] Lee, Jessica. "Democrats' Daschle quietly making some noise" *USA Today.* May 8, 1996. p. 6A

[10] Daschle, Tom (with Michael D'Orso). *Like No Other Time.* New York: Crown, 2003. p. 81.

[11] Lott, Trent. *Herding Cats: A Life in Politics.* New York: Regan Books, 2005. p. 135.

[12] Kiely, Kathy and William M. Welch. "Managing 50-50 Senate up to an Odd Couple" *USA Today.* March 1, 2001.

[13] *Like No Other Time*, p. 52-53.

[14] Interview with Senator Tom Daschle. *The News Hour With Jim Lehrer.* December 18, 2000.

[15] Daschle, Tom. Remarks on Nomination of Tom Daschle. *Congressional Record.* January 30, 2001. p. S686-S688.

[16] Lowry, Rich. "Daschle's Love Affair with Arsenic" *National Review Online.* April 27, 2001.

[17] *Like No Other Time.* P. 25.

[18] Brunkow, John R. "Tax cut better than paying down debt" *Argus Leader.* March 1, 2001.

[19] Kranz, David. "The president came to S.D. to pressure Democratic senators to endorse his $1.6 trillion tax cut." *Argus Leader.* March 10, 2001. p. 1A.

[20] Leiserson, Greg and Jeffrey Rohaly. "The Distribution of the 2001-2006 Tax Cuts: Updated Projections, November 2006". Tax Policy Center. November 2006.

[21] *Like No Other Time*

[22] *Herding Cats: A Life in Poliltics.* p. 223.

[23] Cited in *The New York Times*, October 1, 2001.

[24] *Congressional Record. P. S10572-S10575.* October 11, 2001.

[25] Rothschild, Matthew, "Russ Feingold Interview" *The Progressive.* May, 2002.

[26] Transcript, US Department of Labor. http://www.dol.gov/_sec/media/speeches/20011004_President_visit_to_DOL.htm

[27] *Like No Other Time*, p.190

[28] Savage, David G. and Janet Hook. "Stakes Are High in Push for Latino Court Nominee" *Los Angeles Times.* April 11, 2002. p. A1.

[29] Dewar, Helen. "Senate's Stimulus Bills Die; Jobless Benefits Extension Passes" *The Washington Post*, February 7, 2002. p. A4

[30] Waltman, Scott. "South Dakota Senator Responds to Criticism" *Aberdeen American News*, February 22, 2002.

[31] Kinnard, Meg. "Johnson Reaches Out to Both Parties" *National Journal.com.* November 11, 2002.

[32] "Senate Passes Energy Bill" *The Bulletin's Frontrunner.* April 26, 2002.

[33] Mitchell, Alison. "Democrats, Wary of War in Iraq, Also Worry About Battling Bush." *The New York Times.* September 14, 2002.

[34] Waltman, Scott. "South Dakota Politicians Reflect on Sept. 11" *Aberdeen American News*, September 10, 2002. p.

[35] Johnson, Tim. Senate Floor Statement on Iraq Resolution. September 26, 2002. Congressional Record, p. S9361.

[36] Daschle, Tom. News Conference Transcript. Federal Document Clearing House. October 10, 2002.

[37] Ifill, Gwen. "Newsmaker: Tom Daschle" *News Hour with Jim Lehrer.* September 17, 2002.

[38] Glodt, Jason. Personal Interview. South Dakota State house, Pierre, SD. February 9, 2007[39]

U.S. Public Interest Research Group. "The 2004 Energy Bill: Bad for Public Health, the Environment, Ratepayers." January 11, 2004.

[40] Barbaro, Michael. "If It's January, It's Time to Lobby" *The Washington Post.* January 5, 2004.

[41] Geman, Ben. "Lights Out" *TomPaine.com* November 24, 2003.

[42] http://www.dailykos.com/story/2003/11/20/63338/091

[43] Ross, Denise. "Virginia Senator a Player in S.D. Politics" *Rapid City Journal.* November 25, 2003.

[44] Victor, Kirk. "Second-Guessing Daschle" *National Journal*, December 13, 2003.

[45] Madden, Mike. "Changes in Medicare" *Argus Leader*, November 23, 2003.

[46] National Republican Senatorial Committee. "Pretty Smart" from Glazer, Gwen. "Partisan Rhetoric Ramps Up in South Dakota Senate Race" *National Journal*, September 30, 2004.

[47] Cited in Victor, Kirk. "Fighting for His Life" *National Journal*, October 15, 2004.

[48] "Meet the Press" *NBC News.*

[49] MSNBC. Senate Exit Poll 2004. South Dakota.

Nancy Pelosi and the Democrats of 2006

[1] Anna Eshoo quoted in Breslau, Karen, Eleanor Clift and Daren Briscoe. "Rolling With Pelosi." *Newsweek* October 23, 2006.

[2] Sandalow, Marc and Erin McCormick. "Pelosi's goal: Democrats back on top" *San Francisco Chronicle.* April 2, 2006.

[3] Kady, Martin II. "Party Unity: Learning to Stick Together." *Congressional Quarterly.* January 9, 2006.

[4] Block, Melissa. "Former NFL QB Heath Shuler Gains House Seat." *All Things Considered.* November 9, 2006.

[5] *The Washington Post* Votes Database (http://projects.washingtonpost.com/congress/members/s001171/).

[6] Lakoff, George. "Building on the Progressive Victory" *Rockridge Institute.* December 15, 2006.

[7] Jansen, Bart. "Bush Success Rating at Historic Low" *Congressional Quarterly.* August 31, 2007.

[8] Boehner, John. "House GOP Unveils Report Chronicling Democrats' Top 100 Broken Promises"

[9] Kessler, Jim. "The Kennedy-Kyl Bill and Winning the Immigration Debate" (Memo to Senate Offices). May, 2007.

[10] Reid, Harry. Debate on Comprehensive Immigration Reform Act. *Congressional Record.* June 27, 2005. p. S8580.

[11] Preston, Julia and Connelly Marjorie et. al. "Immigration Bill Provisions Gain Wide Support in Poll." *The New York Times.* May 25, 2007.

[12] Bush, George W. "Statement by the President on the Emergency Supplemental." April 3, 2007.

[13] Pelosi, Nancy. "No yielding on war funding as Bush proposes talks" *CNN.* April. 10, 2007.

[14] Bush, George. "President Bush Discusses Iraq War Supplemental, War on Terror" Fairfax,

Virginia. April 10, 2007

[15] Blitzer , Wolf. Interview with Barack Obama Transcript. *CNN Late Edition*. April 1, 2007.

[16] Ferrechio, Susan. "Democrats Set Stage for Next War Debate" *CQ Today.* May 23, 2007.

Conclusion: Courage Rising

[1] Galston, William and Kamarck, Elaine C. "The Politics of Polarization" *The Third Way Foundation.* October, 2005.

[2] Kohut, Andrew et. al. "Trends in Political Values and Core Attitudes: 1987-2007 – Political Landscape More Favorable to Democrats." The Pew Research Center for People and the Press. March 22, 2007.; also author survey of most recent issue polling from *PollingReport.com*.

[3] The Pew Research Center for People and the Press. "The 2005 Political Typology: Beyond Red vs. Blue." May 10, 2005.

[4] CNN/National Election Survey Data.

[5] Bush, George W. "Remarks in Dallas." November 2, 2004. Federal Document Clearing House Emedia.

[6] Jamieson, Kathleen Hall. *Electing the President 2004.* Philadelphia: University of Pennsylvania Press, 2006. p. 151.

[7] Based on FEC Data: "2004 presidential Campaign Finance Activity Summarized," February 3, 2005; "Party Financial Activity Summarized for 2004 Election Cycle," "Congressional Candidates Spend $1.16 billion During 2003-2004", June 9, 2005; and Toner, Michael. "The Impact of the New Campaign Finance Law on the 2004 Presidential Election" in Sabato, Larry J. (Ed.) *The Divided States of America.* New York: Pearson, 2006. p. 193.

[8] CNN/National Election Survey Data. http://www.cnn.com/ELECTION/2004/pages/results/ states/US/P/00/epolls.0.html

[9] Campbell, Angus; Converse, Philip E.; Miller, Warren E.; and Stokes, Donald E. *The American Voter.* Chicago: John Wiley and Sons, 1960. p.120-145. *and* Bartels, Larry M. "Beyond the Running Tally: Partisan Bias in Political Perceptions" in *Political Behavior.* Vol. 24, No. 2. Special Issue: Parties and Partisanship, Part One. June, 2002. p. 117-150.

[10] *New York Times* Exit Poll Data, 1972-2004.

[11] Jennings, Kent M., Gregory B. Markus and Richard G. Niemi. "Youth-Parent Socialization Panel Study, 1965-1982: Three Waves Combined" [computer file]. Ann Arbor, Mich.: University of Michigan, Center for Political Studies/Survey Research Center [producers], 1983. Ann Arbor, Michigan.: Interv-university consortium for Political and Social Research [distributor]. Cited in Green, Donald; Bradley Palmquist and Eric Shickler. *Partisan Hearts and Minds: Political Parties and the Social Identities of Voters.* New Haven & London: Yale University Press, 2002.

[12] Aldrich, John H. *Why parties: The origin and transformation of political parties in America.*

Chicago: University of Chicago Press, 1995.

[13] Bartels, Larry M. "What's the Matter with *What's the Matter with Kansas*" *Quarterly Journal of Political Science.* 2006, 1: 201-226.

[14] Page, Benjamin I. and Shapiro, Robert Y. *The Rational Public.* Chicago: University of Chicago Press, 1992. p. 62-63, and 68.

[15] (Reprinted from Page & Shapiro - *The Rational Public,* University of Chicago, 1992, p. 63)

[16] Carville, James and Begala, Paul. *Take It Back.* New York: Simon & Schuster, 2006. p. 243.

[17] Miller, Zell. "Text of Zell Miller's RNC Speech." CBS News.

[18] Bennett, James. "The Next Clinton" *The New York Times Magazine.* May 30, 1999.

[19] Yglesias, Matthew and Sam Rosenfeld. "Con – Hillary Clinton for President? An American Prospect Debate" April 4, 2007.

[20] Bacon, Perry. "Giuliani Offers Pledge of Fiscal Restraint, a Vow to Beat Clinton." *The Washington Post.* October 13, 2007.

[21] Sirota, David. "Mr. Obama Goes to Washington" *The Nation.* June 7, 2006.

[22] Jones, David W. Transcript of Presentation from "Democratic Spenders" in *Electing the President, 2004: The Insiders' View.* Ed. Kathleen Hall Jamieson. Philadelphia: University of Pennsylvania Press, 2006. p. 230-236.

[23] Toobin, Jeffrey. *Too Close to Call: The Thirty-Six Day Battle to Decide the 2000 Election.* New York: Random House, 2001.

[24] Gore, Al. "Remarks." December 13, 2000.

[25] Blum, John M. *The National Experience.* New York, 1973. I: 216.

[26] Institute of Politics, Harvard University. *Campaign for President: The Managers Look at 2000.* Hollis, New Hampshire: Hollis Publishing Company, 2002. p. 248-249.

ACKNOWLEDGMENTS

This book would not have been possible without the Democratic Party. Though, as I chronicle here, its leaders can be craven, its principles weak, and its message unconvincing, I also believe that it's worth writing about: its direction and its leadership will play a major role in determining not just the future of our country, but also the planet as a whole. For all my criticisms, I am passionate about helping it achieve success: it is the only American political party that can currently deliver peace, justice, and planetary survival. It is vital, therefore, that we correct its failings and bolster its strengths. So, thank you, Democrats great and small, progressive and reactionary, cowardly and courageous. You made this book possible.

Turning to some markedly non-craven people, my parents William and Mary Hurowitz deserve enormous credit for this book. Not only did they provide a wonderful education, political and otherwise, they also provided valuable feedback on the book. Mom and Dad, thank you and I love you. Thank you to my grandmother Angela Canning, who, along with my late grandfather Denis and many of my relatives in Ireland, exposed me at an early age to a different and colorful political culture – helping me appreciate politics as entertainment, an appreciation that I hope lends this book the occasional comic relief.

My wife Amanda was the single individual who helped shape the broad outlines of the book the most. She offered clear, simple, and insightful suggestions throughout the whole process of researching and writing and had an eagle eye for making much-needed cuts, crossing out large, extraneous sections with confidence and aplomb. And she was cheerful and loving as this book went from glimmer in my eye to words on the page. Allison, Harris, and Fran Fisher also provided vital support throughout.

I could not go further without recognizing my dog Calliope (her name is that of the Greek muse of epic poetry) and she, muse-like, indeed inspired me with her big brown eyes, wagging tail, and wet kisses and kept me a happy literary warrior throughout. Calliope's biggest contribution, however, was in giving me reason to hang out in our neighborhood dog park. While walking there one day, I met Gregory P. Nini and his wife Becca (and their labradoodle Bear). Greg, now a professor at Wharton, turned out to be a statistical whiz eager to help with analyzing the complex data underpinning the ideas discussed in the book. He and I spent countless hours fine-tuning the regression analyses that, I think, help separate this book from so many works of political anecdote and speculation. Greg is indefatigable, indispensable, and a genius.

I am extremely grateful to my agent Susan Ginsburg for having faith and persistence in this book and in me. Her edits, along with those of her Writers House colleague Emily Saladino, transformed this book into the punchy, readable, and hard-hitting work you find in your hands now. She is a champion and an extraordinary asset to any author.

My research assistant Deirdre Fulton brought her considerable talent as a journalist to bear on important portions of this book; not only did she conduct most of the interviews for the chapter about Tom Daschle and spend time in South Dakota doing research, she also wrote the first draft for much of the chapter. Deirdre also did a great deal of exploratory research into another chapter that didn't make it into the final version of the book; I can offer no higher tribute to her honesty and perceptiveness that she was the first to voice doubts about whether the chapter would work as part of this book. I am also grateful to Soyoung Ho for her work.

My best friend Neal Kemkar provided not only trenchant feedback on the book, but also much needed diversions from the looming deadlines, keeping my spirits high. My college roommate Ethan Youngerman was not only a source of mirth throughout, but provided wisdom and specific suggestions that were always spot on; he deserves a lot of credit in particular for the shape of the chapter on Paul Wellstone. David Edeli, Herb Allen, Adam Gordon, Sam Goldman, Darin Dalmat, Jess Champagne, Yen Cheong, and Isaiah Wilner improved the writing, structure, and ideas of the book and helped me navigate the publishing world. Jenna Perry Leschuk was an extraordinary copy editor, coming through on a very tight deadline with a thoroughness and knowledge of the finer points of English grammar that amazed me.

Thanks also to Cindy Kang, Naomi Roth, David Rossini, Jesse Littlewood, Kirsten Collings, Leslie Samuelrich, Antha Williams, Heather Smith and the entire Green Corps class of 2002 (especially Kate Smolski, Margie Klein, Roger Smith, Nick Getzen, Mark Hays, Melissa Waage, Megan Rising, Natalie Foster, and Johanna Neumann) for their help on the book and for teaching me how to be a political organizer and how to transform my love of Nature into action on its behalf. Thanks also to David Lipowicz and Rose Garr for helping make Democratic Courage a reality. Aimee Wood and Shannon Ryan are extremely talented designers who made the book jacket and the DemocraticCourage.com website so appealing.

This book was originally supposed to have a chapter dealing with courage in international progressive politics. However, I came to the conclusion that the politics of other countries are too diverse and too different from those in the United States to include them under the same theoretical framework. However, I did spend several months researching and writing a chapter, about Bolivian president Evo Morales that didn't make the final cut. I am grateful especially to Bolivian Ambassador Gustavo Guzmán Saldaña for his time and assistance in setting up interviews in Bolivia, as well as to Annie Murphy, Tom Kruse, and other members of the overworked Morales administration who gave their time to this project. Above all, I am grateful to William Powers, whom I contacted after reading his brilliant and engaging book *Whispering in the Giant's Ear.* Working deep in the Bolivian Amazon, Bill ran the world's first pilot project to engage international polluters and developing nations in protecting tropical forests – work that won him a major prize in environmental innovation from Harvard's Kennedy School of Government, and, more importantly, protected 3 million acres of rainforest in Noel Kempff National Park in Bolivia. Bill was generous in his time and inspiring in his commitment and charisma. We ended up collaborating on an op-ed that was published in *The New York Times* in June 2007 about the importance of saving tropical forests as part of any solution to the global climate crisis.

I would also like to thank some people who, though they weren't directly involved in the book, have been friends, supporters, and planet-savers: the brilliant and biting Matt Stoller, who has nurtured my career in the blogosphere by promoting my writing with incredibly kind words – and who deserves credit for, above all else, pushing the Democrats to be more courageous. Thanks to Sam Rosenfeld and Ann Friedman at *The American Prospect*, David Roberts at *Grist* and Jessica Wakeman at *The Huffington Post* for giving me the opportunity to air many of these ideas in print before publication of the book. Arianna Huffington deserves enormous credit for first exposing me to the description of Democrats as "spineless weasels."

Finally, thanks to Robert Merrill at Maisonneuve Press for having the faith and vision to take on this project.

And thank you, reader, for picking up this book and making it to the end of the acknowledgements section. I hope you enjoyed it!

Hatch, Orrin 63
HCA 92
Health care 7, 8, 14, 16, 18, 30-1, 60-1, 67-8, 77, 80-2, 84-5, 87-98, 109, 213-4, 229, 234-5, 244
   insurance industry 87-90, 92, 96, 235
   single payer 92, 235, 247
   universal coverage 80, 90, 92, 94
Head Start 95, 178, 237
Heller, Branch 172
Helms, Jesse 99, 177
Henry, Marty 40
Heritage Foundation 13, 222
Hollings, Fritz 124
Holt, Terry 154
Hormel, James 182
Horton, Myles 44, 231
Hussein, Saddam 50-3, 146, 154, 190, 192-4, 226
Hyde, Henry 126

I
Ideology 15, 18, 49, 100, 177, 218
Immigration 17, 63, 85-6, 188, 209-11, 219
   border wall 211
Impeachment 22, 64, 119, 122-6, 130, 134-42, 146, 170, 220
Inflation 39, 69, 70, 75, 96
Influentials, The 16, 160
Inslee, Jay 147
Insurance industry 87-90, 92, 96, 235
Iraq War 15, 17, 21, 51-2, 54, 146-7, 149, 151, 154, 163-4, 166, 168, 170-1, 193-4, 204, 207-8
Iron Range, Minnesota 40, 42, 46
Israel 51, 81, 112
Issue positions (as influence on vote choice) 16-8, 218-20

J
Jackson, Jesse 13
Jefferson, Thomas 231, 233
Johnson, Haynes 87, 92
Johnson, Lyndon B. 147, 175, 227-8, 233
Johnson, Tim 176, 185-6, 191-2
Johnston, J. Bennett 38, 63
Jones, Paula 117-8
Jones, Wes 123
Jordan, Vernon 121, 123
Judis, John 229

K
Kahn, Rick 54-5
Kamarck, Elaine 19, 20, 218
Kantor, Mickey 81

Kefauver, Estes 44
Keller, Ed 16
Kemp, Jack 113
Kennedy, John F. 185, 231
Kennedy, Robert F. 47
Kennedy, Ted 50, 176, 178, 198
Kerrey, Bob 75
Kerry, John 17, 150-1, 154, 159-61, 164, 170, 183, 199, 219, 222, 228, 242-3
Kessler, Jim 210
Keynes, John Maynard 69
King, Peter 137
Kirkland, Lane 79, 87
Kirkland & Ellis 117
Kizer, Kenneth 34
Kosovo 112, 127, 140
Kristol, William 93-5

L
Labor
   law 40
   unions 38-9, 44, 78-9, 82, 84-5, 89, 91-2, 128, 132, 159, 196, 208, 210, 220, 234, 244
Labor, Department of 85
Lakoff, George 8, 205-6
Lamont, Ned 165-6
Lapic, Tom 54
Larsen, Rick 147
Levin, Carl 212
Lewinsky, Monica 116, 118-23, 127-8, 140
Lewis, Peter 154
Lieberman, Joe 20, 50, 123, 135, 140, 150, 164-6, 245
Linder, John 137
Lobbyists 12, 29, 37-8, 47, 91, 133, 137, 191, 197, 204, 239, 241
Lofy, Bill 30, 56
Long, Huey 75
Lott, Trent 54, 99, 176, 179-80, 188, 190, 192
Luntz, Frank 189-90
Lux, Mike 140-2, 149
Lynde and Harry Bradley Foundation 13
La Colline Restaurant 37-8

M
MacArthur, James 84
Mack, Connie 36
Magaziner, Ira 80, 90-1
Maki, James R. 43
Manufacturing 39, 79, 85, 96, 112
Matzzie, Tom 146, 156-7, 163-5
McCain, John 140, 154, 170
McCurdy, Dave 97
McCurry, Mike 124